Elements
&
Evolution

The Spiritual Landscape of Astrology

Eric Meyers, M.A.

Elements & Evolution
The Spiritual Landscape of Astrology

Published by Astrology Sight Publishing
Asheville, North Carolina

ISBN Number: 978-0-9747766-4-4

Printed in the United States of America

www.SoulVisionConsulting.com

email: eric@soulvisionconsulting.com

Cover art derived from Albert Bierstadt's, "Sunset on the Coast."

Graphic design and interior illustrations by Bill Streett, except for spiritual iconography in chapter 9, from Wikimedia Commons.

Back cover photograph taken by Josh Levin.

Lyrics to "Exactly" by Amy Steinberg printed by permission.

Dedicated to Sajit Greene,
for seeing me.

Also by the author:

Uranus: The Constant of Change
(2008)

Between Past & Presence:
A Spiritual View of the Moon & Sun
(2006)

The Arrow's Ascent:
Astrology & The Quest for Meaning
(2004)

The seed of God is in us. Given an intelligent and hard-working farmer, it will thrive and grow up to God, whose seed it is; and accordingly its fruits will be God-nature. Pear seeds grow into pear trees, nut seeds into nut trees, and God seed into God.

–Meister Eckhart

Contents

Introduction   11
Chapter 1 – The 4 Elements   15

    Fire   15
    Earth   18
    Air   21
    Water   24

Chapter 2 – Neutral and Charged Elements   29

    Consensus and Non-Consensus Realities   30
    Levels of Intensity   31
    The Charged Elements: Water & Fire   32
    The Neutral Elements: Earth & Air   33
    Charged & Neutral Interactions   34
    Charged and Neutral Elements in Astrology 41
    Regarding the Planets   44
    Venus as Neutral   46
    Renewing the System   47

Cyclical Evolution

Chapter 3 – The Evolutionary Cycle   51

    The Modalities   52
    The Evolutionary Cycle   54
    Sequence of the Stages   73

Chapter 4 – Aspects & Evolution Part I: 75
      Oppositions & Trines

    Aspects   76
    Oppositions   79
    Trines   88
    Shadow Trines   97

Chapter 5 – Aspects & Evolution Part II: 99
      Squares & Sextiles

    Squares   100
    Sextiles   113

Chapter 6 – Aspects & Evolution Part III: Quincunxes   123

    An Interconnected System   134

Progressive Evolution

Chapter 7 – The Evolution of Consciousness   143

    Enter Astrology   145
    Resolving the Moon   147
    Choosing the Past   148
    The End of Separation   149
    A Spiritual View of the Luminaries   150
    Spiritual Fire   153

Chapter 8 – Elemental Levels   155

    Earth: The Physical Level   155
    Water: The Emotional Level   157
    Air: The Mental Level   160
    Fire: The Soul Level   165

Introduction

Evolutionary astrology is based on a spiritual view of the human experience. We are each seen as being, in essence, a soul that lives through many incarnations in order to learn and grow. Astrology can be used to understand and provide guidance for this evolutionary process. My intention is to contribute to the building of a philosophical consensus that would help this exciting field be as engaging and useful as possible. Astrology is an incredibly powerful tool that can expand our self-awareness, help us have compassion for others, and reliably guide us through the most challenging arenas of our lives. Making the spiritual component more explicit can make it even more potent.

Consensus is best found by building on what is already most agreed upon. The main contributions of this work stem from two universally recognized ideas, one from science and the other from religion.

Science informs us that there are two distinct ways in which we approach the world. Although brain functioning is very complex with notable variation, there is a general trend. The left brain analyzes bits of information through rationality. It logically dissects with its objective razor, cutting through any sentiment to get to facts. Realms of language, mathematics, and reason appeal to its precision.

In contrast, the right brain functions in ways that aren't so linear. Intuition, inspiration, artistry, and emotion all color its subjectivity. It naturally flows with a sense of timelessness and engages with the ethereal and the transcendent. These realms, which also include dreams and expansive contemplation, evade the meticulous clockwork of left brain sensibilities.

This is the fundamental duality of our world: content and process, science and art, structure and essence, objective and subjective. Most anything can be split up using this left/right dichotomy—business and pleasure, technical merit and aesthetic presentation, the masculine and the feminine.

Although these pairings seem obvious to the modern mind, the tradition of astrology we've inherited has not included this division, and understandably so. Astrology is far older than our knowledge of brain hemispheres and their respective functions. In the West, the world was approached more subjectively before the so-called Enlightenment; the objectivity of left brain perspectives wasn't yet part of the picture. In the last few hundred years, science has aggressively pushed the pendulum toward the rational/objective end of the continuum. As a result, we have advanced technologically, but we have marginalized and discounted the validity of right brain functions. Collectively, we are currently finding a greater balance between these two necessary and complementary approaches.

We are at a time in history when many people are learning to honor and skillfully employ both left and right brain functions. Now is a good time to incorporate this basic division into the field of astrology. The left/right dichotomy adds new layers of meaning to some of the components of the astrological system. By classifying earth and air with the left brain as neutral elements, and water and fire with the right brain as charged elements, new perspectives emerge that can impact and vitalize the entire system of astrology.

The second universal idea that this book is rooted in comes from religion and the world's wisdom traditions. Although there has been a plethora of divergent spiritual views expressed throughout history, there has in fact been some significant agreement. There is a central idea held in common that God or Spirit (call it what you will) divides from oneness into separateness and then gradually learns to reconnect the separateness back into Oneness. Furthermore, this process of division and subsequent re-unification involves movement through the distinct levels of the physical, emotional, mental, and spiritual. Spirit descends through progressively denser levels and then ascends and evolves back through increasingly lighter levels on its journey back to unity. This idea is found in all of the major religions and within many other spiritual paradigms. It has been termed the "Perennial Philosophy" and has been commented upon by numerous philosophers and religious authorities for centuries.

Correlating the physical with earth, the emotional with water, the mental with air, and the spiritual with fire is a framework that's well-known by most astrology students. However, conceptualizing each of the elements as a level of reality is not a part of the usual discourse. Astrology has been widely understood as a symbolic system, which is within the mental (air) domain. This book expands on this traditional understanding and offers a multi-leveled philosophy which addresses these four levels of reality.

The charged-neutral division can be thought of as adding to the breadth of our philosophical understanding of astrology, and the levels of reality can be seen as adding to the depth. Both of these new ideas feature the elements as the central players. Earth, water, air, and fire interact in dynamic and fascinating ways. We will examine how they structure and catalyze both cyclical and progressive evolution.

The first half of this book addresses cyclical evolution. There is a procession from Aries to Pisces (thematically consistent with the motion through the twelve houses), which conveys an evolutionary path for each of us to travel. The various aspects (opposition, trine, etc.) connect the twelve stages and thereby provide specific evolutionary lessons.

The second half of the book concerns progressive evolution—the development of consciousness through the elemental levels. From the inspiration of fire (soul), to the understanding of air (mind), to the embodiment of water (emotion), to the materialization of earth (physical), Spirit manifests in our everyday world. And as part of evolution, we develop from matter (earth), to life

13

(water), to advanced cognition (air), to spiritual realization (fire), as we liberate Spirit from separateness and realize Oneness. These manifesting and liberating channels inhale and exhale in a continual rhythm of evolution.

The elements are everywhere, all around us as well as within us. They are the building blocks of life. They dance with each other, support, challenge, synthesize, and transform, never leaving us for an instant. The four elements similarly permeate the astrological system, giving articulation and meaning to all of the planets, signs, and houses. The elements encompass all facets of our experience by creating, and partaking in, our evolutionary circumstance. Together, they combine to illuminate the spiritual landscape of astrology.

Chapter 1

The 4 Elements

In this opening chapter, each of the elements will be introduced in terms of their general characteristics, relationship to humanity, and basic evolutionary contribution. Later chapters will provide more detail about their evolutionary importance, including the roles they play in relationship with each other to stimulate evolution.

Fire

Planets: Mars, Sun, Jupiter
Signs: Aries, Leo, Sagittarius
Houses: 1, 5, 9
Appearance: Nonphysical
Classification: Yang, Charged
Evolutionary Purpose: Provides life force, energy, awareness, creativity, intuition, soul realization.

Characteristics

The fire element contains *light* and *heat*. Its light illuminates the darkness, bringing the potential for awareness and clarity. Personal darkness can induce feelings of disorientation, isolation, and fear. Fire's light can replace these feelings with connection and inspiration, enabling productive interaction with the world and the growth of consciousness.

Fire's other component, heat, equates to *vitality*, the sustaining energy of the life force. Heat radiates outward, ready and eager to spread its lively energy. Fire concerns *presence*—it brings us out of the dark and cold and lights and warms our way.

Both light and heat have various *levels of intensity*. As we notice at sunrise and sunset or when adjusting a dimmer switch, there are innumerable shades of brightness. And temperatures easily rise and fall. Fire at low intensity can manifest as a single, small candle. At high intensity it can be a raging inferno. It can spread wildly and without concern, or be contained and harnessed for beneficial use.

Fire is *metaphysical*. As we see with flames, it can shape shift in a dazzling way. Fire is the energetic vibrating movement within all material, the continual buzzing at the atomic level. It is potent and crackling with *creativity*.

Fire is *active and lightning fast*. It is the quickest of the elements. Like a lightning bolt, it can seem to come out of nowhere to awaken us, to suddenly gift us with a "Eureka!" moment of insight. Fire pertains to *intuition* and *spiritual awakening*.

Our Relationship with Fire

In the human realm, fire is full of desire and passion, highly motivated and often urgent. It wants to enliven and brighten. It burns with conviction to attain its goals, seeking the highest levels of fulfillment. It can also be oppressive or invasive and overrun all sense of restraint or reason.

Fire is initiating and arousing. The signs and houses it's associated with have to do with beginnings. Aries is the first sign of the zodiac and concerns the singular spark of personal autonomy away from the oneness of Spirit. Leo is the first social sign and deals with the development of character on our own terms. Sagittarius, the first collectively-oriented sign, aims to develop a mission which motives the life path. Each of these sign's related houses (the

1st, 5th, and 9th, respectively) also begin the personal, social, and collective sectors of the chart.

In the classification being used here, fire is discussed as a *charged* element, which indicates that it rises and falls in levels of intensity. Our passions awaken and diminish depending on a multitude of factors. Anger, lust, motivation, or attention-seeking can be aroused by our attention, or these passions subside if the fire is not fed. Just like maintaining a campfire, this element requires our interest and effort.

Fire's *yang* quality is seen in its instigating, restless, energetic disposition. When emphasized in a person it manifests as extraversion. It can be flashy, macho, or even abusive when it's out of balance.

Evolutionary Contribution

Fire is related to the spiritual level of life—our soul connection to the oneness of Spirit. From the unified fire source, individual souls venture forth into physical form to gather unique experiences and live out a particular life mission. We can picture Spirit as a gigantic blaze of fire, with each soul being analogous to a candle. As autonomous beings we are learning to consciously reconnect our candles with the larger, singular flame of Spirit. The passion of fire seeks an outcome, motivating souls to participate in evolution, which has personal as well as collective importance. Fire is the genesis of creation which sets it all in motion.

With or without the separation into individual life forms, the conditions of fire endure like the proverbial eternal flame. The speed of light is considered a mathematical constant, just as Spirit is universally pervasive. The constancy of fire is described by the law of the conservation of energy. Despite the endless energetic transformations that take place between matter and energy, including the birth and death of entire stars, the *totality* of energy in the universe remains the same. These conditions lead to the conclusion that fire is everlasting.

Earth

Planets: Venus, Mercury, Saturn
Signs: Taurus, Virgo, Capricorn
Houses: 2, 6, 10
Appearance: Physical
Classification: Yin, Neutral
Evolutionary Purpose: Provides foundation, substance, structure, sensuality, resources, manifestation.

Characteristics

First and foremost, earth is a *physical* element. We can also call it *matter* or *substance*. It is sensual, tangible, and obvious. As a base or container, earth is *stable and solid.* As the structure of the physical world, it is the great foundation that we live on. Earth is enduring, unmoving, and reliable, a pillar of strength. Earth has the quality of *stillness*, sitting idly until it's utilized. Since it's receptive in this regard, earth is considered a *yin* element.

Natural resources are provided by earth—shelter, clothing, and food. Earth is literally the soil and terrain in which things grow. Nature has provided us with everything we need to live life comfortably and sustainably. Since resources play this valuable role in maintaining a comfortable society, earth assumes *worth.* Houses, vehicles, and possessions are valuable commodities.

By itself, earth is just matter—barren, indifferent, and dead. Imagine a desert or an asteroid. In order for life to exist, water, the other physical element, is necessary. Although earth can support life, this element is primarily responsible for structuring the world. Earth is *impermanent.* In contrast to the eternality of fire, earth is only a temporary crystallization of energy. And like anything that has tangible, physical form, it will eventually cease to exist. Although earth is durable and solid, in the long view it is also fleeting.

Earth is what it is. There's nothing to disagree about. It's rational, orderly, and neutral. It provides the *physical content* to our existence. Earth is the "bare bones," or the "bottom line."

18

Our Relationship with Earth

Earth provides structure, the reliable container in which things can grow. And people with a strong earth emphasis also play this role. Earthy people are pragmatic and results-oriented. They are dependable and grounded in common sense and simplicity. Their priority is maintaining what already works as opposed to engaging in the hypothetical or the speculative. And since they respect what has survived over time, earth types tend to be conservative or traditional. Earthy people pride themselves on being solid—the loyal friend or dutiful employee who shows up to work on time each day.

Humans have created a physical basis of civilization in the form of agriculture, transportation systems, housing, and all the other various components of infrastructure. Earthy people oversee how things work in society. They are adept at engineering and management.

Our relationship to the physical world assigns various value judgments to earthy materials. Gold is worth more than lead; trees are more valuable than sand. These designations depend on human preferences, which in turn are usually based on scarcity and utility. While earth in itself is neutral, we relate to it in subjective ways. We standardized value through systems of money and currency, which also have physical forms.

Taurus, the personal earth element, is connected with our body, possessions, sense of security, and self-worth. When we consolidate and secure what we have, we build a reliable foundation. Virgo is earth's social sign and deals with issues of service, crafts, training and skill-development, workplace relations, apprenticeship, and mentoring. The third Earth sign is Capricorn, which relates to the arena of vocation and societal identity. Through dedication and diligence we can become skillful at managing earth and climb toward our chosen summit of achievement. Capricorn is about contributing to, and becoming pillars of, society—those who occupy places of influence.

Due to its basic nature, earth is prone to oversimplify things. It also must guard against preserving the status quo at the cost of progress. Earth may have the tendency to stifle necessary innovations with the attitude, "If it ain't broke, don't fix it." An overemphasis on earth can also lead to materialism, workaholism, and gluttony. The physical world is abundant with gifts. The pitfall is to forget or neglect that we are also made from the stars.

Evolutionary Contribution

Earth is the foundation for our evolutionary circumstance. It serves as the broad container which carries the potential to host life. Matter is the basis for the long evolutionary motion back towards realizing the unity of Spirit. Without membership on the physical level, there is no way to tangibly experience soul lessons.

Since matter is a temporary crystallization of energy, the forms that earth take are fleeting. From a spiritual perspective, the body is seen as a vessel for the soul. Likewise, all material serves as a host for spiritual processes. In a sense, everything physical is *borrowed* and must eventually return to intangibility.

Due to its solidity and obviousness, earth contributes to our consensus reality. We all more or less agree about the material world. A tree is a tree, a stone is a stone. Earth sets up a complete physical landscape on which we rely, a structure whose importance is often neglected. The objects that surround us give us a sense of home and help us maintain our orientation to life. Where would we be without planet Earth?

We must take care of *Mother Earth* in order for evolution to proceed. The Earth itself is an externalized reflection of the collective human psyche. Our bodies are made from the substances on this planet, and we are in a direct relationship with nature. Spiritual teacher Deepak Chopra says, "The tree is my lungs; the earth is my body; the waters are my circulation. It's not environment; it's your extended body. It's you."

Air

Planets: Mercury, Venus, Uranus
Signs: Gemini, Libra, Aquarius
Houses: 3, 7, 11
Appearance: Nonphysical
Classification: Yang, Neutral
Evolutionary Purpose: Provides the spiritual "nervous system," intellect, communication, socialization.

Characteristics

The air element is a massive openness which contains all experience. Another word for it is *space*. Air allows us to get distance from things and thereby gives us *perspective*. This element has no tangibility (like earth and water), and it is not energetic (like fire). Its vast expanse may seem simple. However, air may in fact be the most complex of the elements as it serves as a *metaphysical structure*.

The air holds innumerable *connections and networks*. We hardly ever consider it, but there is a huge range of radio and satellite transmissions filling the space around us all the time. If we had the right antennae we would be bombarded by it all.

Quantum physics informs us that there are nonphysical connections between everything. These connections occur non-locally, meaning they connect phenomena regardless of distance or even time! At the quantum level, the "empty" space is endlessly busy beyond our usual comprehension. Everything is metaphysically interconnected, and air is the element that hosts it all.

Air is orderly and rational. Systems of language, mathematics, and logic are part of its scope. Whereas the earth element categorizes the physical realm, the air element is how we categorize facts and figures. Just as a rock is a rock, and no arguments apply, 2+2=4, and there is no dispute. Air is classified as a *neutral* element because of its cool, dispassionate, irrefutable reason. Like a list of statistics, a dictionary, or phone book, air is *informational.*

Air is considered a *yang* element due to its expansive nature, as opposed to the inertia of earth or the settling of water. Absent

21

the friction and gravity of earth, movement proceeds through space without resistance. The ungrounded quality of air lends itself to the concept of *freedom*. Air brings us to possibilities, which can be mental as well as spatial. There is room to wander, unknown vistas available when we explore its openness.

Our Relationship with Air

Air brings us out of the limitations of a more general animal consciousness into the complexity and opportunities of an advanced intellect. The higher mind has the capacity to understand the conceptual or symbolic worlds. There is an appreciation of aesthetics, beauty, and refinement. Air provides the content for schools, universities, and all forms of learning.

The mental realm allows for human ingenuity and all the technology that it creates. Air thrills us with unlimited possibilities and invites us into the unknown. There is an excitement when something gets "off the ground" or "takes off."

Air relates to perception. There is clarity in the air, a sharpness of vision when views are unobstructed. The ability to perceive clearly allows us to study and learn from the environment. Although we tend to flavor all of our perceptions with our biases, air is the closest we get to being objective. The neutrality of air allows us to develop an agreed-upon reality.

There is a social component to the air element. As the space that envelops everything, it serves as the means for connection, akin to a colossal chat room. Air involves networks and community—any form of social organization.

Knowledge is exchanged through the various methods of communication: writing, teaching, studying, and all forms of learning. Air is the medium which hosts communication and any transmission of sound. Through the complexity of language, music, and the continual symphony of sound all around us, airwaves are constantly busy. The refinement of language leads to comedy, satire, and spoof—sophistication and subtlety that is absent among "lower" animals. Air is the most rarified of the elements.

The three air signs all address the advancement of intellect and socialization. The personal air sign is Gemini, which pertains to the evolution of the human mind and the endless learning available to us. Libra is the social air sign and has to do with diplomacy, justice, equity, and romance—the development of civility and harmony in human relations. The collective sign Aquarius is both social and intellectual. It relates to how nature itself is intelligently organized and how all participants within nature are joined together in the same unified web.

Air draws us out of instinct and into infinite possibilities. There is a risk here of losing the human touch, of prioritizing freedom to the extent that relational bonds are undervalued and destabilized. An insistence on rationality may lead to a robotic disposition and a tendency to unwittingly harm others through the trappings of cold logic. This detached style can ultimately lead to estrangement. Air types may endlessly ponder possibilities without committing to a plan. Some become ivory tower intellectuals who lose sight of the "real" world.

Evolutionary Contribution

There is literally nothing to grab hold of in the air element. This emptiness on the physical level contrasts with the fullness that air has metaphysically. It's like an invisible nervous system that connects everything. We can think of air as a gigantic mind, full of endless, fascinating options. At the spiritual level, air is the nervous system of the cosmos.

The optimal way to manage air is to adopt an attitude of non-attachment instead of detachment. With non-attachment, there is a suspension of personal preference, a willingness to allow and connect with anything and everything. All possibilities are preserved, while we are able to engage fully with what is actually happening. In contrast, detachment leads to withdrawn observation and a lack of participation. Air teaches us that we can move beyond the ego (the identity of being a separate self) and the suffering produced by being attached to its desires. This element informs us of our transcendent nature.

As an organizational element, air structures the spiritual intelligence which is woven through everything. Astrology is an airy discipline which examines the patterns of this intelligence. Indeed, the study of astrology can lead to seeing how intelligence extends beyond our humanity—we are like nerve-endings in a larger brain. This larger brain encompasses—at one end of its continuum—the billions of enormous galaxies that are spread through the universe. At the other end of its continuum, we find the confounding carnival of sub-atomic activity at the quantum level. What an extraordinary scope of phenomenon! Air puts us in our place; we are limited and enveloped in something far bigger than we can fathom.

Water

Planets: Moon, Pluto, Neptune
Signs: Cancer, Scorpio, Pisces
Houses: 4, 8, 12
Appearance: Physical
Classification: Yin, Charged
Evolutionary Purpose: Provides depth of consciousness, emotion, autonomy to life forms, reproduction.

Characteristics

In addition to earth, water is the other physical element. Looking at a globe, we see continents (earth) surrounded by water. It is shapeless and fluid, malleable in relation to the solid structure of earth.

This lack of definition illustrates how water concerns *process* rather than content. Water can assume solid (ice), liquid, or gaseous (vapor) forms depending on the temperature. It eludes constancy; water is always in a process of change. In a still pond, the slightest movement sends ripples through it. Water is *sensitive to its environment, continually adapting* to its surroundings.

Water has various *levels of depth* to it. From superficial surface layers all the way down to the farthest depths, water acts as the

24

metaphor for levels of *consciousness* (defined here as awareness in the separate self). A common expression is that we experience or express a *stream* of consciousness. When consciousness connects with others, it has collective relevance, with the metaphor being an *ocean*. As the prerequisite for life, water pertains to living beings and their entire spectrum of consciousness—from simple vegetative states all the way to the transpersonal.

Water is a *yin* element as it tends to move downward and settle. The well of the unconscious similarly holds and consolidates experiences. As we interact with life and the broader world, we are impacted and changed. We then need to integrate our experiences in order to maintain inner homeostasis, a sense of balance. Water concerns this process of recalibrating through introspection, sleep, retreat, or other methods and reorienting ourselves to what is most essential and personally meaningful. Water relates to how we extend care to ourself and others, supporting both survival and nourishment.

Our Relationship with Water

Earth provides the structure, and water nourishes life. This activation of life, the development of some form of consciousness, leads to *sensitivity, the need for protection, and endless subjectivity.* Water correlates to *emotion*, which is energy in motion. In contrast to the inertia of earth, water is perpetually in a *state of flow.* And where there is movement, there is also some type of process. Process sets up the exchange of energy and impacts all involved in subjective ways. We see the connection between water and emotion in many bodily processes. Sadness or great joy generates tears; fear produces sweat; anger triggers adrenaline.

Water is a *charged* element, which means it has levels of intensity. In contrast to the neutrality of earth, water is personally moving and has a wide spectrum of expression: from deep upset, hurt feelings, and heartache, to love, empathy, and a reverence for life. One person's internal process or experience can never fully be understood by another. The inherent *irrationality* of emotions and water is constructive, allowing us to approach life on our own

25

terms, to be moved in ways that are unique. Being in our heart, in all of its wild perturbations and uncertainties, gets us in touch with our humanness. As beings composed mainly of water, it is our task to learn how to manage it.

Cancer is the sign of our personal connection to water—the inner depths, heart, familial roots, and style of nurturing. It sinks into what really matters at the most personal level. The social water sign is Scorpio, which relates to forming emotional, psychological, or other meaningful connection with others. It deals with underlying interpersonal dynamics, which may include sharing resources, sexuality, or business transactions. Pisces is the collective water sign, bringing emotions into the broadest expression. This sign of transcendence and selflessness involves compassion, altruism, and the quality of consciousness where we experience oneness.

Watery people tend to be soulful, deep, and in touch with both the strength and vulnerability of the human condition. They are filled with an innate capacity to feel, connect, empathize, and nurture both the self and others. Like all of the elements, however, water's energy can be out of balance. With sufficient activation, water can rage out of control in the form of tirades and acts of fury, or collapse inward into depression and apathy. Watery people can be excessively needy, intrusive, or self-absorbed, lacking sensitivity and concern for others.

Evolutionary Contribution

An evolutionary purpose of water is the establishment of autonomous life. It thereby provides access to the great drama of biology—survival, reproduction, and the formation of ecosystems. Having some form of consciousness along the spectrum from vegetative to animal to human allows for participation in the great web of interconnected life. Autonomous beings learn evolutionary lessons appropriate for their level of consciousness. Everything at the biological level ultimately contributes to the evolution of the collective consciousness.

Through its emotional nature, water stimulates us to care about our evolutionary situation. There is a genetic investment to

26

see offspring flourish. Our meaningful connection with nature also compels us to care for the broader spiritual health of our collective evolution. Water sets up a vast system of life forms which ultimately may realize our shared interconnectedness. The more conscious we become, the more we unify Spirit. From the transpersonal view, we see how others are actually us. In the end, there is only One.

Water concerns the well of the unconscious—the depth of the individualized soul which is evolving towards greater completeness and awareness. The more life is lived and lessons are addressed, the more that the depth of the soul condition is understood. As we become more conscious, we're increasingly freer of the limitations of the separate self and more able to flow with life.

Chapter 2

Neutral and Charged Elements

The elements are conventionally organized by pairing water and earth as yin/negative and fire and air together as yang/positive. This yin/yang format of pairings deals with the vertical dimension. Earth and water are physical elements—they conform to gravity and take tangible form. In contrast, air and fire are nonphysical, being neither tangible nor grounded. So on a vertical axis, we can picture air and fire as located above earth and water.

These pairings are as valid as they are enduring. And yet, as stated earlier, by using an additional classification, new perspectives of meaning and nuance emerge. How else can we divide the four elements? What similarities can we find? What other pattern could be there?

Looking at the elements on a horizontal axis creates the new grouping. In fact, this division into left and right fits perfectly, as the elements will be organized into what is widely discussed as left-brain and right-brain categories. The left side addresses content, and the right goes with process. Content is termed "neutral," as it pertains to structure or information—there is nothing loaded or subjective about it. And process is termed "charged," because it is loaded with emotion, desire, opinions, or preferences. So this new pairing classifies air and earth as "neutral" and fire and water as "charged."

This fuller categorization of the elements results in the following: Earth is receptive (yin) and neutral, and water is receptive (yin) and charged. Air is active (yang) and neutral, while fire is active (yang) and charged. Earth and water are, respectively, the neutral and charged elements of the *physical* world. Air and fire are, respectively, the neutral and charged elements of the *nonphysical* world.

	Neutral	Charged
Yang	Air	Fire
Yin	Earth	Water

Element Organization

Figure 1

Consensus and Non-Consensus Realities

This division between the neutral and charged elements can be understood by equating the neutral elements with *consensus reality*, and the charged elements with *non-consensus reality*. Consensus reality consists of the common understanding of how our shared reality is organized. In contrast, the charged elements are involved with subjective processes, which are unique to every individual and can never be fully experienced by another.

Regarding the earth element and the physical world, consensus reality includes all physical objects, materials, and their tangible qualities. One object may be scratchy, while another is smooth. Although the internal *experience* of it may differ, there is universal agreement about the relative feel of these two objects. We all say that a shirt is a shirt. No one sane would seriously say that it's a staircase.

The air element structures the nonphysical world. Its scope includes language, mathematics, logic, and communication. There is consensus that 2 + 2 = 4, or that grass is green. The factual world has order just like the physical world—we just don't see it. Ask 100 relatively sane people how many days there are in a week, or how many inches in a foot, and you'll get a unanimous answer. Air relates to how time, space, calendars, etc. are objectively organized. There is also a structure and order to sound, as in a musical score. We've organized the notes from A to G in a precise system of musical communication.

In the realms of non-consensus reality, water is the element equated with the physical world. Each of us has a highly subjective relationship with the physical world, processing sensation and responding to it in our own unique ways. Something fuzzy, for example, might make one person comfortable and another person irritated.

Fire is the subjective element at the nonphysical level. It deals with interpretations, opinions, theories, speculations, intentions, and our relationship to energy, auras, and other nonphysical realities. Fire has to do with the *quality* of energetic experience, enjoying, for instance, a particular form of music or aligning with a certain philosophy. In contrast, air, in its objectivity, makes no such distinctions—music is just sounds, and philosophy is nothing more than words and ideas. With fire, we are activated and then make choices based on our preferences.

Levels of Intensity

Another way to understand the difference between charged and neutral is to address the factor of intensity or quality. Earth provides structure, and air provides content. They can change in terms of quantity—you can have more or less possessions (earth) or sentences in a paragraph (air). However, they cannot increase or decrease in intensity or quality. A logician will tell you that the factual statement (air) "Grass is green" is not a better statement than "The sky is blue." A statement can either be true or false, but this does not make it *better* or *worse*.

Meanwhile, the charged elements carry various degrees of intensity or quality since they deal with subjective process rather than objective content. Preferences can be rated on a scale of intensity. For instance, on a scale from 1 to 10, with 10 being the best, someone may give corn flakes a 4, oranges a 6, and ice cream an 8. We can also have subjective preferences for objective sounds (air). On paper, the musical scores for rap, pop, or classical music are not qualitatively different—they're just selections of notes in different arrangements. However, using the scale from 1 to 10, someone may *dislike* (charged) rap and rate it a 3, but enjoy classical music very much and rate it a 9.

The factor of intensity carried by water and fire is clearly seen in the natural world we inhabit. There are quiet streams and raging seas, moderate climates and blazing hot deserts. These elements may rise to levels of high excitation. The same can be noticed in people. You can sense a marked energetic difference in someone enthusiastic (fire) or sad (water) compared to someone who isn't activated by any charge.

The Charged Elements: Water & Fire

Water is involved with emotional processing. As a yin or receptive element, it takes in all of the stimulation we encounter and stores in the unconscious whatever makes the greatest impact. Just as physical water settles lower compared to what is nonphysical, our emotions settle in us and tend to reside deeper than our awareness (fire). Water motivates behavior from beneath the threshold of awareness, that is, from the unconscious. The development of greater awareness facilitates emotional or spiritual growth in part by making this unconscious material conscious.

Water is potently charged, so emotional management becomes one of the biggest challenges of human life. Identifying, understanding, and using emotional stimuli skillfully is necessary for successful relationships and inner peace. Sometimes what's needed is greater neutrality. People who have a lot of water may have difficulty turning off their emotional faucets and fail to see how full of charge they are. They are prone to being sensitive, insecure, and having large fluctuations in their moods. Water can consume by its power and force when its intensity rises. Our emotional nature could rage like a tidal wave. Other people drown in their sorrow.

As an active or yang element, fire ignites the life force and gets our juices moving. It initiates action, expressing itself as inspiration, enthusiasm, and displays of power. It is daring, prone to thrill seeking, and impulsivity. And due to the range of intensity its charge carries, it can become harmful in excess, manifesting as hot tempered, aggressive, and even brutal.

Fire is the element with the most outward impact. Our first impressions of people are due to the ways they channel fire. As we get to know someone more, we encounter their deeper (water) levels. Fire is overt, while water is more hidden.

The charged elements are responsible for how we really come to know ourselves and others. They create the wide spectrum of human character, desire, preference, and attachments. Life—the joy, the misery, and everything else in between—becomes *meaningful* through the charged elements. With their dynamism and intensity they challenge our growth with necessary evolutionary processes.

The Neutral Elements: Earth & Air

Together, earth and air combine to form our consensus reality. Earth gives us the structure of the physical world, while air pertains to the nonphysical content of the invisible world. Earth is analogous to the skeleton, while air is like the nervous system.

As a neutral and receptive element, earth responds and comes alive when charged energy activates it. Like a lump of clay, it is waiting to be used. Each of us may have a unique relationship to earthy objects. An heirloom owes its sentimental value to the charge carried by water. A temple may become a holy site for a person who brings a fiery charge.

The air element provides spaciousness, inviting movement and novelty. Its apparent emptiness can actually be seen as structural. Just how the notes of a song are given meaning by contrasting with silence, the space between objects allows them to have definition. Without air, there would be no room! Air creates the space for all things to exist in the realm of separateness, and everything has a distinct boundary. Without air, we wouldn't be able to distinguish one thing from another.

To bridge the separation created between humans by air, we communicate and socialize. Sound travels through the medium of air just like neurological information moves speedily across synapses. Air is a spacious expanse for us to move in, while earth is a durable foundation to move on. The neutral elements provide the physical (earth) and nonphysical (air) structures that support the processes of the charged elements.

Charged & Neutral Interactions

There are three possible types of interactions between the elements: charged-charged, charged-neutral, and neutral-neutral. Here we will briefly explore these various combinations as they play out in both the physical and psycho-spiritual realms. In later chapters, this elemental understanding will reveal its full value when applied to the study of astrological aspects.

In terms of addressing the strength of a charge, there is no distinction as to it being "positive" or "negative," or whether it's handled consciously or not. The only concern is its *level of intensity*. When a charge is weak, say a 1 or 2 on a scale from 1 to 10, it's unable to have any staying power. An example would be a conversation between people who have nothing in common. Without the stimulation of interest, they will quickly end the interaction and move onto something more interesting.

A moderate charge (a 5 or 6 on the scale) compels interaction. Here, there is interest and curiosity, a wondering about what else might be in store. An example would be listening to a sales pitch for something we are considering purchasing. There is a willingness to invest some attention to see if the charge could rise to reach a peak, which, in this case, would mean buying the product. Moderate charges are the most prevalent. We generally go through life willing to give interactions and experiences a chance before either moving on and diminishing the charge, or moving further in toward an increase in the charge.

A powerful charge is restless and urgent. It seeks to bring experience to a peak. Imagine a woman who loves the art of Van Gogh. She would be delighted were she to receive an original Van Gogh as a gift. The charge would fly off the chart. She might jump up and down and shout with pleasure. The peak of a charge always includes some form of release. With water, the release is emotional and with fire it's energetic.

Charges are always temporary. Eventually, thrills subside, emotions settle, energy dissipates. It is foolhardy to try to maintain a charge indefinitely because time is the great neutralizing factor. Some charges are as fleeting as a mild arousal while passing an attractive person on the street. Others maintain longer, but they too will eventually subside.

When charged energy is in relationship to other charged energy, there is the most amount of activity. Since levels of intensity (1 through 10) continually fluctuate, this combination is marked by instability. An example of this type of situation occurs on a first date when two people have a moderate charge (let's say 5) about each other. There are a number of possibilities. He may increase his charge (increase to 7) as the evening progresses. His date might match his charge (at 7), which would then encourage and further raise his charge. They might continue to feed off each other's energy and end the night swooning from the pleasure of their time together.

Or, alternatively, his date might feel that his increasing charge is unwanted and hers may decrease. He can maintain his charge and continue pursuing in hopes of elevating hers, or match her at the more reduced level. If he chooses to persist, she may develop a different kind of charge which motivates her to tell him to back off. In response, he might reduce his charge, which would likely lead them to part ways. Charged in relation to charged is like a dance, a process with movement, response and adaptation.

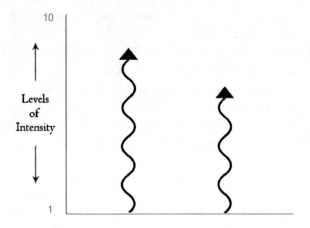

Charged-Charged Interactions

Figure 2

The relationship of the charged elements in nature portrays this wild interplay. An increase in the charge of fire heats water, putting it into motion and raising its charge. The hotter the fire, the more volatile the water becomes. Eventually the building of charges reaches a *peak*—in this case, the water boils.

When water's charge builds, setting it in motion, it is capable of dominating fire. A crew of fire fighters puts out a fire by dispersing water through hoses. In a similar way, emotionally expressive people tend to dominate others through sheer force. Water seeks to make an impact or have its needs met in some climactic way, after which it's better able to settle down. Water added to fire could produce steam, which can actually exaggerate its potential harm.

Fire can also dominate water. With enough intensity, heat will evaporate water. When fire is highly active (as seen in a burning building), it takes time for water to have an effect. This is analogous to the hostile person (fire) who is gradually calmed by the care (water) and attention of a friend or counselor.

36

Although either of the charged elements may dominate the other, the most optimal result is to find a balance between them. Examples include the skillful management of fire and water to cook or to bathe at the best temperature. Just as we continually have to adjust the stove or the faucet settings, finding the right balance between water and fire can be delicate.

Fire brings a *positive* charge to water as it heats and activates it, while water brings a *negative* charge to fire, as it cools and extinguishes it. Again, positive and negative are used in this context not as value judgments, but rather to indicate active (yang) or receptive (yin) energy. Being a physical element, water's absorptive nature adds weight and pulls processes down. Fire's nonphysical quality burns material and rouses energy up.

The dynamic process between the charged elements involves the variable of quantity in addition to intensity. No matter how hot a furnace becomes, if it's thrown into a lake it will fizzle out. No matter the speed or range of water shot from a squirt gun, its quantity is too limited to put out a forest fire.

Interaction between the neutral elements deals with content and structure. One example would be when two computers exchange information about a complicated mathematical problem. There's a lot of activity without any emotion (water) or opinions (fire). There are no hurt feelings (water) or judgments (fire) about the other computer's abilities. One computer doesn't look the other in the eye and say, "I really love working with you; it means so much to me," or "Go get an upgrade if you want to talk to me, you dinosaur!" There is no emotional *process*, just the sharing of content.

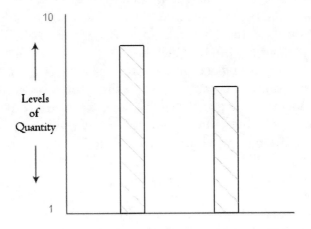

Neutral-Neutral Interactions

Figure 3

Whereas the charged elements may dominate by way of both intensity and quantity, the neutral elements function only in terms of quantity. The neutral-neutral exchange may have disparity based on the amount of *content* each side contributes. For instance, a book can have fifty pages or five thousand. One side of the neutral-neutral interaction may dominate the other through sheer volume. Consider a pot of soil where the amount of earth fills up the entire space. Here, earth dominates air. On the other hand, imagine a solitary planet out in space which is tiny in the broader expanse—air far exceeds earth. In both of these scenarios, there isn't a dynamic process between the neutral elements. They coexist without charges.

38

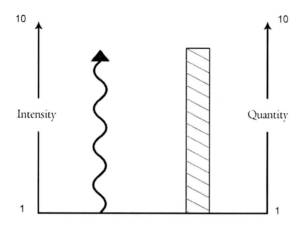

Charged-Neutral Interactions

Figure 4

  Charged in combination with neutral has an entirely different dynamic. In this case, the charged element expresses its intensity in relation to the neutral element which remains stable. There are three possibilities here: 1) The charged element passes a *threshold of intensity* and dominates the neutral; 2) The charged element does not rise in intensity, and the status quo of the neutral element prevails; 3) The charged element rises in intensity to connect with the neutral element on equal terms.

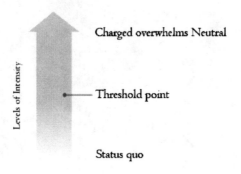

Charged overwhelms Neutral

Threshold point

Status quo

Levels of Intensity

The Threshold Point

Figure 5

In the first instance, a significant charge topples the stability of the neutral status quo. An example would be someone who strongly dislikes the remodeled décor of their cherished house. As their charge rises, it overwhelms the neutral with its force, compelling dramatic and possible destructive changes. Tables might be overturned; curtains could be ripped off the wall. An urgent charge often leads to impulsive behavior.

In the second instance, the status quo prevails. The décor is more or less accepted—there isn't sufficient urgency to instigate any change. The third possible situation is the most complicated. Here the charged element rises in intensity and meets the neutral element in a delicate relationship that is free of any dominance. There is neither the aggression of a dominating charge, nor the static acceptance of a dominating neutral. In this case, the dislike would motivate a person to handle the situation in a level-headed manner.

Again, this dynamic between the charged and neutral elements is seen in nature. With the physical elements, earth sets up a neutral container. Depending on the intensity of charge carried by water, it can settle into the earthy container and rest in stable form. Or it might rise in intensity and disrupt the container. An example of this is seen with a tidal wave. The contours of the land create a

40

structure for water. When the waves become too forceful (increase charge), they encroach and flood an area. When the seas are calm, the earthy status-quo prevails.

In the form of rain, water moves through the air, which holds the space for it to travel. In the event of a hurricane (increase charge), water can dominate this space, essentially using the air to soak everything. When the storm settles, air holds the status-quo of no active charges. When these two elements are in balance, air is the medium that hosts water for evolutionary purpose—rain travels from clouds to the earth to nourish life and then back up as vapor to again form clouds.

Fire has a similar relationship with the neutral elements. Usually the land (earth) isn't actively ablaze (fire). Earth maintains a steady state until a significant charge disrupts it. When a fire continues to build, at some point it will cross the threshold. It will then dominate the land until its power diminishes. Working in harmony, fire and earth are balanced effectively for maximal use. Heat warms the ground, which is then able to sustain plant life.

Air serves as a neutral container for fire to spread. One way to see the dynamic between these two yang elements is through light. Imagine a confined room with no light source—complete darkness. With the introduction of a light source, the air is filled with light, and we are able to see. However, with too much intensity, we are blinded. The fire—here in the form of light—takes over the space until its intensity subsides. When a light bulb burns out (an example of decreasing intensity), the room returns to darkness. In balance, light is neither too bright nor too dim, but rather at a comfortable level which allows us to easily see.

Charged and Neutral Elements in Astrology

Charge and neutrality in the form of process and content, respectively, is found throughout the astrological system in the common groupings of planets, signs, and houses. In order to help discuss each grouping's theme, they are given a voice and a representative statement. Keep in mind that when we interact with the neutral elements, we tend to have charged emotions or opinions *about* them, but this doesn't make them inherently charged.

The charge of Aries, the 1st House, and Mars is quite easily seen within the issue of free will. Behavior is governed by instinct and impulse. We are strongly motivated to satisfy our various hungers. Aries declares, "I will do what I want!" which conveys its desire to live life on its own terms.

In contrast, Taurus, the 2nd House, and Venus are neutral. The theme here pertains to what the self has—its money or belongings. It may say, "I have a house, a car, and $15,000 in my bank account." Although we may have feelings about these things, ownership of items is neutral. The only charge about money is what we add. Remove this added emotion and money is left as just paper; possessions are simply physical items. All of the materials we own belong to the neutral, physical world.

Gemini, the 3rd House, and Mercury are logical, intellectual, and informational. As in the dictionary or the phone book, facts are simply organized. Gemini says, "3 x 4 = 12," a neutral statement void of a charge. We may have favorite numbers, but that's our charge, not theirs.

Cancer, the 4th House, and the Moon's charge is noticed in any feeling state. "I'm fed up with you!" is loaded with an unmistakable emotional quality. The strength of this upset may be mild or strong depending on the person and the situation.

The charge of Leo, the 5th House, and the Sun is evident in the expression of personality. Everyone radiates themselves in a different way. In a moment of delight, Leo may declare, "I'm the king of the world," which has no relevance in consensus reality.

The neutrality of Virgo, the 6th House, and Mercury is apparent in its connection to how things function. The round peg goes in the round hole, not the square one. There is no debate and no charge, unless we inject one. Virgo may say, "Quitting smoking reduces the chances of having a heart attack." This is a scientifically proven fact about health, just the way the world works.

Libra, the 7th House, and Venus are also neutral and relate to the social organization in consensus reality, including customs and norms. Libra could say, "It's conventional for men to propose marriage," a factual statement about our customs. Although the ways in which social realms are organized may change, the organization in itself remains neutral.

The charge of Scorpio, the 8th House, and Pluto are seen in the exchange of emotional truths. "I have strong feelings for you, and I want us to be more intimate" is loaded with personal desire. This theme pertains to our deepest passions, wounds, and interpersonal psychology, all of which are filled with extremely subjective emotional material.

Opinions also have a charged component. Sagittarius, the 9th House, and Jupiter may proclaim, "My religion is the closest to God." There is no consensus here, just a subjective viewpoint. The charge of this theme is also evident in what stimulates the expansion of experience, which is unique to each person. One person has a peak experience sky-diving, while another prefers gardening. We all "get high" in our own ways.

Capricorn, the 10th House, and Saturn's neutrality are seen with physical or structural organization. It may say, "The United States Government is split into executive, legislative, and judicial branches." This compartmentalization creates a neutral framework.

Another type of neutrality is carried by Aquarius, the 11th House, and Uranus. Among many things, the theme here relates to groups, community, or sociology—any large-scale system. You can look at the demographics of a society and see its composition. You can observe the entire cosmos and understand its objective arrangement. Aquarius may calmly assert, "There are forces in nature which form discernable systems."

Pisces, the 12th House, and Neptune territory includes dreams, longings, meditation, and transcendence. As experienced nightly, what happens in a dream is completely unique and will never be understood in consensus reality. This theme also deals with our subjective relationship to spirituality. Pisces sings with sweet emotion that, "Spirit is beautiful."

Regarding the Planets

There are a couple of issues to address with the planets in this method of classification. First, there are six charged planets (Sun, Moon, Mars, Jupiter, Neptune, and Pluto) and four neutral (Mercury, Venus, Saturn, and Uranus). This apparent imbalance is corrected by the fact that Mercury and Venus both rule two signs. Since it's an interconnected system in which planets, signs, and houses all contribute, the ways in which charge and neutrality play out is balanced. Below is a simple graph which illustrates this.

	Neutral		Charged	
Yang	Mercury — Gemini		Mars — Aries	
	Venus — Libra		Sun — Leo	
	Uranus — Aquarius		Jupiter — Sagittarius	
Yin	Venus — Taurus		Moon — Cancer	
	Mercury — Virgo		Pluto — Scorpio	
	Saturn — Capricorn		Neptune — Pisces	

Planet and Sign Organization

Figure 6

Although there is this overall balance, the Sun and Moon, the two central energies in the system, are both charged. What are we to make of this?

Since charge concerns engagement with alive and dynamic process, it must be the primary condition for evolution to proceed. We live in a *participatory* universe. Due to the range and levels of intensity to the charged energies, we are positioned to have a subjective, and therefore meaningful, relationship with the universe. If our fundamental disposition were neutral there would be less individua-

44

tion and uniqueness. Having the Moon and Sun as charged provides us with the optimal situation to further our spiritual growth.

The Moon absorbs and processes experiences. It has to do with the soul's past and is influenced by emotional conditioning. Its charged quality is seen in its reactivity, subjectivity, and the intensity of its emotional needs. We evolve by becoming aware of how we instinctually receive life. Saturn (neutral) is the natural agent of balancing the Moon as seen with the polarity of Cancer/Capricorn. Through experience, maturity, and wisdom (Saturn), we develop the clarity and skill that enables healthy management of our emotions.

Further spiritual development incorporates individual creativity and strength of character, which allows us to grow into ourself in the present (Sun). If the Sun were neutral, we would all converge in conformity. Connected by the polarity between Leo and Aquarius, the Sun has a unique connection with the planet Uranus. This dynamic entails the use of the life force (Sun) as a vehicle for a broader, non-attached truth (Uranus). While the Moon/Saturn dynamic deals with the resolution of prior conditioning, Sun/Uranus moves us toward realizing a new, non-conditioned existence. Uranus is neutral—similar to an astrology chart, it's a set of intentions. Then, the ways in which the life force expresses these intentions is open to endless personal creativity (Sun).

From the geocentric perspective, Mercury and Venus are always seen as near the Sun. This arrangement parallels how their neutral energies accompany and inform our being (Sun), as we connect with others in consensus reality. These inner planets not only orbit nearest the Sun, they each rule two astrology signs. Our connection with consensus reality is so close to us that our inherent charged orientation (the Moon and Sun) naturally and automatically connects with it. It is easy to see how Mercury is a neutral energy, as witnessed in the objectivity of math or science. Venus' neutrality, on the other hand, tends to be more difficult to see.

45

Venus as Neutral

How could Venus, the Goddess of Love and Beauty, be neutral? Isn't Venus passionate, sensual, and seductive? The best way to understand this situation is to think of Venus as a mirror, similar to how the 7th House (the other) mirrors the self. Venus has much to do with projection. What we think we see in others is really parts of ourselves in disguise—our charges come back to us through Venus.

Astronomically, Venus is the closest planet to Earth. It is known as our "sister" planet due to its similar size and close proximity. Because it's so close to us, it's easy and natural for us to charge it with our subjectivity. However, it serves the function of mirroring to us parts of the self we have disowned.

The Libra side to Venus includes aesthetics, ideals, and living in harmonious civility. Concepts of fairness, balance, and diplomacy are untouched by the distortions (charged) of souls learning by trial-and-error. The neutrality of Venus invites us to reach a more refined way of being, to smooth out (or neutralize) our rough edges through engagement. Civilization is the attempt to move beyond the drama of the survival game in which our hair is often on end (charge).

The Taurus side to Venus, the physical world, just is. How we interact with materials, money, and possessions determines their value. Without judgments on our part (charge), the material world is neutral. When we do interact with the physical world through our senses (Venus), we immediately bring our biases. We may be pleased by the delicacy of touching something velvety or the taste of something sweet. These subjective reactions have more to do with the likes and dislikes of the Moon. There are a wide variety of preferences—some like chocolate, while others may prefer vanilla. Since we cannot categorically say that chocolate is preferable to vanilla, then one is not "better" than the other. Therefore, they are neutral, and it is we who determine their worth.

For some reason, the neutrality of Libra and Taurus is more easily understood than that of Venus. The folklore involving this planet of love and beauty really charges us up! When we see that is

46

it our *reaction* to Venus which gets us going (increase charge) then we can appreciate its neutrality.

Renewing the System

This book aims to bring a renewed perspective to the astrological system, one that has a broad and transpersonal relevance. Transpersonal means "beyond the personal," so this perspective is from a removed vantage point. The usual way we engage with astrology is from the ego, and the entire system becomes charged by our participation with it.

If astrology has come this far without the charged-neutral distinction, do we really need it? If we charge everything through participation, why does this categorization even matter?

The charged-neutral division can assist in our philosophical understanding of astrology and the psycho-spiritual realms it describes. Since neutrality vanishes upon interaction, it has been difficult to perceive. The awareness of charge and neutrality allows us to use them both more skillfully. When we notice the interplay between them, we can witness our emotional reactions and desires. Also, we can choose to move into charges with greater awareness of their fleetingness and therefore really appreciate and better navigate them. The increasing intensity of a charge is like an opportunity for a surfer on a wave. Skillfully managing the waves is incredibly advantageous in creating a satisfying life.

Managing charges skillfully helps resolve unprocessed psycho-spiritual material. We can find confirmation for our healing process in the arrival of neutrality. When we no longer get triggered (charge), we can maintain our center. Then, we can *consciously* engage charges instead of unconsciously reacting. Once we attain the knowledge of what charges us, we can choose healthy ways to work with the energy. The neutral-charge distinction gives us a broad perspective; we see more clearly how the personal self is spending so much time and energy in working out the charges of emotions or ego-preferences.

Anything that instigates a charge in us is relevant to our soul, either for the resolution of prior wounding, or by inspiring us

47

to move forward. This program of growth is not about deleting the personal story and all of its charges, but rather about being able to skillfully manage them. The goal is integration and non-attachment—being able to view the personal story from a transpersonal perspective, while also participating in it fully. We can increase our level of joy and appreciation of the subtleties and gifts of all facets of life, both charged and neutral. This elemental division is an additional tool to assist our spiritual growth.

Cyclical Evolution

Chapter 3

The Evolutionary Cycle

We will first discuss evolution in terms of its cyclical motion. Nature is full of cycles. There's the rotation of the Earth which brings us the alternating rhythm of day and night. The Moon travels around the Earth in its monthly dance, while the Earth marches around the Sun in its annual revolution.

Plants burgeon forth in the spring and then either die or go dormant in the frigid winter. As if directed by an internal clock, birds know exactly when to fly south, completely in tune with the cycles in nature. We humans are also intimately connected to nature's cycles, moving through the stages and cycles of life also on a discernable schedule. Of course, all of this activity can be found within the cycles of the planets and is described by the astrology system.

Cyclical evolution is based on time. There is an orderly procession of stages and cycles. Astrology does an impeccable job of describing 12 essential processes which compose a complete cycle of spiritual evolution. These stages constitute a cohesive storyline if the lessons of each are grasped correctly. There is certainly no guarantee that growth will occur through the journey, for that is our responsibility.

In this chapter we'll explore these 12 stages, each of which provides evolutionary opportunities as well as challenges. A keyword will be offered as a way to encapsulate and remember the

51

essence of the various themes. Keep in mind that the complete evolutionary cycle envelops all of life so the selection of a keyword is meant to be only a loose guide. Since the entire dictionary would fit somewhere in the system, these words could not possibly be all-inclusive of the territory of each stage.

The Modalities

Each of the 12 stages has an elemental quality as well as an attunement with one of the modalities (cardinal, fixed, or mutable). The title of each stage consists of its combination of these two variables—*fixed fire* or *mutable water*, for example. The modalities are crucial in understanding the cyclical motion of evolution.

We can conceptualize any event or process as having a beginning, middle, and an end. With a cyclical understanding of nature, endings lead into new beginnings. Spiritual teacher Deepak Chopra has said that if GOD were an acronym, it would stand for "Generation, Organization, and Distribution," which fits precisely with the astrology modalities.

The cardinal modality is the beginning phase of any cycle. It is the generation of energetic direction. Cardinal initiates, insti-gates, and establishes, setting sail with a specific bearing. The cardinal quality *directs* the spiritual work to follow. The cardinal signs of the zodiac are Aries, Cancer, Libra, and Capricorn. These signs respectively concern the establishment of autonomy, family, part-nerships, and career. The development of these areas is necessary in order to have a base of power from which to operate. They are immediate and essential to the human condition and must be addressed before more complex matters.

The fixed modality concentrates and solidifies the power established in the cardinal phase. In this middle phase of the cycle, energy is deepened and given more focus. There is the sensation of slowing down to allow for maximal utility. The fixed modality has the greatest strength and durability. Taurus, Leo, Scorpio, and Aquarius are the fixed signs relating, in order, to personal resources, creative self-expression, interpersonal intimacy and shared re-sources, and a systemic collective vision. All of these areas involve

52

challenges which require sustained investment and persistence. Work performed in the fixed phase creates a sturdy center that eventually leads to a beneficial energetic dispersal in the mutable phase.

The mutable modality carries through with the energy by building bridges and engaging in experience designed to raise consciousness and find some sort of completion. The final stage has an accelerating quality as it leaves behind the stationary energy that preceded it. Mutable prepares for endings and eventual rebirth by maximizing its reach, and have the most variety and possibilities. Gemini, Virgo, Sagittarius, and Pisces are the mutable signs. They represent, in order, the endless realm of ideas, the varieties of earthly manifestation of these ideas, the movement toward meaning and purpose, and the returning to sources of spiritual power by integrating understanding into consciousness.

Combining the four elements with the three modalities results in a rich and complex system of interactions between the stages. In the following chapters, we'll connect the stages together through the various aspects. For now, a discussion of each of these stages sets the scene.

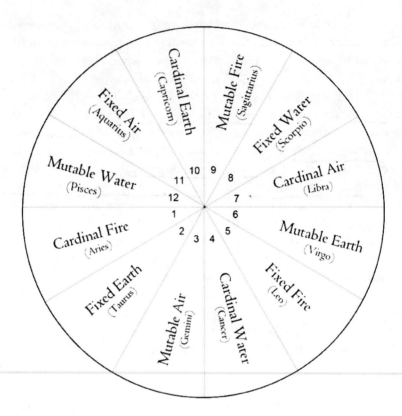

The Astrology Wheel

Figure 7

The Evolutionary Cycle

Stage 1: **Cardinal Fire**

Related Planet, Sign, House: Mars, Aries, 1st House
Evolutionary Task: Developing free will; establishing an orientation to the world; making behavioral decisions.
Hurdles: Behaving unconsciously or without clarity; impulsivity; brashness.
Keyword: Autonomy

The cardinal fire stage is the initiation of the individual into the great evolutionary cycle. Like a newborn emerging from the womb, there is a clear and dramatic new start. However, this new beginning is influenced by what came before. Stage 12 (as we'll see) is where soul experiences are processed and serves the function of a cocoon or chrysalis. A new vision is established in that transpersonal stage, and now it's time to act upon it. As life begins anew, the experiences that came before have been forgotten or at least temporarily hidden in the unconscious. Now there's an upsurge of fiery energy—but how should it be managed?

Enthusiasm exceeds knowledge of how to act at this stage. The cardinal fire quality compels us to go for it and to trust that the momentum being established will work itself out over time. This is the stage where we align with intentions. There is a trial-and-error quality. We figure out our natural behavioral inclinations by seeing how the world responds to us. Ultimately, we learn the best way to *orient* to the surrounding world. Sometimes given the metaphor of the rudder of a boat, the Ascendant (along with Mars and Aries) is how we choose to navigate. This function may behave instinctually, but with greater self-awareness we can learn to direct behavior consciously, increasing our effectiveness in the world.

Stage 1 is selfish by necessity, hungry, and in touch with personal desire. There are correlates to survival and the "fight or flight" response. In the survival-of-the-fittest game, we ensure viability by being up to the tasks at hand. In the broader view, the evolutionary question is whether we are up to *the task of incarnation*. At a fundamental level, we either choose the role of predator pursuing our goals or hindered by indecision and weakness and so become the prey. Choosing unwise areas to exercise these predatory tendencies is a hazard to avoid—we may end up running roughshod over others. We learn as we go, so these experiences do help to calibrate the compass a bit better. This stage is about the willingness to venture forth into the unknown.

So, what do you want to achieve? How potent can you be in that pursuit? How much will behavioral choices further, or sabotage, your aims? What unintended consequences will there be for immature behavior? The arrival of a soul into the personal condition carries significant consequence. The wheels of *samsara* (the cycle of birth, death, and rebirth) are renewed for another lifetime. By embracing our autonomy we see that we are responsible for our actions and our impact on the world.

Cardinal fire is eager and driven. Its restlessness easily propels it into situations which call for improvisation. Analogous to a New Moon, the journey has begun but it's unclear what will happen. The evolutionary cycle begins with an initiating (cardinal) spark (fire) to live it out. As fire pertains to the soul, membership in the evolutionary cycle as an autonomous being originates from spiritual processes beyond our usual comprehension. Trusting that we can develop the awareness to align with soul intentions equips us with the *courage* to proceed.

Without a broader spiritual understanding to inform behavior, it becomes easy to accumulate *karma* (the consequences of our actions) which will eventually have to be addressed. For many, it's unclear what we have gotten ourselves into. This is the universal condition of human evolution—we grow over the course of many lifetimes and learn to balance the energetic books. Stage 1 is a burst of energy fueling us to give it another go.

Stage 2: **Fixed Earth**

Related Planet, Sign, House: Venus, Taurus, 2nd House
Evolutionary Task: Committing to the self; gaining inner peace, self-worth, safety, and security.
Hurdles: Stagnation; indulgence; self-doubt; hoarding; over-simplifying.
Keyword: Resources

It follows that some degree of tranquility is needed to temper the often restless cardinal fire of Stage 1. Solidifying (fixed) available resources and settling (earth) into the self assists in attaining composure. The "dog-eat-dog" quality of the world can be rough. We are supported and bolstered by taking the time to reduce the pulse rate and get in touch with the sensory self. Then, we can decide what is *worth* doing. Finding some inner peace is enormously helpful.

In this stage, soul intentions become more embodied. We accept the strengths and limitations of who we are, and what we have for the evolutionary journey. Fixed earth has the quality of being sturdy. This stage is about responsibility—the *ability to respond* and to do so most effectively. In Stage 2, we ideally develop self-confidence. The inward (yin) movement allows us to be receptive and restful, to establish our resolve.

Owning things can be part of securing an inner foundation. When we are fortified with enough resources (money, possessions, know-how, confidence) we feel prepared to meet challenges. This stage is about preparation and having all available resources organized for maximal usefulness. Success here includes conquering self-doubt, spending money wisely, and gaining a sense of security. One common pitfall is the temptation to hoard resources or inflate the importance of money due to self-doubt. We can also get caught in stagnation and self-indulgence. It can be easy to fall into the trance of believing we are only physical beings. We then become stuck (fixed earth) in the drama of our life situation and over-identify with our bodies and possessions.

The evolutionary task of Stage 2 is to develop a solid commitment to the self. This investment makes us unperturbed by the challenges which lie ahead. We know full well that we can handle anything and that there is no need to worry. Poor navigation of this terrain results in an insecure base of operations for the rest of the evolutionary cycle. On the other hand, whatever is properly "earthed" in this stage becomes a fixed sense of who we are and what we're capable of.

Fixed earth solidifies spiritual intent in the body, grounds us in this life, and compels us to show up. Resistance to this process creates some form of insecurity: anxiety, self-doubt, dissociation. If we can be rooted in trusting who we are and what we have, we venture forth willingly, with openness and curiosity.

57

Stage 3: **Mutable Air**

Related Planet, Sign, House: Mercury, Gemini, 3rd House
Evolutionary Task: Forming hypotheses; gathering knowledge and experience.
Hurdles: Confusion; overstimulation; becoming trapped in logic; over-promoting/over-attachment to intellect.
Keyword: Mind

Part of being human is learning about the circumstances we find ourselves in. This is the terrain of Stage 3, which addresses the development of the intellect. The first two stages orient us to our biological awareness, first in the outer world and then the inner. Now, we have access to a dizzying array of new stimuli which stimulates cognitive development. In this phase we study the environment around us in a more refined way as we move away from Aries the Ram and Taurus the Bull and their more primal energies.

The mutable modality is the most diffuse and flowing. Similarly, the air element is unrestrained and open. Mutable air produces the combination most interested and open to new experiences. It is curious about everything and lacks any judgment about what it learns. There is no end to the human mind's fascination. It is full of questions and hypotheses. Here we learn to orient our minds to the immediate environment and develop our unique style of perception.

Mutable air uses logic and reason to form an approach to the world. However, this stage is still early (the 3rd of 12), so it's unsure of what to do with its knowledge at this point. Confusion arrives when ideas substitute for actual experience. Reading an informative book is far different from directly experiencing the subject matter. One hazard of this stage is being pedantic—having knowledge but lacking wisdom. In this stage, we are *students of life*, and it's appropriate to question and wonder. Forming conclusions is premature.

The purpose of Stage 3 is to bask in youthful fascination and figure out what we're interested in. We can then begin to approach the world from a place of conscious choice rather than merely strategizing for survival. We step into our uniquely human position of having advanced intellects and begin the process of maturation that follows. When we begin to see how wide open life really is we become stimulated to grow. In this stage, we may become aware of the immensity of the existential situation we are in.

The modern mind tends to think that education can prepare us for anything. However, this view overlooks the fact that the present builds from the behaviors of the past—there are karmic consequences to what we do and to what we did. Without this view of soul evolution, the possibilities of mutable air can persuade us that developing the intellect is the singular formula for success. However, the pursuit of mastering nature through the mind may actually be a trap that binds us in the egoic prison of the separate self. In this stage we can become intellectually convinced that humans control nature instead of seeing that we are a part of it.

In order to learn the lessons of this stage we must refuse the tendency to grant authority to the mind's limited knowledge. Remaining open-minded allows us to discover what our souls intend for us to do in this life. Along the way we can enjoy our sense of wonder at everything there is to learn. As the evolutionary cycle continues, our curriculum next takes us inward.

Stage 4: **Cardinal Water**

Related Planet, Sign, House: Moon, Cancer, 4th House
Evolutionary Task: Developing awareness of soul and its patterns; connecting with and establishing family; deepening emotionally.
Hurdles: Regression; hiding; any harmful influences from family; enmeshment.
Keyword: Heart

On the astrology wheel, this stage is at the bottom. It's the anchor that roots us. Initially, we might think that this stage should come first in the evolutionary cycle since family seems to be our initial orientation to this world. However, in an evolutionary sense, it's 4th because we must first have self-orientation and the ability to think before we can understand our roots. The first 3 stages address the evolutionary goal of personal differentiation, a necessary gathering of experience that serves as a precursor to deepening. Stage 4 gets us in touch with the soul condition, the *familiar* themes of evolution—and these are played out in *family*.

None of us have completed our soul growth. We make contact with much of the spiritual curriculum of our current lifetime in the emotional dynamics of our early home life. This curriculum stems from the soul's attachments and unfinished business in prior lives. The role we play in our families often illustrates these unfinished, unconscious themes. Ideally, experiences are *processed through* to completion—emotions released, misguided beliefs corrected, lessons learned—and the experience is left in the past. Any leftover material remains in the unconscious, and it must eventually be addressed. In Stage 4, we get our wake-up call.

In this stage we have the opportunity to touch in with the unprocessed hurt or pain in the soul. The cost of not doing so is to blindly repeat old dynamics that preclude further growth. This can be a very challenging stage, as the pull of past conditioning is very strong.

Developing "heart" involves the nurturance of love that family ideally provides. It also involves the evolutionary task of developing awareness about our spiritual vulnerabilities, which provides the impetus to vigorously pursue (cardinal) emotional growth and spiritual healing (water). Successful navigation of Stage 4 can result in self-knowledge and an authenticity that gives us a stable internal foundation. It's up to us to move out from its sheltering—and potentially inhibiting—familiarity so that we can individuate into our full and unique selves.

Cardinal water is a powerful combination as it initiates the flow towards wholeness. From the evolutionary view, it is the personal heart, in all of its beautiful incompleteness, which reincarnates for further development. Cardinal water bonds us to the self, our loved ones, and ultimately the wider world. When we agree to feel, we can move forward from a place of integrity towards novel things which enliven us.

Stage 5: **Fixed Fire**

Related Planet, Sign, House: Sun, Leo, 5th House
Evolutionary Task: Experiencing and expressing joy, our unique personality, and the social self; participation.
Hurdles: Self-absorption; naïveté; untamed or extravagant behavior; hedonism.
Keyword: Character

Building from an emotional foundation, the momentum of the cycle moves to finding uniqueness in the radiance of the present. Stage 5 addresses the specialness of individuality. If the 4th stage is like a seed, the 5th is akin to the flower. Here we enter the social dialogue in a distinctive way. No longer preoccupied with survival or our roots, the movement is toward enjoyment and basking in the goodness of life.

Recreation provides the opportunity to learn about personal preferences, to follow our whims in the exuberance of the moment. In Stage 5 we try things on (sometimes literally) to see what we like. Developing a unique personality and a social self allows us to meet life on our own terms. We learn to show up in the present moment with our full vitality, spontaneity, and trust in life. Ideally we become thrilled to be alive, which motivates us to eventually deliver our unique gifts most radiantly.

The fixed quality of Stage 5 concerns the development of character, which becomes strong and enduring. Having some degree of charisma or radiance gives potency to the life force. We make a compelling impact when a solid sense of self-awareness is cultivated. In Stage 1, we feel the fire of the individual spark. In Stage 5 we have the poise and strength to show it to others.

If Stage 4 was poorly managed, if we haven't sufficiently contacted and processed our emotional terrain, then Stage 5 is approached unconsciously. Our behavior may become wild; we tend to "act out" inappropriately. This me-first orientation naturally finds outlets in the extraverted 5th Stage, sometimes in overcompensating or hedonistic ways. Fixed fire offers the greatest sense of sheer recreational release in the cycle thus far, so we need to be aware of the tendency to get carried away. Another struggle in this stage is to shy away from life and remain contracted. This protective stance could inhibit the expression needed in future relational and vocational endeavors.

This stage has correlates to children, both in terms of being one as well as having them. The broader purpose is to renew a sense of purity and gratitude for life. We can enjoy the simple things and take some time just to enjoy being alive. This renewal and fresh appreciation for life supports us as we move on to face the trials of maturation that follow.

Fixed fire suggests the eternal nature of Spirit. It may seem like a contradiction that this stage deals with the development of an impermanent character in a fleeting lifetime. But this is where the magic happens. At the spiritual level, our presence in the drama of life resonates forever. When we see that our radiance bridges the worlds of separation and unity, we accept our roles as powerful collaborators in the glorious dance of evolution. With this knowledge, we become aware of and deeply inspired to graciously contribute our unique gifts.

Stage 6: **Mutable Earth**

Related Planet, Sign, House: Mercury, Virgo, 6th House
Evolutionary Task: Passing social tests; developing skills, expertise, and routines; maturing.
Hurdles: Subservience; ineffectuality; health issues; anxiety.
Keyword: Competence

While the fixed modality carries a concentrated energy, the mutable modality enjoys diversity. Apply that to earth and the result equals endless possibilities of ways to manipulate the tangible world. Imagine the various ways someone can work with a lump of clay or a pile of lumber. Stage 6 involves skill-development and mastering a trade. It is also a relational stage, though the types of relations here are purposely unequal: a master teaches an apprentice, or a technician assists a client.

Ultimately, this stage is about maturation. While Stage 5 can feel like childhood, Stage 6 correlates to adolescence when we are tested and pay our dues. Social interactions often have a feel of measuring ourself in relation to others and jockeying for status. The next stage concerns equality, but Stage 6 is organized hierarchically, how we position ourselves in the social pecking order. The first earth stage (Stage 2) offered the test of self-worth. The challenge here applies to our efficacy in social situations. Negotiating unequal relationships such as rankings in peer groups, starting at the lowest position in a new job, or learning a skill from an instructor allows the developing self to learn by example. We figure out ways to improve our standing, to develop and demonstrate competence.

Stage 6 asks us to take the necessary steps to ensure that the soul is healthy, viable, adept at the details of daily living and dedicated to improvement. There may be trials and tribulations in health, social, and skill-development areas to get a soul focused on its development. Successful management of these lessons allows us to proceed to the next stage feeling capable and able to connect with others on equal terms.

Mutable earth pertains to the variety of earthy ways in which we can utilize Spirit. We have yet to scratch the surface of what is possible on this planet. This stage has to do with the ingenuity, methods, and mastery that display the precision of Spirit as it is expressed through our hands. Selecting the proper craft, service, or skill to perfect helps distribute (mutable) creative impulses tangibly (earth).

Without the knowledge that we serve as Spirit's hands, we are prone to stay in immature patterns. A pitfall here is selecting a trade or skill which is irrelevant to our growth such as mastering video games or the fine points of emulating celebrities. This is a critical phase which prepares us for more worldly participation. Staying in adolescent routines or underachievement keeps the entire world from evolving. When we mature, we are able to enter the world ready for more sophisticated socialization and adult connections.

Stage 7: **Cardinal Air**

Related Planet, Sign, House: Venus, Libra, 7th House
Evolutionary Task: Participating in social culture; forming partner-
ships; cultivating interdependence.
Hurdles: Co-dependence; orbiting around others; phoniness; pro-
jection.
Keyword: Relationship

When we reach Stage 7 half of the cycle is complete. The
latter 6 stages are more publicly-focused and increasingly concern
worldly issues. The processes that relate to self-orientation (Stages
1-3), and learning of the self in youthful arenas (Stages 4-6), now
give way to mature connecting. The first stage of this hemicycle is
cardinal air: the initiation of relationships. These relationships
include marriage and other romantic connections based on interdependence, but also business partnerships, significant social contacts,
personal friends, and any important "other" where there is mutual
support.

We form these relationships in order to build a social foundation that supports evolution in public spheres. A spouse or life
partner ideally serves to buttress our continued spiritual advancement. Friends, social contacts, and other associations help us
broaden the scope of our potential impact through involvement and
networking. Learning the skills of refined socialization (being able
to schmooze a bit), allows us to enter the prevailing social culture.
In this stage, we learn to see clearly (air) the ways to join with others
in creating civility. We learn of the social interdependence which
unifies civilization.

We move beyond the self by forming associations based on
equality and diplomacy. If the prior stage (6) was managed well, we
emerge into the world relatively polished and eager for socializing.
If not, then insecurity is injected into associations in the form of co-
dependence, focusing on trying to please others, phoniness. The
hazard of relinquishing our individual power to a marriage, or
another form of relationship, is that it may undercut the collec-
tively-focused evolutionary processes awaiting us in subsequent

stages. Ideally, this stage sets our orientation to the public world and provides a springboard for our contribution to it.

Cardinal air gifts us with the beginning of perspective. From the spiritual view, this could mean really getting it that we are connected to others. The term "sacred mirrors" has been used to describe this interconnectedness. From the perspective of oneness, others are a part of us. This is usually hidden by the more obvious and superficial relative vantage point. A lesson of Stage 7 is to treat others like ourselves, because that is exactly what they are.

If we don't integrate this spiritual perspective, we play out the drama of our separate selves—the ego dream—in our relationships. We may see things as unfair, the "other" as somehow wronging us in some way. The parts of us that we do not own are projected, which may eventually lead to working through the underlying psychological dynamics in Stage 8.

In Stage 7, the context of relationships is established: the terms of connecting, expectations, and style of communication. This is the first stage which tests our maturity in worldly realms. The relationships that will become instrumental for more advanced growth are established (cardinal) here. Navigated well, we are ready to handle a deeper level of process.

Stage 8: **Fixed Water**

Related Planet, Sign, House: Pluto, Scorpio, 8th House
Evolutionary Task: Developing facility with interpersonal processes; sharing resources; attending to reproduction and death.
Hurdles: Everything abusive and underhanded we do to each other; perpetuating our own misery.
Keyword: Power

Stage 8 is a crucial test designed to weed out anything that inhibits us from claiming our authentic power. Interpersonal in focus, it's about how we make an impact on each other. These energetic exchanges help us become conscious of our underlying psychological landscape: our desires, motivations, and blind spots. Whereas Stage 7 mirrors (air) who we are, Stage 8 involves doing the emotional work to reach greater wholeness.

65

There are two ways to deal with the reflection of self provided by others. The first is to fail to recognize ourself in it. We then view our partners in a negative light, and some form of tug-of-war ensues. Stage 8 deals with all the various ways in which we struggle with others in the pain of developing greater awareness. On the way, our shadow material involving dramas of manipulation, abuse, and secret-keeping tend to be on full display.

The more mature way to manage this stage is to take what we perceive as distasteful in the other and find it within ourself. Once we see that the psychological dynamics involved are necessary and helpful for growth (rather than a pain to deal with), our prospects to work through issues are far better. It's possible to use connections as important catalysts, like a necessary lancing of wounds to release energy and heal the soul.

By doing this deep inner work we become able to contribute to evolution from a place of wisdom. This stage is often associated with death, which can be literal, but more often this applies to the parts of us that need to die in order for us to evolve. This type of psychological death brings with it a rebirth. Poor management of this stage results in playing out our unaddressed wounding in public arenas.

Fixed water addresses emotional connections which have a lasting impact. The first water stage (4) dealt with our roots, our biological inheritance. In Stage 8, we may reproduce and further these genetic bonds. Reproduction involves the exchange of fluids (water) and requires sustained emotional investments (fixed). Sexuality and deep emotional exchanges lead to the most meaningful levels of bonding, regardless of the choice to have children. Stage 8 is a relentless confrontation (fixed) with the psychology of the soul (water).

This stage asks us to create satisfying intimacy, which sets the stage for the deepest learning in the interpersonal arenas. We gain greater self-knowledge along with its attendant responsibilities. And we confront realities of soul wounding in need of healing. We learn what we are capable of, both for good or ill. The evolution available is nothing less than ridding the forces of stagnation or regression which hold us back from our highest potential. Successful management of this stage readies us to broaden and develop a specific purpose.

Stage 9: **Mutable Fire**

Related Planet, Sign, House: Jupiter, Sagittarius, 9th House
Evolutionary Task: Developing our belief system; life mission; collective orientation.
Hurdles: Righteousness; aimlessness; missionary zeal; narrow life path.
Keyword: Direction

After the confrontation with our shadow and the wisdom gained through interpersonal bonding, we're rightfully interested in expanding into the world. The degree of readiness to address global issues is determined by how consciously the previous stage was navigated, but evolution proceeds regardless. Ideally, a life mission germinates from the depths (Stage 8) and is ignited by the fire of purpose.

Stage 9 begins the process of using the individual self as a vessel for collective evolution. As in Stage 3, there is an expansion of experience and discovery, but now we learn to focus on specific goals—to see how our purpose can fit into the bigger picture of evolutionary unfolding. Therefore, we address a larger vision of life, eternal questions, and the cosmos as a whole. Traveling through this stage requires that we figure out what we believe in and what we want to dedicate our life to.

Our experience in Stage 8 strongly impacts our journey here. At the extreme of having mismanaged the previous stage, we can be unconsciously stuck in a hellish existence and unwittingly bring others into it. This drama may take the form of becoming a mouthpiece for dogma and embodying the very things that have hurt us. Ideally, the uplifting expansiveness that is available in this stage can help free us of these dynamics.

Mutable fire pertains to the variety of ways to discover the great reach of Spirit. Broadening our horizons in fiery ways can be accomplished in many forms. We might undertake physical travel, study some form of higher learning, or develop our intuitive skills.

The ultimate goal here is to find a true spiritual path to travel. The mutable quality calls for adaptations on this path as we continually gain more experience.

Many of us get caught up in expansive experiences; we become the constant travelers, the excited adventurers, and the endless spiritual seekers. There may be great reward in these pursuits, but the 9th Stage is not the final destination. If we become enamored with experiences that have no utility we may drift aimlessly as a nomad or proceed through life without any real conviction. We can fail to see that the life journey sometimes requires times of industriousness, responsibility, and tough choices.

On the other hand, we may become narrow and rigid about the spiritual path during this stage. A navigational error here is to believe that everyone else should adhere to a particular life direction. Lots of time and energy is then spent justifying this decision and convincing others of its merit. Instead of using the path to inform our life's contribution, we become obsessively identified with our guiding belief system and miss out on the mutable, joyous quality of this stage of discovery.

Mutable fire invites us to have a broad vision and conception of spirituality. Stage 9 can be a thrilling ride of awakening which informs an understanding of this life. Experiences can be used as fuel for a vocational contribution. We become inspired to build on what is discovered, making our work a reflection of uplifting and meaningful experiences and knowledge.

Stage 10: **Cardinal Earth**

Related Planet, Sign, House: Saturn, Capricorn, 10th House
Evolutionary Task: Responding to our calling; doing our true work; claiming authority.
Hurdles: Excessive control and self-promotion; selling out.
Keyword: Vocation

By following personal purpose in alignment with soul intent, we become poised and eager to tangibly contribute to society. In this stage we get in touch with our personal calling and feel a healthy responsibility to it. We need discipline and commitment to give a mature articulation to this calling. We have to put aside any and all distractions that prevent us from rising to the challenge here. Movement from the right side of the wheel (stages 4-9), to the left (stages 10-3) correlates with the return back to self-orientation and personal focus.

Stage 10 is the pinnacle of achievement—the proverbial climb up the mountain or ladder of success in order to reach the summit. Ideally, we become an authority in our professional niche. Every astrology chart points out a set of specific skills and intentions. In this stage we hammer our unique contribution into form. We attain stature in a field and make a significant impact on collective evolution.

This stage carries the energy of cardinal earth, which pairs initiation with the material world. It is authoritative and secure with executive power. Ideally, we handle our worldly roles from a place of integrity. No matter what occupation we choose, we can bring a well-rounded, experienced, and astute vocational offering which stems from our personal growth. The archetype of the "Elder" belongs to this stage, and elders have deep sources of wisdom.

An immature response to the terrain here can harden the fiery passion of Stage 9. Career and social institutions then become the areas in which unfinished, and possibly hurtful processes, are expressed. In this case, we would engage with our vocation as a means to get on a soap box and errantly distribute a misguided agenda. Or we might see career solely as a way to make money or get ahead of others. We would attempt to bolster our deficient self-esteem by becoming controlling, worried about reputation, and continually competing for selfish gain.

Cardinal establishes while earth is structural. This stage is about the tangible creation of social organization, the infrastructure and glue of society. When people join with a common calling, the organization of society houses and reflects this cohesiveness. Cardinal earth is analogous to the skeleton—the bare bones which supports everything.

On the astrology wheel, Stage 10 is located at the zenith. Instead of pointing up and away to transcend the day-to-day, the spiritual meaning is to bring our cosmic nature down and create a

69

spiritual village here. Cardinal earth wants to take the expansive discoveries of Stage 9 and organize them in a worldly way. In Stage 10 we contract, or concretize, an inspired plan.

If this stage is navigated well, career is motivated by our care for collective humanity. We are inspired to use our stature and influence for the common good. We naturally move towards networking and connecting with the broader world family to bring about global changes.

Stage 11: **Fixed Air**

Related Planet, Sign, House: Uranus, Aquarius, 11th House
Evolutionary Task: Tapping into global interconnectivity; claiming the future; embracing change; cultivating allies.
Hurdles: Anonymity; impotence; group-think.
Keyword: Systems

Stage 11 begins the descent down from the pinnacle of the wheel. The manifestation of the personal contribution in Stage 10 gives way to the collective consciousness. The personal self is no longer the focus as collective membership in humanity and progress assume priority. The self was part of oneness the whole time. Now this reality has the potential to be fully integrated consciously. Outward activity here includes networking, building community, and using the stature attained in the previous stage to advocate progressive causes.

This terrain of Stage 11 can be visualized as concentric circles, similar to how rings surround the bull's-eye on a target. Encircling the individual is an immediate group—such as close friends or some sort of fellowship. Moving outwards there are acquaintances and audiences at the next layer, followed then by more distant allies. The outermost rings of the target include society and the global community all the way out to the edges of the solar system, and finally to the farthest reaches of the universe itself. At each of these levels, the social and intellectual (air) culture is organized as a system. Navigating Stage 11 well equates to not only contributing to the healthy functioning of systems, but also to achieving a broader,

70

more cosmic understanding of our place within the larger organization of life and reality.

Fixed air pertains to the interconnected web of energy that connects us all. This web has no beginning or end—it is the eternal intelligence of Spirit. This stage has much to do with the view that we are all made of Spirit, and we're all in this together. Personal concerns for recognition or gain can actually impede the progress toward reaching a vision of our shared interconnectedness. In Stage 11 we are willing to give what we've accomplished as an investment in collective and/or transpersonal causes. The self, having progressed through all its growth up to this point, is now properly used as an impersonal vessel for evolution.

Many people struggle with transcending personal concerns, which makes this stage difficult. The beginning of the dissolution of our strictly personal identity can easily leave us feeling anonymous, marginal, or disoriented. There is the potential to succumb to group-think or become a cog in a system. If we attempt to hold on to the past (an outmoded paradigm, career position, or legacy), there is the potential for great upset and interpersonal challenge as the times have now shifted. If we remain egocentric here, we can become very angry at the world and actually want to sabotage other people's attempts at furthering collective advancement. The ostentatious person who refuses to recycle or reduce his carbon footprint is one example.

This stage inspires us to claim the future. We all do our personal part (thinking globally, acting locally) to live in maximal accordance with nature. Worn-out structures and paradigms are demolished to make way for new innovations. Technological breakthroughs (such as the Internet) and a broad conception of our shared evolutionary predicament join us together. The world becomes plugged into a new reality. We realize that we are like nerve-endings in a magnificent intelligence which both envelops and transcends us.

Fixed air relates to the eternal nature of evolution itself. The mind (air) that envelops us is everlasting (fixed). Spirit will endlessly renew itself. In Stage 11, we may consciously contribute to this sweeping project of Spirit realizing itself. Through the joining of

71

individuals, the world strives to reach interconnectivity. It can be thrilling to live this out consciously. Done well, we move towards the realization of heaven on Earth.

Stage 12: **Mutable Water**

Related Planet, Sign, House: Neptune, Pisces, 12th House
Evolutionary Task: Realizing heaven on earth; bringing things to an end; cleansing; developing compassion.
Hurdles: Holding on to the personal story; disorientation; sorrow; confinement.
Keyword: Mysticism

Stage 12 completes the cycle. Mutable water is where everything is ultimately dissolved and returns to Spirit. Personal attachments are released, and there is a complete immersion into the collective consciousness. We process our journey of incarnation, reflecting on everything that has occurred. We thus become prepared for a new cycle that builds on what has been learned. This stage has the role of finishing the current cycle and also envisioning the next.

Stage 12 is the fruition of what has come in the previous 11 stages, for better or for worse. Like the prior stage, it's an area where we can impact the collective consciousness in a *selfless* way. If evolution has proceeded optimally, this stage is the realization of heaven on earth. A utopian vision reaches its endpoint—life is lived with full consciousness and humanity is healed. Of course, this is the ideal and is rarely manifested. This stage shows us where we have fallen short or missed the mark. It also delivers the karmic consequences for unconscious and harmful behaviors.

Traditionally associated with sorrow and pain, this stage can be experienced like a holding cell or being in our "soul cage." We can't escape who we are or what we've done. It gets reflected to us through others, the world itself, or in dreams. All of this is the unconscious trying to get our attention. Stage 12 is about processing, feeling, and ultimately releasing the impact of the dramas that we have created and absorbed.

Associated with water, this stage deepens our spiritual understanding. All the various lessons are seen as having been necessary, resulting in compassion and gratitude. There are tears shed for what needs to be let go of. There is a special connection between this stage and the next—Stage 1—where the cycle begins anew. This connection is like an interface between the collective and the personal, an open channel of dialogue between the self and Spirit in order to review the lessons learned (and not learned) along our journey of personal evolution.

If we resist the ending of the cycle, we set ourself up for the perpetuation of existential pain. Mutable water requires that we flow and release attachments. And if we don't cooperate, we're sure to lose our bearings and become disoriented. This is the realm of ghosts or other beings who are trapped between the worlds.

For those able to swim in these currents, the 12th Stage offers a variety of opportunities for spiritual growth in the development of mysticism. Any spiritual practice which loosens the ego and orients consciousness in the transpersonal direction qualifies. Meditation, yoga, dreamwork, rituals, and ceremonies are some examples. Handled with proficiency, the self is able to powerfully channel or radiate Spirit and increasingly become a form of the yogi or master.

Mutable water indicates the quality of Spirit's nourishment—flowing everywhere, without limitations, distinctions, or judgments. The abundance of Spirit's love and compassion is universally available to the extent that we can drop our resistance to it. Ultimately, we are able to experience this level of intimate interconnectedness. Everything enters the flow of the river which returns to Source. The 12th Stage dissolves the personal story—a surrender in order to rejoin with oneness.

Sequence of the Stages

The motion of the evolutionary cycle follows this rhythm: fire (charged), earth (neutral), air (neutral), and water (charged). There is the alternation of yang (fire, air) and yin (earth, water); and there is a pattern of charged-neutral-neutral-charged. Usually just

73

the yin-yang motion is noted, but the additional charged-neutral dimension gives added perspective to the unfolding evolutionary dance.

The cycle starts with an upsurge of energy (Aries, 1st, charged), moves to solidifying, calming, and securing (Taurus, 2nd, neutral), learning through choices and action (Gemini, 3rd, neutral), and then integrating and processing (Cancer, 4th, charged). There are 3 repetitions of this 4-part advancement: individual, social, and collective. The alternation of yang and yin provides the cadence of breathing in and out as the stages advance. Instead of a simple alternating of charged and neutral, charged processes are at the beginning and end of each 4-part (fire, earth, air, water) sequence. Fire with its positive charge always begins, while water, with its negative charge, comes at the end. What goes up must eventually come down. In between, we are involved in practical (earth) and learning (air) issues on our way toward integrating lessons. With successful evolutionary movement, there's deepening (water) before further advancing (fire).

Chapter 4

Aspects & Evolution Part I
Oppositions & Trines

The Evolutionary Cycle portrays the stages of spiritual growth, from personal to social to collective in a circular pattern. Ideally, consciousness develops with each run through the cycle, and so when we return to Stage 1 we do so at a higher level of evolution. The growth process, therefore, brings in the vertical axis as well as the horizontal, creating the shape of an ascending spiral rather than a flat circle. This evolutionary movement is an eternal process, a blueprint for our spiritual experience.

These next chapters will address how the various stages interact with each other. In addition to the cyclical movement from Stage 1 to 12, each of the stages has a series of different connections with the rest of the system. Instead of using the term "stages" at this point, we'll often use the associated signs as familiar shorthand.

Using simple geometry, the circle of the zodiac can be cut into pieces like a pie. The divisions of the pie represent evolutionary lessons. The fewer the cuts of the pie, the more basic or fundamental the lessons are. And as the pie is cut into more pieces, the lessons become more advanced or, in some cases, more peripheral. In these next chapters, we'll address the division of the pie into 2, 3, 4, and 6 sections which correspond respectively to the opposition, trine, square, and sextile. For reasons which will become clearer as we go, the quincunx will also be addressed.

The discussion here looks at *pure* aspects, which occur naturally between the various stages. For instance, Aries is opposite Libra. In an actual chart, though, there can be an opposition between a planet in early Aries and one in late Virgo. These "over the sign" aspects will not be addressed.

This presentation aims for a "big picture" view of the astrological system. The focus is on the *general* evolutionary purposes of the interchanges. *It is not designed to be directly applied to chart analysis.* In natal charts, all the information is specific to the individual's unique soul condition. Natal charts have many aspects, and therefore many lessons being simultaneously addressed. Just as we are more than our Sun sign, so too are we more than any particular aspectual interchange. We are the sum of many parts.

There are four issues to address for each of the various aspects. First, what is the *evolutionary purpose* of the exchange? Second, what is the *shadow* possibility? This is different than simply failing to take advantage of the evolutionary gift. It's a darker, often twisted, use of the energy that leads to problems and devolution. Third, what happens if *one side dominates* the other and, lastly, the situation created when the other side dominates?

Aspects

The first aspect is the *conjunction*, which only involves one stage. Therefore, it's concentrated in a particular evolutionary process, and is the most basic of the aspects. When two planets are in a conjunction, they strongly energize one of the stages, but there is no interrelating with any other stage. The relevant information, therefore, has already been discussed in the previous chapter.

The *opposition* cuts the pie in half, forming polarities, or dualities. The oppositions reveal six fundamental balancing acts which catalyze universal issues. Traditionally considered a "hard" aspect, there is a dramatic tension with the opposition—the continuum of possible expression here includes a tug-of-war struggle on the one end, and a cooperative coming together on the other. The paired signs always share the same modality. Like two people vying for the same role, there is competition. When aspects feature

76

differing modalities, the respective sides have different roles, which produces cooperation.

The neutral-charged elemental division presented earlier springs into action with the opposition. Since the earth signs oppose the water signs, and air signs oppose fire signs, an opposition always feature a charged element opposed a neutral one. This aspect provides the clearest illustration of how the delicate balancing act of charged and neutral actually plays out.

The neutral element sets up a status quo, or consensus reality, with which the charged element interacts. If the status quo is acceptable, the charged element complies and doesn't see the necessity to overturn it. If it is deemed unacceptable, the charged element rises in intensity and overpowers the neutral element. This dominance throws the opposition out of balance which then requires further process or negotiations to reach a resolution. Ultimately, a balance between the two sides is necessary to learn the evolutionary lesson.

The *trine* is the next division. When the pie is divided into three sections, personal, social, and collective themes interact with each other in supportive and harmonious ways. Trines always occur between signs of the same element, but of differing modality. Classically, it's considered a "soft" aspect because there is no crisis or urgency here. Rather, there is great potential for collaboration.

Cutting the pie into quarters yields the *square*. This "hard" aspect has an ominous reputation. Squares always involve the same modality. As seen with the opposition, this involves a clashing of wills. Furthermore, a yin sign (earth, water) is always square a yang (air, fire), which also introduces a frictional component. Squares relate to more advanced lessons, and their friction or discord helps catalyze dramatic spiritual evolution. Using the charged-neutral elemental classification, there are actually three distinct types of squares (charged-neutral, neutral-neutral, and charged-charged), each of which will be reviewed in detail.

The *quintile*, a relevant and compelling aspect, takes the shape of a star when the 360 degree circle is divided into five sections of 72 degrees. This aspect is the wild card, as it is the first instance in which the segments do not divide cleanly by the number

77

12. It may point to an intelligent order beyond our usual perception, asking us to go beyond what is neat and familiar in order to see other patterns. Many astrologers ignore this aspect, but as five comes before six, the quintile may be more fundamental than the sextile. Discussing it in detail, though, poses a significant problem. With 72-degree sections, we cannot discuss the quintile in connection to the signs. The quintile pertains to genius, paradox, and things that evade easy categorization. It points us in the direction of transcendence and mysticism. The planet Uranus and the sign Aquarius would be the most relevant correlations to this confounding aspect. Unfortunately, the quintile is too complex to adequately include in this book.

The *sextile* divides the circle into sixths and forms a hexagram. Like the trine, it's a "soft," or supportive aspect. It connects earth to water (yin-yin) or air to fire (yang-yang). The hexagram surrounds, rather than runs through the center of the circle, so it can be construed as a peripheral aspect. Its energy deals with forming alliances and providing assistance. It's usually seen as stimulating and simplistic, but when the charged-neutral dynamic is added, it takes on greater complexity. Finally, we'll review the *quincunx*, which emerges as a fascinating aspect that has great evolutionary import. Additionally, more complex aspect configurations are later presented in the Appendix.

As with the evolutionary cycle, there is a keyword given for each aspect. These words are not meant to be definitive or comprehensive. Rather they are suggestions that represent a sort of snapshot of the aspect's essence.

Oppositions

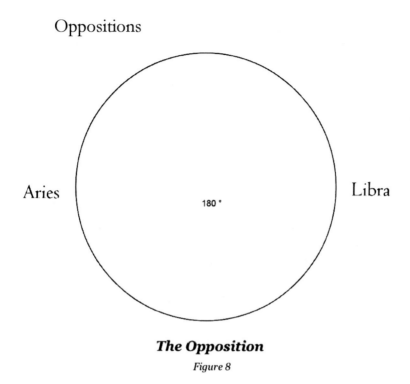

Aries   Libra

180°

The Opposition

Figure 8

Aries opposite Libra

Cardinal fire opposite cardinal air. This opposition deals
with the fundamental tension between self (Aries) and other (Libra).
Aries is assertive and self-orientated. The check on its impulsiveness
is Libran social norms and concern for others. Libra also includes
laws, which are often necessary to curb Aries imprudence. When
laws are broken, the scales (Libra) of justice are employed as a
balancing agent.

The issue here is ***behavior***, how we conduct ourselves with
others. The evolutionary purpose is for an individual (Aries) to
learn through the process of socialization (Libra). Others provide a
mirror for self-reflection. We develop an awareness of self in relation to others, and learn to behave with respect for both. The
shadow potential is incivility, coarseness, offensiveness, or any form
of indecent conduct.

When Aries becomes charged it tends to disregard Libran etiquette or laws. With sufficient motivation (charge) such as getting to a hospital or meeting an urgent deadline, we readily ignore the posted speed limit. Depending on the situation, overriding civility may be disruptive and offensive, or it could be heroic. Absent a charge produced by an immediate concern, we generally choose to conform to societal standards which govern behavior.

Libra also involves romance. When we're turned on (increased Aries charge), there is motivation to make connections with others. There must be sufficient desire to override the social norm of courtesy and general decorum (Libra), to take the risk (Aries) in declaring our passionate desire to another.

Libra sets up rules of relating which establish peace and satisfaction in relationships. If personal needs are not met by an agreement, then we become motivated to do something about it (Aries). We may try to negotiate a change in the relationship, or, if that fails, we may choose to end it.

There can be an imbalance in the Aries direction if we act as if our needs are more important than the other person's. Consider a traditional marriage where the man is the chief decision-maker. He sets the terms of intimacy and sees his wife (who takes his name) as subservient. This arrangement shows how Aries can dominate Libra by sheer power. In this situation, greater fairness is only possible if the wife increases her Aries charge. If she doesn't, then the dynamics stay the same as she tacitly agrees to the rules.

The maintenance of relationship (Libra) can also neutralize individual desire (Aries). Libra's call for compromise and harmony may quell the individual members of the pairing into routine and peacefulness at the expense of increased aliveness. Then, relationship becomes imprisoning—a storybook cover that belies the deadening of passion within. Change will only occur when a sufficient charge builds that is capable of toppling the complacency.

Aries/Libra is a continual negotiation between self and other. Ideally, we learn to cultivate the delicate balance of passion and compromise in our behavior. Cardinal fire and cardinal air socialize the individual.

Taurus opposite Scorpio

Fixed earth opposite fixed water. Whether discussing personal (Taurus) vs. shared (Scorpio) resources, or having the sturdiness (Taurus) to engage in deep processes (Scorpio), this opposition concerns issues of substance. Taurus and Scorpio are fixed signs—they dig into material and psychological realms. Bridging this opposition successfully requires a "stick-to-it" attitude, a willingness to sink into what is significant. The evolutionary purpose is to achieve *endurance*. The shadow is entrenched control dramas and inflexibility.

Taurus/Scorpio is the tension between inertia and change. "If it ain't broke, don't fix it," is a good example of the salt-of-the-earth Taurus mentality. Taurus wants to solidify and preserve in an uncomplicated way, while Scorpio wants to catalyze some kind of transformative process. Scorpio is willing to be disruptive in its investigative pursuits, a complete reversal of Taurus values. Scorpio becomes charged by the prospect of deeper intimacy, by revealing the hidden or taboo, and by sharing in emotional experience. Taurus's neutrality resists all of this dynamism, keeping it at bay until the charge of Scorpio's urgency dominates it.

This polarity addresses personal resources vs. shared resources. Taurus includes the ownership of possessions, and Scorpio involves merging resources as done in a marriage or a business venture. We surrender autonomy (Taurus) when we take a risk in pooling resources (Scorpio), and declare, "What's yours is mine, and what's mine is yours." In order to enter such a contract, we must be adequately charged with the desire to do so.

Merging has literal connotations with sexuality, another Taurus/Scorpio province. Taurus pertains to the body while Scorpio relates to how bodies are shared. For most of us, the intensity of sexual pleasure is greater with a partner than just with ourself. There is also greater risk (disease, entanglements, unwanted pregnancy) in sexual sharing, which is absent for those comfortable with non-involvement (Taurus). We only choose to engage in intimacy when the intensity of a charge is stronger than the perceived risks of venturing forth.

81

If the intensity of the Scorpio charge diminishes, so do the reasons to continue connecting. We then may choose to reorient our desire to what makes us content and secure as individuals (Taurus).

Imbalance in the Scorpio direction shows up as manipulation, psychological demands, or abuse. The pain and suffering that result strongly disrupt the solace and internal peace which Taurus prioritizes. When Scorpio's charge overwhelms Taurus, connecting turns into a roller-coaster ride that eventually becomes exhausting.

On the other hand, if Scorpio's passion stays quiet, the Taurus status quo reigns. There is no sense of intimacy, excitement, or healthy conflict. One result could be endless hours of small talk or watching television. Maintaining the balance between intimacy (Scorpio) and internal contentment (Taurus) is negotiated in this polarity. Learning to be steadfast and unflappable (Taurus) in the face of stressful (or ecstatic) circumstances (Scorpio), brings poise and endurance. Fixed earth and fixed water is a commitment to connecting.

Gemini opposite Sagittarius

Mutable air opposite mutable fire. Gemini and Sagittarius deal with the evolutionary program of *learning*. Certainly every sign involves an education in some way, but these two specifically deal with broadening our intellect to inform a life philosophy. There is an accumulation of experience which helps us make sense of this existence. The shadow emerges in being naïve and uninformed but claiming expertise—not really knowing what you're talking about.

This polarity concerns the dynamic between facts (Gemini) and opinions (Sagittarius). Our knowledge base (Gemini) generates our belief system, the ways in which we connect the dots and see the bigger picture (Sagittarius). This belief system then points us to where we find meaning and a sense of purpose in life.

Sagittarius is a fire sign, full of passionate ideology that sometimes overrides any sense of reason (Gemini). One example of imbalance in the Sagittarius direction is seen with the religious fanatic who disregards scientific facts (Gemini). In moments when

82

the charge of beliefs and opinions lowers, we can open up to new information (Gemini) that can alter our world view. If we believe we know it all already, there is no room, or inclination, to adapt.

On the other hand, Gemini data may dominate any sense of meaning. One example is post-modern thinking, which argues that no belief system is better than any others, just different. This stance negates that a philosophy of altruism may be more conscious than a philosophy of malice. This leveling of the intellectual playing field disregards that consciousness evolves. It would deny that we are able to approach things differently based on higher (more conscious) perspectives.

Another consequence of Gemini facts dominating Sagittarian meaning is losing a connection to the fire of life. The world is seen as a series of digits, sounds, and an array of other sensory stimulation. Nothing is better or worse, thrilling or exhausting. Being stuck in neutral, there is no impetus to make a difficult decision or take a stand for something worthwhile. Without a Sagittarian charge, an existential crisis eventually takes hold, and the eternal question, "What's the point?" loses its answer.

The success of integrating this opposition is contingent upon managing the charge of Sagittarius in balance with an openness to learn new things. Ideally, increased knowledge (Gemini) leads to wisdom (Sagittarius), while being wise includes openness to new data. Mutable air and mutable fire inform an approach to life.

Cancer opposite Capricorn — Impact —

Cardinal water opposite cardinal earth. Family vs. career, private vs. public life, the inner child vs. the seasoned elder—this opposition deals with the tension between our roots (Cancer) and growing into greater potency in the world (Capricorn). A commonality of these signs is influence, which takes form in raising children (Cancer) or impacting the world (Capricorn). The evolutionary purpose is to develop *importance*. The shadow is claiming authority prematurely and exhibiting immaturity.

Traditionally, this polarity has been divided along gender lines with women playing the Cancer role and men, the Capricorn.

83

Nowadays, this gender delineation is not as evident as an increasing number of men and women are interested in having both active family and career lives. The intensity of charge on the Cancer side determines how this combination is managed. For some people, the urge to have children is so strong that vocational concessions are gladly made. For others, having children is a lesser priority, and they choose not to. Or the parenting agreement may be that their partner will assume much of the responsibilities.

Being cardinal signs, the Cancer/Capricorn opposition serves as a central issue in the course of development. We choose a career path (Capricorn) based on what is emotionally satisfying (Cancer) to achieve. If the internal charge does not motivate, we may end up in a career of drudgery or routine, just clocking in and getting a paycheck. This may stimulate us to go within to find a true calling. Then, the increased Cancer charge serves as a motivation to find a heartfelt vocation.

If the early home influence is strong (high charge), it can dictate our vocational choices through heavy-handed expectations. When we attain maturation (Capricorn), there is greater control of our career as the charge from family influence never rises to the point of governing our choices. Successful management of this polarity involves awareness of our Cancer roots along with self-management (Capricorn) of autonomous choices.

An example of neutral (Capricorn) holding the status quo is seen with the structure of work. Capricorn excels in routine: for instance, working eight hours a day in a five-day work week. This is disrupted if Cancer increases its charge in the form of a family emergency or anything at all that requires parental attention. When mommy (or daddy) gets a phone call from school telling her that her child has been hurt, she drops everything and rushes to the rescue. If everything is ok with the children (no charge), then the work day proceeds as scheduled.

A heightened (and unbalanced) Cancer charge can get in the way of work performance. When we act overly emotional, it's impossible to focus on productivity. In order to balance this polarity we must grow out of immature tendencies while also staying connected to the heart. Then, handling positions of importance from a place of centeredness is possible. Cardinal water and cardinal earth establish the impact we make.

Leo opposite Aquarius

Fixed fire opposite fixed air. The polarity between Leo and Aquarius concerns the interplay of the personality with collectivity—how an individual is part of the larger world community. These signs address involvement with life. Each of us holds a special uniqueness (Leo), and, at the same time, we are anonymous faces in a sea of billions (Aquarius). The evolutionary purpose here is *participation*, to join the individual with humanity. The shadow is subverting healthy participation for our own amusement.

Every performer (Leo) needs an audience (Aquarius). The world validates our talent through applause and is warmed by our unique contribution. Standing in front of the world and expressing our gift requires a healthy sense of confidence (Leo). In order to participate, Leo needs a sufficient charge. When it reaches the necessary threshold we are acknowledged by the group's response.

Another facet of this polarity is the animation (Leo) of ideas (Aquarius). The archetype of Aquarius, with its ruling planet Uranus, is like a gigantic matrix of possibilities. This interconnected web of energy is neutral and awaits our activation. When we become charged by certain possibilities, the Aquarian matrix enters personal domains (Leo). Through our participation, the vastness of this intelligence becomes accessible.

Leo/Aquarius concerns our relationship with social conditioning. Aquarius deals with group processes and dynamics, which tend to have particular norms. We can choose to abide by these dictates or increase our personal charge in order to find our own way. With an excessive charge, there is a narcissistic takeover—we believe we are larger than life (and the most important thing in it!). This is seen with charismatic athletes, politicians, or celebrities who are addicted to the limelight. The collective tends to want these people to experience some kind of fall as a check on their narcissism. This fall corresponds to a reduction in the Leo charge.

On the other hand, with no Leo charge at all, there is blind conformity to group-think. If we lack a personal charge sufficient to pass the threshold point, then our orientation to life is based solely on being an observer or a "cog in the machine." At the extreme, we may feel like a "nobody" or a failure. This distancing from Leo's majesty can make us either envious or judgmental of those who are more recognized.

Although most people do not become famous, many of us do attain some degree of visibility or recognition for making a contribution. Successful engagement with this polarity gives us a sense of joining with others. We're not larger than life, but also not overlooked or forgotten. Fixed fire and fixed air affirm our presence in the world.

Virgo opposite Pisces

Mutable earth opposite mutable water. Although all the signs deal with issues of development, the Virgo/Pisces axis specifically address how we handle our personal growth and also heal our wounds. Both signs want to realize a more advanced state of being, though they go about it very differently. Virgo develops through diligence, perfecting skills, and taking concrete steps to advance in life. Pisces develops by raising consciousness, absorbing lessons into the soul, and releasing what holds us back. The purpose of this polarity is *improvement*. The shadow is strengthening regressive patterns through deflecting responsibility, or directing this energy outward and trying to "fix" others.

Virgo compares, while Pisces transcends comparisons to realize oneness. As an earth sign, Virgo is methodical and practical. Breaking things down, analyzing, and getting into the "nitty gritty" certainly has its place. All of this dissection of the physical world doesn't erode the underlying spiritual unity unless we let it. Creating dualities and comparing one thing to another is a useful exercise. In fact, that's what we are doing in examining Virgo and Pisces! When consciousness develops in the Pisces direction, we can experience the underlying unity to all things.

Virgo is associated with everyday reality, the neutral, mundane existence defined by order. With Pisces, we enter the world of timelessness and transcendence. Virgo efficiently and precisely categorizes the phenomena of this world. From the Pisces view, the world appears more like a dream. The Pisces charge is increased through meditation and other spiritual practice. When we are fully present and experiencing the world in "flow," the apparent separation between things is temporarily transcended while this charge dominates. Note that substance use of many varieties can distort "reality"—there is also a reckless side to Pisces.

Virgo pertains to the specifics and details of our work, while Pisces includes the inspiration that can be put into it. Ideally, an increase of a Pisces charge opens a channel to divine inspiration. If the Pisces charge becomes excessive, the result is great, inspired intentions without any accomplishments—the dreamer who never applies himself.

On the other hand, in the absence of sufficient Pisces charge, Virgo maintains the status quo in which work is just work. Tasks feel difficult, tiring, even boring. And if Virgo is even more entrenched and discounting of any possibility of transcendent levels of consciousness, we may succumb to the most difficult components of Virgo: anxiety, drudgery, and servitude.

To balance this polarity, the inspiration of Pisces must be in harmony with performance. We are then able to bring dreams into reality. We improve by raising our consciousness (Pisces) and acting in accordance (Virgo). Mutable earth and mutable water inspires us to work toward our ideals.

Trines

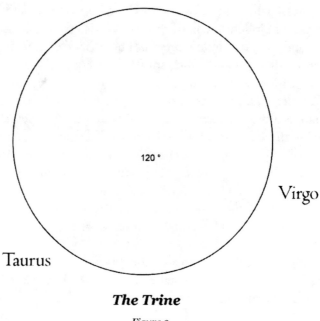

The Trine

Figure 9

The next way to cut the pie is into thirds. Here we take a step beyond the most basic level of interaction of the opposition. The trine illustrates four evolutionary programs derived from the four elements. There is a progression from personal to social to collective themes in each of the elements. The trine connects the cardinal, fixed, and mutable modalities. Any two signs trine to each other will share their charge or neutrality, so they can reinforce neutral or charged tendencies for better or for worse. The focus is on strengthening the connection between signs of the same element rather than on negotiating the balance between charged and neutral as seen with the opposition.

Fire Trines

The fire trines build from Aries (personal) to Leo (social) to Sagittarius (collective). There is a procession from free will to creative radiance to the development of purpose. The phases build on, complement, and strengthen each other through an easy flow (trine) of energy. Aries is cardinal, initiating the will of the self. Leo is fixed, where we find solidity in character, and Sagittarius is mutable, dispersing our energy into selected causes. Although not the primary focus of the trine, there is still the issue of charge-neutrality. In the case of the fire trines, we must be aware of the potential for the unchecked charge to be overly excited and create trouble. When the fire charge is managed consciously, the gift is that our soul's intentions are able enter into the world.

Aries trine Leo

Cardinal fire trine fixed fire. Aries concerns the declaration of autonomy and the exercising of free will. We feel ignited with energy and eager to venture forth. Leo's terrain is the evolution of the social self that engages with others and shares who we are. We can radiate a unique personality, develop a talent, and enjoy recreational pursuits. The spark in Aries can be channeled into social (Leo) settings.

The evolutionary task of Aries trine Leo is developing *valor*, the ability to behave with, and radiate, courage and boldness. Both of these signs have animal correlations, and we can take note of their power as it shows up in nature. Like a ram (Aries) or lion (Leo), self-alignment and fierceness enable us to meet the world on our own terms. The shadow is brashness or unnecessarily dominating others. With excessive Aries, aggression is likely, while an overly-intense Leo produces macho attention-seeking. Cardinal fire ignites the spark and fixed fire maintains it.

89

Leo trine Sagittarius

Fixed fire trine mutable fire. The next leg of the fire triangle addresses worldly issues. Sagittarius deals with finding a mission and channeling our potency into a life path. Here, our character (Leo) provides the "oomph" to the life purpose.

The successful combination of Leo's radiance and Sagittarius's broad perspective produces ***grandeur,*** which enables us to proceed through life with optimism and a nobility of character. This trine connects the social self with the collective, so rallying others to meet a purpose is part of the program. Sagittarius amplifies and encourages the warmth of Leo; our confidence becomes inspiring and contagious. This positivity and charisma is eager to take on any challenge. The shadow is grandiosity. With a more intense Leo charge, this combination turns toward conceit—taking undue credit for our contribution. An error in the Sagittarius direction is over-confidence, losing awareness of our limits. Ideally, evolution is accelerated when we are ignited to make a difference and join with others with the attitude of "Yes we can!" Fixed fire solidifies mutable fire for dispersal into the world.

Aries trine Sagittarius

Cardinal fire trine mutable fire. Aries and Sagittarius bridge the personal with the collective. Perhaps more than any other interchange in the astrological system, Aries/Sagittarius is "pedal-to-the-metal" adventurousness. Although many adventures end up with little results, and some risk-taking ends up in emergency rooms, the evolutionary task here is to simply "go for it."

This trine concerns individual *conquest*—having specific goals to achieve in the world. Here we extend our personal fire into large arenas of life. The challenge is to choose the right battles to wage. The shadow of this combination is choosing the wrong battles, which can lead to destruction. We might then launch warheads instead of an authentic contribution. If Aries is off balance in leading the charge, the error may be in lacking foresight—forging ahead without a strategy. This behavior often creates conflict and

90

pain in the world. An error in the Sagittarius direction would be getting stuck in too much policy and not enough decisiveness. There is arrogance without the action to back it up. Cardinal fire and mutable fire broadens our reach.

Earth Trines

The earth trines are entrepreneurial. The evolutionary task of earth is to create tangible evidence that evolution is proceeding. The metaphor of the "field" is appropriate in discussing the earth trines. There is a procession from soil (Taurus), to gardening (Virgo), to being a master of our chosen field (Capricorn). From resources (fixed) to crafting (mutable) to management (cardinal), the earth elements address responsibility and skill in using the physical realm. When these trines are worked well, Spirit evolves on this earth plane through our mastery. A pitfall is that the neutrality of earth can be mutually reinforced and thereby squelch innovation or change. These trines have to do with getting down to business to make workable structures in our world.

Taurus trine Virgo

Fixed earth trine mutable earth. Taurus includes earthy materials and substances but also inner resources such as self-worth and poise. Ideally, we establish a healthy foundation from which life can grow. Virgo connects to the process of maturation and caretaking. Once plants sprout from the soil they require care and attention to thrive. If the Taurus stage is like soil, Virgo is the gardening.

Combining Taurus and Virgo brings **productivity**. Resources are put to work in a variety of ways: pruning, sifting, tending, plowing, assembling, crafting, tinkering, and any other activity designed to produce something of value. A hazard here is to enter mindless repetitive routines which churn out a supply that has no demand. The resistance to changing production techniques keeps consumers, and ultimately society, in the past. What's the current demand for an abacus, a top hat, or a girdle? The shadow is wastefulness. An error in the Taurus direction is excessive material without making products—the gears of the machines slow down and stagnation results. An imbalance in the Virgo direction has technique superseding supply, resulting in scarcity. Fixed earth and mutable earth transform raw materials into useful products.

Virgo trine Capricorn

Mutable earth trine cardinal earth. Capricorn pertains to the management of resources, excelling professionally in the wider world, and attaining stature. The cardinal quality defines a public image and aims to contribute to society. The lessons learned in Virgo around skill development reap material gain with Capricorn. The cardinality of Capricorn has its eye on promotion and success, while Virgo's mutability is the know-how that allows it to happen.

The central theme of connecting Virgo and Capricorn is *industry*. Capricorn deals with infrastructures, markets, and business, while Virgo relates to the specialized skill-sets required for production. Workaholism is the shadow here, which can lead to exhaustion and depletion, discontent and pessimism. Overdoing the Capricorn energy produces exploitation—the heavy-handed boss who dishonors his workers. An imbalance on the Virgo side would result in industriousness without management, a leaderless bunch of workers without direction, their products never arriving on the store shelves. Cardinal earth provides management to mutable earth efforts.

Taurus trine Capricorn

Fixed earth trine cardinal earth. Both of these signs are self-oriented. Taurus wants to attain personal security, while Capricorn is more sophisticated with a broad reach into public venues. How do we incorporate resources into a vocational contribution? Making money is part of the curriculum here, which can be beneficial both personally and collectively if it's done well. Fixed earth is the materials that cardinal earth promotes into society.

92

These signs join to form *success*. Capricorn's skillful career management bolsters the bank account (Taurus). And through success, we increase our self-worth. A shadow possibility is greed, having a career solely as a means for financial gain. An excess of Taurus results in gluttony and indulgence like an entitled tycoon demanding only the best. Tipping the scales in the other direction, Capricorn domination results in success at all costs—an addiction to status and the rewards of privilege. Fixed earth and cardinal earth achieve prosperity.

Air Trines

The air trines involve the process of creating an advanced civilization. The sequence from personal to social to collective begins with the mutable mode here. Our individual minds (Gemini) are open to conceive of unlimited possibilities. We communicate with others (Libra) to find what is suitable for everyone and establish (cardinal) social norms. These norms are brought to the collective through the development of culture (Libra/Aquarius). The fixed intelligence (Aquarius) of Spirit is able to be brought into personal domains (Gemini) though the channel of genius. The air trines provide movement, make connections, and engage the mind as a tool for evolution. If these channels are functioning well, we learn how to civilize the planet in accordance with the intelligence that envelops us. If the neutrality of air is blindly reinforced, then the ways that we civilize may be out of touch with our inherent humanness.

Gemini trine Libra

Mutable air trine cardinal air. The first air stage, Gemini, relates to the development of the human mind through curiosity, perception, and hypothesis. Libra takes this open-ended learning and ushers it into dialogue, socialization, negotiation, and diplomacy. Information (Gemini) is transferred into interpersonal contexts (Libra). Mutable air considers a wealth of content, while

93

cardinal air sets up the dynamics for how this content can be shared.

The teamwork of Gemini and Libra produces *communication*—sharing our thoughts (Gemini) with another (Libra). By communicating in social domains, each individual voice becomes part of a larger chorus of ideas. Ultimately, these ideas set up the basis for education, culture, and other arenas where ideas are communicated. The shadow for this trine is lying. Gemini can lack a moral compass, and Libra wants to please others—the pitfall is to fill communication with untruths, which in this case stem from a naïve, rather than manipulative, place. An imbalance in the Gemini direction shows up as talking over others, while an error in the Libra direction is excessive agreeableness to what others have to say. Mutable air and cardinal air exchange information.

Libra trine Aquarius

Cardinal air trine fixed air. This pairing brings the interpersonal dynamics of Libra to the collective scale with Aquarius. The theme here is sociological—how we can all harmoniously get along on this planet. In particular, the issue is how interpersonal connections (Libra) and group dynamics (Aquarius) mutually impact and inform each other. What does society teach us about relating? How can our associations promote global civility? Cardinal air establishes social norms, while fixed air solidifies these agreements for the collective.

The integration of this trine produces *culture*—the collective agreements, customs and behavioral norms that serve as social glue. The shadow of Libra/Aquarius is conformity. If everyone (Aquarius) is expected to act in ways that maximizes fairness and civility (Libra), individual expressions of dissent would be unwelcome. Too much Libra takes the form of high-brow refinement and snobbishness, instead of what would be acceptable to all (Aquarius). Overdoing Aquarius, on the other hand, looks like the collective lacking sophistication, an insipid culture without a sense of art or a tasteful aesthetic. Cardinal air and fixed air develop the collective social milieu.

Gemini trine Aquarius

Mutable air trine fixed air. The intellectual, rather than social, facets of air are most relevant in this exchange. The personal, intellectual focus of Gemini connects with the transpersonal dimensions of Aquarius. The individual is able to be a vessel for extraordinary ideas. Fixed air, the everlasting intelligence of nature, is brought into mutable dispersal through individual minds.

The integration of this trine is found in *genius*. Individuals tap into the larger intelligence through ingenuity and flashes of brilliance. Distortion in these channels of mental interconnectivity can lead to the shadow, which is erratic or chaotic cognition. At the extreme this would be some forms of mental illness. An imbalance in the Gemini direction is quite common. This occurs when we think that we are more advanced than the universe. We are then prone to assert a human agenda onto nature to control it. An excess of Aquarius is also quite common. We think that God is too advanced for us to fathom, leading to agnosticism, alienation, or apathy about a larger order in nature. Mutable air connected to fixed air downloads brilliance.

Water Trines

The water trines portray the cycle of attachment. Cancer, a cardinal sign, concerns family, identity, and the establishment of personal attachments to loved ones. Scorpio's domain includes how we attach to significant others in intimate ways. Scorpio governs the fixed evolutionary conditions found in nature—attraction, reproduction, menstruation and other natural rites of passage, and death. Pisces releases its mutable water into the collective. Personal attachments and intimate relationships reach completion and give way to a broader love for all. A challenge is that water's charge can build in unchecked ways in these aspects, creating insatiable emotional demands. With the water element, we bond with life, perpetuate it, and increase consciousness by processing it through and learning our deep lessons. Water allows evolution to enter into biology and allows life to flourish with meaning and depth.

95

Cancer trine Scorpio

Cardinal water trine fixed water. With Cancer, we get in touch with our personal needs for love and attachment. Scorpio connects us to others through intimate sharing. The associations with water here are rich. Cancer is connected to family—our blood relations, and Scorpio intimacy includes the exchange of bodily fluids. Cardinal water pertains to the depth of the individual, fixed water maintains our genealogy through our lineage.

When there is self-acceptance (Cancer), we are better able to have meaningful intimacy (Scorpio). The result of the partnership of these two water signs is *bonding*. Our genetic roots and identity (Cancer) forms the biological, emotional, and psychological background which influences mate selection (Scorpio). The shadow component arises when there's a lack of acceptance, for both ourself and the other. The emotionality of these signs can then turn dark in the form of unconscious emotional abuse. The water element typically functions below the surface, so when we act in such ways we don't even realize the damage. Increased intensity of Cancer over Scorpio results in neediness, while an excess in Scorpio leads to taking advantage of others love. Cardinal water and fixed water connects the individual to the human species.

Scorpio trine Pisces

Fixed water trine mutable water. Pisces is collective. It has compassion, an altruistic love for everyone. Connecting this to Scorpio is to bring boundless (mutable) love into intimacy. As a fixed sign, Scorpio concentrates and gives staying power to the elusive quality of Pisces. There is the potential for open-hearted, unconditional love in our most precious connections.

The integration of these water signs is *sacred union*—deep connecting infused with transcendent love. Many people get hurt in realms of intimacy (Scorpio) and are in need of attaining closure. Through the wisdom and heightened perspective of Pisces, our unresolved emotional dramas (Scorpio) are able to find release. The shadow possibility is the loss of self in some type of obsessive dynamic: stalking, endless fantasizing or inappropriate devotion, indiscriminate sexual boundaries. If Pisces dominates this trine, there is the codependent enabling of others. Compassion at the expense of accountability (Scorpio) gives people permission to hurt us. An imbalance in the Scorpio direction is the application of severe punishments, even emotionally victimizing others who we are deeply connected to. Fixed water solidifies the expansiveness of mutable water.

Cancer trine Pisces

Cardinal water trine mutable water. The water that connects us to family (Cancer) may extend further and compassionately connect us to the world family (Pisces). This is where we can learn to love everyone. This trine has to do with the ability to familiarize the self with the widest range of emotion. Pisces wants to break the personal heart (Cancer) open.

The integration of this trine is found in ***empathy***, which furthers evolution by connecting us all through our shared emotions. The shadow is naïveté or gullibility. The empathy of Cancer/Pisces may want to hug everybody, so it can be a pushover. An imbalance in the Cancer direction results in dissatisfaction. The self has emotional requirements for the broader world to meet. If the Pisces charge dominates instead, then we are reduced to ineffectuality. The personal roots that ground us are weakened, and we become spineless. Cardinal water brings the boundless nature of mutable water into the immediacy of the personal self.

Shadow Trines

The glamorization of the trine has hidden its other, darker possibilities, leaving them virtually unexplored in astrology discourse and literature. The common view is that if the great benefits of trines are not seized, the only down side is a missed opportunity—nothing to worry about.

The consciousness with which any aspect is met determines its expression. Trines are supportive, with no resistance to the

97

exchange. This easy flow between the two sides can fuel healthy growth, or it could simply connect two signs that are not functioning well on their own. If Virgo and Capricorn are both struggling, the trine doesn't improve the situation, as it's just their means of connecting. There can certainly be a *harmonious* connection between control (Capricorn) and servitude (Virgo). The shadow of exploitation easily arises in this example. So trines do carry the potential to reinforce unconscious patterns and thereby stifle evolution.

Additionally, since trines connect signs of the same element, the nature of the element in question is amplified—in positive or in negative ways. Among the many challenges of each element is: earth can be stuck, water can be labile, air can be detached, and fire can be explosive. When you combine two signs of the same element, these tendencies can be exaggerated. Viewing the trine as exclusively positive—or any aspect for that matter as solely "good" or "bad"—would be a great error in seeing clearly the evolutionary gifts and shadows, both of which exists throughout the system. This perspective is important to keep in mind as we shift now to the next aspect in our exploration, the square. The evolutionary tasks of this so-called "hard" or "bad" aspect are of the highest importance.

Chapter 5

Aspects & Evolution Part II
Squares & Sextiles

Classically considered a "hard" aspect, the hallmark of the square is friction. There are two reasons why this aspect is difficult to manage. First, signs in a square dynamic always share the same modality, which fuels competition/conflict. In our discussion about the trine, we saw that differing modalities are supportive: "I'll be the manager (cardinal), and you can be the messenger (mutable)." When signs share the same modality, however, they each want to perform the same role.

The second reason why the square is so tough to manage is because a yin sign (earth, water) is always paired with a yang (air, fire). The instability created by these different approaches and agendas calls for negotiation and, hopefully, cooperation. If not, then they remain at cross purposes, and the aspect becomes destructive.

Every component of astrology has an evolutionary purpose, and the square is no different. In fact, because this aspect is so pressing, the reward for finding integration is more valuable. The six oppositions deal with *fundamental polarities*. The trine is defined by *elemental cooperation*. With the square, the *management of evolutionary crisis* takes center stage. The growth is equal to the tasks at hand.

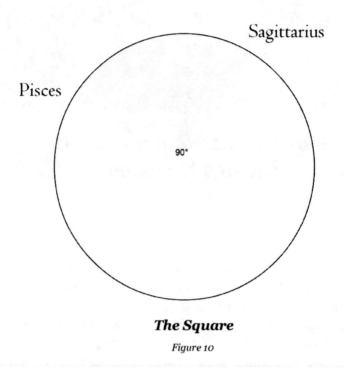

Pisces

Sagittarius

90°

The Square

Figure 10

The charged-neutral division, as always, brings another variable, one that takes on increased importance with the square aspect. Instead of there being just one type of square, there are now three, each with their own energetic dynamics: charged-charged, neutral-neutral, and charged-neutral.

Charged square Charged

This type of square pairs the fire and water signs. It's the most rambunctious of the squares because there is no neutral component. There is often restlessness, competing agendas, and the opportunity to exaggerate differences and build antagonism. When one side increases its charge, the other may follow. Eventually, things reach some type of peak. Managed consciously, there is potent breakthrough. Managed poorly, there are severe conflicts.

Aries square Cancer

Cardinal fire square cardinal water. Aries asserts the needs of the self, while Cancer advocates for the good of the family unit. This combination deals with fighting for, or defending family and/or loved ones, **protection**. Aries gives Cancer assertion and Cancer gives Aries the emotional connections to defend. An emotionally intelligent (Cancer) use of force (Aries) shows the integration. The shadow here is overprotection—initiating preemptive attacks in the name of defense.

When highly charged, Aries becomes reckless, while Cancer becomes hysterical. Aries is involved with the "dog-eat-dog" mentality, doing whatever it can to be victorious. When activated, it chooses fight or flight. In contrast to the aggressiveness of Aries, Cancer is defensive. Like a mother grizzly bear defending its young, it will fiercely meet any perceived threats. The escalation between these charged signs continues to build to some sort of definitive conclusion—fighting to the death, retreat, or a detente. Aries square Cancer is a drama of survival with the highest of stakes.

If Aries dominates Cancer through the power of its attack, the predator nabs his prey. There are winners and losers in the great survival game. An example of Cancer having the upper hand is smothering—parental control (Cancer) inhibiting autonomy (Aries). In these very different scenarios, the common denominator is behavior that is highly emotional and urgent. In either case they quickly find themselves in hot (Aries) water (Cancer).

Finding balance between charged signs is a tall order. Ideally, Cancer stimulates Aries to be more sensitive in its assertion, and Aries catalyzes Cancer to be more forceful in its emotional expression. This collaboration can be supremely competent in seeing to survival. Cardinal fire and cardinal water fight for what is most important.

101

Leo square Scorpio

Fixed fire square fixed water. Charge combined with the fixed modality brings concentrated passion. Leo wants the spotlight, to spontaneously enjoy the moment in all of its glory. Scorpio functions in the dark, behind closed doors, and in secrecy. Leo shares, while Scorpio wants to exchange. Integration is found when Scorpio is open and Leo is noble. Being able to *trust* is the evolutionary goal. Leo may shine on Scorpio and bring what is hidden into the light. Scorpio catalyzes Leo to behave with greater depth. Together, they can merge in passion that is as life-affirming (Leo) as it is deep (Scorpio); there is a wonderful, playful intimacy available here. The shadow is suspicion of, and harming, others. Operating darkly, we may hurt the very people we most care about.

There is a negotiation for power, a test of wills. Both signs are stubborn, potentially ruthless, and equipped to kill. If the Leo charge becomes excessive, its narcissistic focus shuts down the interactive process. Scorpio doesn't feel respected and loses interest since its desire is to merge in reciprocal union. Feeling wounded by Leo, it may retaliate through underhanded means. With an overemphasis on intimate revelations and poignant processes (Scorpio), Leo feels forced to yield its light, which is anathema to the Lion's desire to live large. Feeling dominated, Leo roars and becomes self-righteous, exposing its immaturity and fueling the drama.

This square connects what the self needs in relationship (Leo), with what is emotionally required (Scorpio) for a partnership to work. Upon successful balance, there is trust and spirited (often steamy) exchanges. Fixed water and fixed fire create lively intimacy.

Sagittarius square Pisces

Mutable fire square mutable water. Charge motivates, and mutable seeks. Together they want to discover what is meaningful. Sagittarius is on the proverbial quest, while Pisces is the mystic who travels through the inner realms. The goal is to connect spiritual learning (Sagittarius) with experiences (Pisces), thereby forming (a broad definition of) *religion*. The shadow is any delusional, misguided or fanatical religious fervor.

Sagittarius concerns the development of knowing through panoramic vision, while Pisces undoes knowledge in order to just be in experience. Whereas Sagittarius likes to have a destination, Pisces is about the journey. There is often a marked friction between declarations of truth (Sagittarius), and what is found through mystical means (Pisces). Most religions have a branch that favors orthodoxy or tradition. They also tend to have a branch of adherents who throw off the shackles of rigidity and embrace the primacy of direct experience. The Gnostics (Christianity), Hasids (Judaism), and Sufis (Islam) are examples from the monotheistic religions.

If Sagittarius overpowers Pisces, it might dismiss it as deceptive, gullible, impotent, phony, or downright delusional. Sagittarius could strong-arm Pisces into a submissive role. This movement makes Sagittarius increasingly rigid, bombastic, and domineering. This imbalance would certainly benefit from Piscean compassion, surrender, and grace. When the Pisces charge dominates, it retreats from the dictates of Sagittarius altogether and finds solace in meditative states, dreams, trances, and any type of spiritual practice. This retreat may devolve into escapism, removing Pisces from any healthy participation with the mundane world. The remedy is to come down from the proverbial mountaintop and act on the mission, purpose, or vision that is discovered (Sagittarius).

Without the mystical or spiritual essence (Pisces) that informs belief (Sagittarius), there is indoctrination. Without philosophy, teaching, and goals, there can be a nebulous and unstructured sense of Spirit. Both Sagittarius and Pisces must increase their respective charges to become meaningfully motivated. When there is direction towards experiencing the divine, these mutable signs powerfully work together in developing religion. When in balance, the common purpose shared among humanity (Sagittarius) is fueled by the loving embrace of Spirit (Pisces). Mutable fire and mutable water challenge us to match beliefs with experience.

Neutral square Neutral

This type of square involves the earth and air signs. Instead of a charge rising and falling as it catalyzes process, recall that the neutral elements are associated with content and structure. As with all squares, each side of the neutral-neutral aspect holds a truth in itself. And, as always, imbalance results if one side dominates. Upon balance, a major evolutionary lesson for the structure of society is attained.

Capricorn square Libra

Cardinal earth square cardinal air. The initiating spirit of the cardinal modality combined with neutral structure sets up *civilization*. Capricorn involves institutions, the structure of government, and other social systems. Libra adds laws to bring about fairness, social norms, diplomacy, and outreach. An air sign, Libra deals with concepts such as liberty, equity, and judiciousness—ideals to strive for. Capricorn cements these concepts into form. The shadow is complacency, the preservation (Capricorn) of social norms (Libra) which are not advancing humankind.

Capricorn provides the necessary executive decision-making in order to make social structures most effective. An excess results in the concentration of power—institutions become controlling rather than fair (Libra). Tradition is preserved at the expense of refining our social laws and customs to match modern realities.

If Libra dominates the conversation, then the structure of civilization is unreliable, constantly trying to be all things to all people. Like a board meeting without a leader setting the agenda, there can be endless dialogue, unproductive open-mindedness, and well-intentioned attempts at collaboration that lead nowhere. Furthermore, the agreeableness invites attack from those outside the governing structure in the form of opposition or even invasion.

The integration of this square sets up necessary boundaries and borders (Capricorn) that are fair and agreed upon (Libra). It invites trade (Libra), while also valuing self-interest (Capricorn). Too much Capricorn leads to isolationism; too much Libra weakens the government. Libra/Capricorn ideally produces sturdy govern-ance which holds to the highest of ideals.

At the personal level this aspect pertains to the competing demands of career (Capricorn) and relationships (Libra). As cardinal signs, these areas are of central importance. With too much focus in either direction, the other is likely to be compromised. When these areas are balanced, we can feel a sense of support (Libra) in sculpt-ing our life's work (Capricorn). Cardinal air and cardinal earth establish social structures.

Taurus square Aquarius

Fixed earth square fixed air. This square brings together matter (Taurus) and mind (Aquarius), the fixed structures of the physical and nonphysical worlds—*nature*. Certainly, with a loose definition, everything in the astrological system relates to nature in some way. However, this square specifically addresses the meta-physical structure of this existence (Aquarius), and the natural, everyday, physical world (Taurus). The visible and tangible earth is like a fertile garden, while the invisible transpersonal intelligence is like a giant nervous system that permeates everything. The shadow is found in artificiality—bringing intelligence (Aquarius) into physi-cality (Taurus) devoid of human processes (charged elements). Imagine robots taking over!

Being fixed, Taurus is like an immovable object and Aquarius is the irresistible force of progressive evolution. There can easily be a clash between these energies. There is often resistance (Taurus) to change (Aquarius). And it's common that, through mis-understanding, the complexity of a greater intelligence (Aquarius) gets naively simplified (Taurus). If Taurus is bolstered and Aquarius is ignored, then the mundane world is seen as the "real" nature. We become increasingly blind to the broader metaphysical reality which envelops us. Advocating being "down to earth" to the exclusion of more open-ended imagination can result in the Taurus problems of inertia, gluttony, and excessive materialism—indulging the senses without a broader awareness.

With an excess of Aquarius, we become enchanted by the future as we speculate or ruminate on what could be. With our "head in the clouds," the realities of the senses and the body, as well as simply being natural and at peace, become elusive. Then, the Aquarian struggles of anxiety, restlessness, alienation, and even dissociation may emerge as the psyche refuses to show up in the "here and now."

Aquarius without Taurus is impotent; Taurus without Aquarius is overly simplistic. When the body and mind engage with and inform each other, we are able to see that nature itself reflects this union. Fixed earth and fixed air connects the visible with the invisible.

Virgo square Gemini

Mutable earth square mutable air. This combination deals with the gathering and utilization of knowledge. Gemini is like the wide-open top of a giant funnel which welcomes anything and everything. Virgo is analogous to the much smaller bottom of the funnel. It sifts through what has been collected and then analyzes, refines, and produces what is most relevant to work with. The top of the funnel is open in the air, and the bottom is planted in the earth. Gemini holds possibilities and hypotheses, while Virgo tests hypotheses and reaches conclusions. Gemini is the data, and Virgo, the analysis. This square pertains to **science**. The shadow is what's been termed "scientism"—the view that only that which can be studied is valid and real, while everything else is mere fantasy.

Gemini is a "busy body," always gathering information, fascinated by everything and always wanting more. When it dominates, the result is irrelevancy. Ideally, there should be a point to all the facts and figures Gemini takes in. People want science to deliver knowledge and technologies that improve our lives. Untamed Gemini has a thousand questions without any answers. Too many options easily leads to indecision. And all this mental energy can be overly idealistic, lacking any regard for practicality.

In its methodical editing, Virgo finds what works best and produces efficient products. This sign's precision, attention to

106

detail, and technical ability is legendary. In excess, Virgo can solidify into dreary routine, become closed-minded, and turn skeptical toward any potential change to what is already working. Eventually it becomes redundant or outdated.

Mercury is the planet of intelligence, reason, language, and cognition. It rules both Gemini and Virgo and in so doing reflects our task of integrating the air and earth components of learning. As we do so, we are able to see the distinction between the things that we think, and the things that we definitively know. The ideal balance here results in intellectual clarity and discipline. We have the mental dexterity to use what we know, while simultaneously being open to new stimulation. Mutable air and mutable earth collect and implement knowledge.

Charged square Neutral

There are two of this type of square: fire square earth, and water square air. As seen with the opposition, there is a delicate dance of the charged element rising and falling in intensity in relation to the neutral. Ultimately, they must find a way to work together, but the dynamic is quite different than the charged square charged scenario. Since the neutral element stays stable, the charged element learns to modify its charge in relation to it. The neutral element provides the structure necessary to maximize the usefulness of the charged.

Fire square Earth

Aries square Capricorn

Cardinal fire square cardinal earth. This is a clashing of the fiery will of the individual with the necessity to sculpt a disciplined vocational contribution. We have desire (Aries) vs. what is actually feasible to achieve (Capricorn). Aries wants autonomy and empowerment but often lacks the patience to see its goals through to the end. Capricorn provides persistence but is prone to enter into rigid routines. The integration here forms *leadership*—being confident

107

and assertive in our public role. The shadow is tyranny, exercising excessive personal will (Aries) with an iron fist (Capricorn).

As its charge rises, so too does Aries's strong desire to get ahead. If the charge exceeds the pragmatics of Capricorn, Aries finds itself in a position of foolery. Its bluster exceeds its mastery, so it appears immature and over-eager. Executive decisions (Capricorn) made from the place of hot-headedness are usually imprudent. These types of leaders tend to lose their followers.

If we become heavy with the practical route of earthy diligence (Capricorn), then the fire (Aries) that initially motivated success diminishes. We get consumed by preserving our status and influence, while obligations continue to pile up. Work hours get longer, and the mountain we so eagerly climbed is now a burden to stay atop of. Our leadership at this point is passionless, overly-conservative, and bound to the past. Our followers lose interest in fighting the same old battles in the same outmoded ways.

Aries injects fresh and bold beginnings that continually renew the spirit of leadership. Combined with the seasoning from experience (Capricorn), a leader can expand into new frontiers with a steady hand on the helm. Cardinal fire and cardinal earth hold power with integrity.

Leo square Taurus

Fixed fire square fixed earth. This aspect deals with the issue of ownership (Taurus) and enjoyment (Leo). We bolster our sense of security by acquiring possessions and feeling solid within the self. Structure is established, an anchor in the form of a bank account or in self-reliance (Taurus). When we are in touch with the sheer joy of life, we naturally want to share and give of ourselves (Leo). The integration of these fixed signs results in *abundance*—having ample resources to both satisfy our needs and share with others. The shadow is hoarding, ostentation, and materialism.

The exchange plays out in how we choose to spend money. In moments of delight (increased Leo charge), it's easy to become extravagant in taste and behavior. Our immediate desire can overrun any realistic appraisal of our resources (Taurus). This is seen

108

with the boyfriend who showers his beloved with gifts he can't afford or with families who overextend for the holidays. The joy is more important than the financial reality.

Earth can smother fire. There are people who don't get excited about anything and never make the impulse buy. Life becomes increasingly flat or boring. If the Leo charge does not increase, then life may enter a status-quo of maintenance rather than having any fun. There may be a mountain of money but absolutely no enjoyment—the archetype of the Scrooge.

Leo's charge is joyful and wants to sustain the heat of the moment. When it's time to relax and calm down we can enjoy the comforts of our good fortune. The integration here has the quality of contentment—having what we love in balance with loving what we have. Taurus can provide substance to Leo, while Leo gives warmth to Taurus. Fixed fire and fixed earth constitute joyful living within our means.

Sagittarius square Virgo

Mutable fire square mutable earth. This interaction addresses the day-to-day implementation of our life path. Sagittarius develops aspirations, and Virgo concerns the application of intent. The integration here is *foresight*—having a prudent strategy (Virgo) for how to manifest our purpose (Sagittarius). The shadow is living a misguided life—structuring everyday activities (Virgo) around dogmatic prescriptions (Sagittarius) and being fanatical about doing everything "right."

Virgo organizes the hours of the day and finds a routine. If its neutrality should squelch the zest for discovery or broader purpose of Sagittarius, life becomes confining, even imprisoning. Life is then lived like a rat running through the same old maze. Virgo can turn to self-denial, a life of limitation, drudgery, and resignation.

With an increased charge, Sagittarius tends to break free from any restraints like a wild horse galloping away. Everything in its path is engaged with gusto—new experiences, higher learning, anything that expands our horizons and informs our broad education of life. However, without some tempering from Virgo's practicality, Sagittarius is prone to errant righteousness. It believes that everyone should live by its example. Sagittarius dominating Virgo results in pomposity, loftiness, and possibly dangerous choices like doing extreme sports without appropriate safety gear.

Ideally, we are able to see the big picture while also reading the fine print. With this foresight, we attain a broad conception of a life mission (Sagittarius), which we then diligently work with (Virgo). Mutable fire and mutable earth find the optimal ways to ground spiritual intentions.

Water square Air

Cancer square Libra

Cardinal water square cardinal air. This aspect addresses the issue of getting personal needs met (Cancer) in relationships (Libra). Cancer is emotional and wants depth and nourishment, while Libra calls for harmony, agreement, and cooperation. Creating a loving home (Cancer) filled with togetherness (Libra) is the promise. The integration is *romantic love*. The shadow is emotional (Cancer) co-dependence (Libra).

Libra sets up the structure of a relationship through expected behavior norms. It establishes common ground that is agreeable to both parties. In order to be a part of something larger than the self, there needs to be negotiation and compromise. When Libra suppresses Cancer, relationships are unsatisfying due to a lack of heart. The relationship structure dries up the emotional juice and evaporates the fulfillment. Concessions are made and a superficial peace is prioritized. The cost is feeling emotionally unsatisfied.

On the other hand, an elevated Cancer charge can hold the relationship captive to its needs. Cancer may use the relationship as an outlet for attention-seeking, care-taking, or any excessively emotional dynamic. With heightened emotions always looming, the natural harmony is disrupted.

Relationship is indeed a delicate balancing act, but romance and love can be successfully combined. Cardinal water and cardinal

110

air challenge us to find relationship models which are emotionally satisfying.

Scorpio square Aquarius

Fixed water square fixed air. This is a potentially explosive combination, as both signs hold fast to their respective truths. Scorpio insists upon exchanging psychological or emotional truth, while Aquarius is unsentimental, even cold about delivering its intellectual or conceptual reality. This square deals with becoming aware of (Aquarius), and engaging with (Scorpio), our deepest lessons. The integration is achieving *wisdom*. The shadow is coldly exposing others to their failings—being oppressive through intellectual means.

Recall that Aquarius sets up the metaphysical organization of nature, an interconnected web of energy. Like a behind-the-scenes coordinator of our spiritual growth, it connects us to people and experiences that will catalyze our growth. As this is a transpersonal process, there is no concern for the ensuing difficulty or discomfort for the ego-based personality. Working through these opportunities offered by Aquarius requires fierceness (Scorpio)—a determined and profound willingness to honestly acknowledge, and subsequently integrate, with our spiritual truth.

In light of the awakenings that Aquarius instigates, Scorpio determines our psychological reaction. How would you react if you were diagnosed with a terminal illness, or learned that a loved one had been murdered? Scorpio's intensity could slip out of control. The creation of conflict or emotional drama makes integration impossible. What we resist tends to persist. Trying to keep unpleasant truths away is a recipe for suffering as the ego is uncomfortably on edge. Life is then lived from a place of fear, dread, suspicion, or victimization. When the charge relaxes, Scorpio is better able to let in the truth that Aquarius presents.

On the other hand, if Scorpio's charge lies dormant, then a state of numbness, detachment, or impotency reigns. There may be alienation and resignation. Absent Scorpio's empowered, warrior energy, Aquarius's impersonal energy can send a shock to our sys-

111

tem, leaving us feeling overwhelmed by the painful enormity of our existential condition.

Soul evolution is not for the squeamish. We nurture and encourage our own wisdom through our willingness to face the realities of all facets of human life, especially the shadow material that most of us choose to ignore or repress. Fixed air and fixed water require us to take an unflinching look at our underlying psychology.

Pisces square Gemini

Mutable water square mutable air. This aspect asks us to use both sides of our brain. Gemini excels at left brain facts, data, and logic, while Pisces swims in the creative, intuitive, non-rational right brain. Through honoring both charged (Pisces) and neutral (Gemini) ways of perceiving the world, a greater synthesis is attained. The integration results in holistic **understanding**. The shadow is confusion—having perceptual distortions and erroneously claiming clarity.

What is more real, an actuary table or a dream? The mathematician surely would say that his methods are clear, understandable, and easily verifiable. The mystic claims that his territory must be *experienced*—you can't approach it using the tools of reason.

As the structure for the factual world, Gemini cannot be argued with. 2 + 2 = 4, end of the story. This logic holds great power because it's self-evident and seemingly irrefutable. Anyone who questions Gemini is considered a fool. When the neutrality of Gemini suppresses Pisces, science alone is seen as valid; intuition is thought to be unreliable or even unreal. This attitude inhibits us from exploring consciousness and also leads to the broader condemnation of spirituality.

Perception changes and consciousness is reoriented when we engage in transpersonal experience. The solidity of the factual world collapses. Enveloped by this mystical charge, Gemini's neutrality is transcended. The apparent orderliness of the world gives way to the numinous. Matter may be perceived as energy. There may be the awareness of non-physical beings. These phenomena

112

cannot be understood through Gemini's intellect. In fact, as soon as Gemini tries to understand Spirit, it reduces it. To paraphrase the Tao de Ching, "As soon as you talk about the Tao, it's no longer the Tao."

An excessive Piscean charge leads to disorientation. Transcendence of the intellect may bring estrangement from the self as well as from others still firmly planted in consensus reality. Without the structure of Gemini's factual world, Pisces is prone to fantasy, escapism, and delusion—not so different than continually being on drugs or asleep!

Ideally we come to see that both left and right brain processes are valid and necessary. With intention and practice we can learn to use them both skillfully, shifting perception from the rational to the non-rational consciously and in accordance with what a situation requires. We *understand* that we are spiritual beings having human experiences and relax into the reality of this delightful complexity. Mutable water and mutable air rely on all modes of perception in gathering knowledge.

Sextiles

Sextiles divide the zodiac into six sections of 60 degrees each. The six points resemble a hexagon or a six-pointed star. There are 12 sextiles in total, and all involve charged-neutral connections. Sextiles are similar to the opposition in that both aspects connect earth and water or air and fire. However, the opposition involves a single modality, which generates its tension. With the sextile, the two signs involved are of different modalities, like the trine, and are therefore complementary.

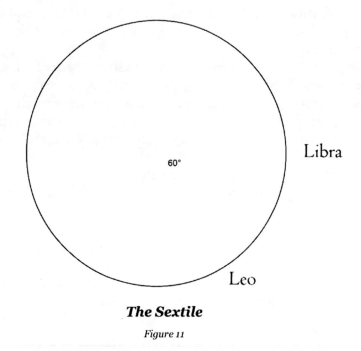

60°

Libra

Leo

The Sextile

Figure 11

Aries sextile Gemini

Cardinal fire sextile mutable air. This sextile gifts us with *agility*—mental alertness joined with behavioral versatility. Gemini's data collection supplies a plethora of options for behavioral choices (Aries). The improvisational nature of Gemini becomes more action-oriented, and the forcefulness of Aries makes Gemini decisive. This combination is highly energetic and would easily find trouble if used unconsciously. There's an impulsive trial-and-error mentality to it. Picture a teenager who is curious about firecrackers and eager to light one on the back of the frog he just caught by the stream. The shadow here is recklessness. The eagerness for experience, though, does serve growth, as it makes us excited about life.

Gemini is like an advisor, and Aries, depending on the intensity of its passion, decides if and how to use this advice. When

Aries is very charged, no amount of reason will calm it. Gemini may say, "You'll go to jail if you kill that guy!" And the charged Aries retorts, "I don't care!" At the other end of the spectrum, the natural impulses of Aries may be so subdued by Gemini's reason that it never takes the risks that it thrives on. When this aspect is working well, Gemini provides needed assistance, and Aries acts from an intelligent place. Mutable air advises cardinal fire's behavior.

Taurus sextile Cancer

Fixed earth sextile cardinal water. The integration here creates *nourishment*. Both Taurus and Cancer have correlations to food, sustenance, and inward contentment. The stability of Taurus supports Cancer's need for love and attachment. Cancer lends emotion to the sensuality of Taurus, while Taurus anchors Cancer into its surroundings. Creating a beautiful home that is nurturing and comfortable is part of the program. The shadow is gluttony, an inordinate reliance on comfort foods.

When emotions (Cancer) dominate, the stability (Taurus) of the home environment is compromised. Picture a house full of hungry children who need attention and care. The atmosphere is restless and anything but nourishing. On the other hand, Taurus introduces a calming influence which may neutralize emotions through its earthiness. When Cancer increases its charge, its needs can be met. The ideal here is creating a home which has both peace (Taurus) and love (Cancer). Fixed earth provides a fortress in which cardinal water finds emotional security.

Gemini sextile Leo

Mutable air sextile fixed fire. This vivacious interchange produces *fun*, in particular experimental, improvisational, and comedic recreation. Although sometimes overlooked, developing a sense of humor is an important evolutionary task. It is helpful intellectually, socially, and professionally. It also supports our physical health and sense of well-being. The unlimited curiosity of Gemini is given a flair for entertainment through Leo. And the

115

developing character (Leo) is encouraged to openly share its speculations by way of having more information (Gemini) of the world to draw upon. The shadow is recreational indulgence—the kid who wants to stay up all night playing video games and eating sugar, or the annoying class clown who won't give it a rest.

Leo may want to shine (increase charge), but not know how. Without being knowledgeable, the Emperor (Leo) may fail to realize he's not wearing clothes. By providing input, Gemini helps Leo avoid being a fool. On the other hand, if we continually strive to learn more (Gemini) in place of stepping forward and participating, then we neutralize the radiance of Leo. Working well, Gemini informs Leo and supports its charm, while Leo excites Gemini to shine. Mutable air and fixed fire develop a sense of humor.

Cancer sextile Virgo

Cardinal water sextile mutable earth. This aspect concerns **health care**. Virgo brings an emphasis on health, and Cancer cares. Together the combination is about developing healthy routines or assisting others. There is support between taking an internal inventory (Cancer) of what needs attention, and actually taking steps (Virgo) toward improvement. The development of emotional intelligence is available here, as precise understandings (Virgo) join with emotions (Cancer). The shadow is hypochondria toward ourself, or excessive care-taking of others who don't require it.

Cancer's emotions may become heightened and overrun practical restraint (Virgo). We could feel a white-knuckle urgency to "do better," and begin a drastic and unhealthy weight loss program. Conversely, when a Cancer charge is lacking, there is pessimism and defeatism—the issues that Virgo struggles with. Healthy measures are then forgotten, and depression may set in. Ideally, we approach life with the determination to find inner contentment. Mutable earth provides methods for cardinal water to be healthy.

Leo sextile Libra

Fixed fire sextile cardinal air. These social signs pertain to *engagement*. Sharing (Leo) supports connecting (Libra), and this sextile lights up interactions in life-affirming ways. The territory here is not exclusively romantic, though the vibe could be like the energy experienced on a successful first date. In social interactions, we often experience harmony and joy when we share who we are (Leo) and feel understood by another (Libra). The art of engagement readies us to be socially fluent in a variety of contexts. The shadow is using others to create a particular social appearance, or to benefit in some other way through the association. Leo is charismatic, and Libra has a smooth touch. Others could be easily manipulated if this aspect is channeled deviously.

We need a sufficient Leo charge to be able to meet others on equal (Libra) terms. Without it, we risk erring on the side of etiquette (Libra), deferring to the other. Too much focus on radiating the self (Leo) leads to blinding others (Libra), which makes reciprocal exchanges impossible. Ideally, there is good cheer (Leo) in personal relations (Libra), a sense of togetherness that is life-affirming. Cardinal air provides social opportunities for fixed fire to shine.

Virgo sextile Scorpio

Mutable earth sextile fixed water. Virgo and Scorpio both like to get to the bottom of things. Virgo wants to analyze, while Scorpio is geared towards psychological process. Using a broad definition, the integration is *therapy*—doing any form of powerful, transformative work. The insistence on risk (Scorpio) supports the skill-development which Virgo seeks. When we are willing to powerfully connect with others (Scorpio), much learning (Virgo) occurs. Tricky but true, the shadow is being caught in the shadow. Virgo's realism can sour into pessimism and view Scorpio territory as an endlessly threatening labyrinth. Expecting the worst, being a "professional patient," or sabotaging progress to reinforce pain, are all possible if this combination is used darkly.

117

In order to progress, Scorpio needs to summon a sufficient charge and lead with an eye toward transformation. Without this boldness, there could be despair, hidden suspicion, or internal stress. The work never gets off the ground. With an excess charge, control dramas and forcefulness reign. By overriding sensible guidelines (Virgo), the process becomes abusive, histrionic, or uncontrollable in some way. The integration of this sextile is to have psychologically intimate exchanges (Scorpio), which supports health (Virgo). Mutable earth focuses fixed water's need for transformation.

Libra sextile Sagittarius

Cardinal air sextile mutable fire. With Libra and Sagittarius, the reach now extends into the broader world. Libra is interpersonal, while Sagittarius seeks direction. The integration is *politics*, again using a broad definition. Collaboration (Libra) supports policy (Sagittarius)—this aspect deals with how people join together to achieve a purpose. The shadow is endless campaigning to get people to agree with you. This is quite evident in U.S. politics leading up to an election. There is a barrage of misinformation or half-truths, promises, and demagoguery.

If a political agenda is passionately advocated (heightened Sagittarius charge), inflexibility overpowers negotiations (Libra). If diplomacy (Libra) neutralizes opinions, it's impossible to get momentum in any certain direction. In balance, an approach that is acceptable to everyone (Libra), is vigorously pursued (Sagittarius). To manage this aspect consciously requires knowing exactly when to compromise without selling out our convictions. Cardinal air opens dialogue about mutable fire direction.

Scorpio sextile Capricorn

Fixed water sextile cardinal earth. These powerful signs integrate as *command*—the judicious wielding of authority. Institutions (Capricorn) support the psychodynamics of power (Scorpio). Scorpio is a catalyst for change, and Capricorn sculpts

118

this intention into workable forms, potentially on a broad social scale. Used intentionally, our public institutions rule society with conscious conviction. The shadow is controlling the collective through manipulation, oppression, and cruelty.

If the need for power (Scorpio) becomes excessively charged, then it corrupts institutions (Capricorn). The internal workings become shady as seen with Fascist regimes or some exclusive secret societies. If Scorpio is suppressed or denied by Capricorn, then the preservation of order or tradition will reign. Healthy balance here leads the dominant factions that govern society to incrementally progress through process and experience. It also leads those who occupy high office or prominent positions to properly understand the responsibility of having this level of command. Cardinal earth structures the power of fixed water.

Sagittarius sextile Aquarius

Mutable fire sextile fixed air. These worldly signs involve the assemblage (Aquarius) of people for a common purpose (Sagittarius)—*congregation.* Interconnectivity (Aquarius) supports direction (Sagittarius)—we are bolstered by allies who share our viewpoint. People congregate for social, political, philosophical, or religious reasons. The shadow here is organizing a cult. The attitude of "our way is best," is reinforced by the group psychology. At the extreme, there's the desire to convert everyone to a belief system or lifestyle through propaganda or brainwashing.

When Sagittarius is coming from a heightened charge, it asserts that one way is right for all. This overpowers the Aquarian neutrality which is more concerned with leveling the playing field than with being right. If the Sagittarian charge remains low, then causes aren't adopted and advocated for. Without any fiery momentum, interest in staying in the group diminishes—there's no compelling reason to show up. Too little passion results in stalling, while too much is overreaching. Ideally, we congregate with others to further noble aims, and the group becomes greater than its individual members. Fixed air provides the space and togetherness for a mutable fire purpose.

119

Capricorn sextile Pisces

Cardinal earth sextile mutable water. The integration of this sextile is found in *charity*. Compassion towards all people (Pisces) is given organizational structure (Capricorn). Capricorn grounds a dream or a vision of how things could be (Pisces). This aspect attempts to bridge transpersonal love and the social fabric. This may lead to problems as recipients of such charity may become overly dependent. The shadow is enabling weakness.

If the Pisces vision is overly charged, then the urge to create utopia exceeds what is actually possible. The potency of Capricorn becomes diluted, and good intentions lose their bearings. Without sufficient charge, institutions reflect an uninspired consciousness and cease to be charitable. Balancing realism (Capricorn) with idealism (Pisces) is a delicate process. Cardinal earth structures the benevolence of mutable water.

Aquarius sextile Aries

Fixed air sextile cardinal fire. An individual (Aries) provides *representation* for a group (Aquarius). Only through the actions of separate individuals (Aries), can the collective (Aquarius) actually progress. We have elections to choose which people are best—in theory, at least—to represent us in larger systems. The shadow is an over-identification as the spokesperson for a group. We lose our individual identity to the pressures of group-think and conformity.

If Aries carries an excessive charge, an individual disregards the consensus of the collective and acts unilaterally as seen with a rogue leader. Without personal empowerment (no Aries charge), a representative fails to behave decisively, and the entire group loses its effectiveness. Ideally, our representatives act boldly on the intentions of their constituents. Cardinal fire gives power to fixed air.

Pisces sextile Taurus

Mutable water sextile fixed earth. This aspect gifts us with **serenity**. Piscean love and inspiration can be brought into the body (Taurus) to produce inner peace. We can learn to sit (Taurus) in Spirit (Pisces), and connect the personal to the transcendent. The shadow here is sloth; an aversion to work or necessary exertion.

With too much Pisces charge we become detached from the mundane world. Practical things are forgotten, and life turns into a series of unrealized dreams. With a deficient Pisces charge, life becomes stagnant. Our body and physical senses dictate experience rather than inspiration. When this sextile is balanced, we are able to be "in the world but not of it." We find serenity by seeing that everything unfolding on the physical plane is in perfect accord with Spirit. Fixed earth grounds the flow of mutable water.

Chapter 6

Aspects & Evolution Part III
Quincunxes

The 150-degree quincunx doesn't neatly fit into the 12-fold division of the zodiac, and it's considered a secondary, or "minor," aspect by many astrologers. The Ptolemaic aspects (conjunction, opposition, trine, square, sextile), are given the designation of being "major" aspects. Another perspective on this aspect, though, is that it seems to suggest complex evolutionary programs that have yet to be addressed by most of us. These lessons are becoming increasingly relevant as our collective evolutionary journey is accelerating.

The quincunx connects signs that are one away from being in opposition, such as Aries and Virgo. Like the opposition, it's a relational aspect, though it has more to do with finding workable solutions than bridging polarities. A common keyword for the quincunx is *adjustment*, which does seem to capture its essence.

Similar to the trine, the quincunx always connects signs of differing modalities, which flavors the aspect in a supportive direction. However, like the square, a yin sign is always paired with a yang sign, and this friction requires negotiation. With regard to the charged-neutral dichotomy, a quincunx connects all three possible types: charged-charged, charged-neutral, or neutral-neutral—this is also similar to the square. The quincunx thus has factors in common with each of these major aspects.

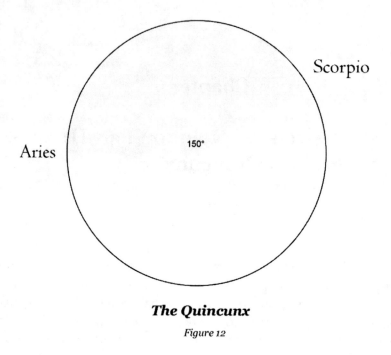

The Quincunx

Figure 12

Charged quincunx Charged

As described in the discussion of the charged squares, the lack of neutrality brings the evolutionary challenge to a crisis point. Since each side of the aspect can raise its intensity, the connection is prone to getting out of hand. The quincunx involves finding a workable solution, and, with the charges clashing, this is quite a tall order! Successful integration brings profound developmental growth. Unsuccessful integration leads to profound difficulties.

Aries quincunx Scorpio

Cardinal fire quincunx fixed water. These signs are perhaps the fiercest in astrology, so when they get together, watch out! Both involve conflict, sex, and hostility. The integration is learning how to manage *passion*. Aries concerns the personal, hot-blooded drive

124

that motivates us to get our needs met. Scorpio's social and psychological focus leads to loaded exchanges with others. The potential here includes both disastrous outcomes as well as a wealth of learning. The shadow is severe malice—being abusive, vengeful, or even violent. This is the combination where rape and murder would show up.

A significant area of overlap here is sexuality. Aries has a libidinous heat, which motivates procreation and ensures genetic survival. With too much eagerness, hunger, or force, the necessary self-orientation of Aries turns blatantly selfish. If its charge dominates, then Aries acts aggressively, torching others with rampant desire.

An excess of Scorpio inflicts psychological damage through vindictiveness, rage, jealously, manipulation, excessive drama, and underhanded tactics. Scorpio holds Aries hostage in its dungeon, playing out its wounded process.

Ideally, Aries can serve as a catalyst in getting the fire started. Scorpio provides the depth of water. When it's working well, this combination is what many of us really want in our private lives—hot, and meaningfully connected, sex! Learning to manage conflict, sorting out differences, and challenging others to be the best they can be are also part of this dynamic. Cardinal fire and fixed water passionately arouse each other.

Leo quincunx Pisces

Fixed fire quincunx mutable water. Leo wants to live in the moment, while Pisces goes with the flow in its otherworldly way, always seeking loftier experiences. Managed well, this combination correlates to having peak experiences. Maintaining clarity of awareness (Leo) in such altered states (Pisces) provides the integration, *spiritual awakening*. The shadow is the elevation of the personality in delusional ways—a messianic complex.

This combination may become hedonistic. Leo likes to party, while Pisces seeks to go beyond limits. The result is revelry, finding Dionysian release. The charge between the two signs can easily escalate toward some consequence. Aside from a simple

125

hangover or acting foolishly, many revelers have landed themselves in car crashes and hospital rooms. Leo is prone to indulgence, and Pisces welcomes ego-obliteration.

A Leo excess is the use of spirituality for self-aggrandizement—enjoying the benefits (fame, money, status) of being some form of the "enlightened master." Pisces dominance is having peak experiences that are disconnected from the core self, such as a substance-induced trip which is neither comprehensible nor beneficial.

Handled skillfully, this quincunx lights up (Leo) the transcendent parts of us (Pisces). We become aware (Leo) of mystical guidance, or the everlasting spiritual presence which envelops us. Bridging this world (Leo) to another (Pisces) is the program: lucid dreaming, vision quests, or anything that pierces the veil between dimensions would qualify splendidly. Fixed fire and mutable water awaken Spirit in us.

Sagittarius quincunx Cancer

Mutable fire quincunx cardinal water. Sagittarius is on the proverbial quest, and Cancer concerns love, family, the home, and our ancestry. The integration produces *self-discovery*—the pilgrimage towards an emotionally meaningful existence. Sagittarius continually likes to see what's around the corner and Cancer wants emotional fulfillment. Together they may search the entire world! The shadow is traveling the world to indoctrinate others. Instead of learning about the self, there is a heightened need to go great distances to convince others of, or force upon them, our views.

If Sagittarius holds the higher charge then questing is restless; we're always on the go in search of some ideal. This is seen in the endless wanderer, the procrastinator, or in other impatient behaviors. If Cancer dominates this dynamic then travel may be for escapist reasons. The driven adventurer may be running away from pain instead of dealing with it.

This quincunx also deals with seeking our roots or the creation of new ones. The inward journey has many moving experiences, an entire landscape to explore. This aspect is about finding

126

(Sagittarius) our emotional centeredness (Cancer), in every way. Mutable fire and cardinal water search for the self.

Neutral quincunx Neutral

Similar to the neutral-neutral squares, these quincunxes combine to form necessary structures for evolutionary advancement. The square is more fundamental—the integration of the neutral squares yields *civilization*, *nature*, and *science*, which are of paramount importance. With the quincunx, an additional evolutionary step is taken, towards *education*, *art*, and *technology*.

Capricorn quincunx Gemini

Cardinal earth quincunx mutable air. The institutional structure of Capricorn combines with the language and learning of Gemini to produce communications systems. In the spirit of Gemini, let's use two points of integration for this one: **education** and **media**. Any organization (Capricorn) housing Gemini activities would be included. As Gemini is a mutable sign, its diversity ranges from linguistics to journalism to broadcasting—anything designed to get the word out. All universities and the entire infrastructure of school systems are included here. The shadow is demanding intellectual conformity to preserve order or tradition.

Capricorn is the Elder, while Gemini is the student. Passing down knowledge to the next generation is a theme between these signs. Our teachers tend to be older, especially so during the formative years. It's easy for Capricorn to dominate this combination as tradition tends to change only gradually over time, and students generally defer to their teachers. An example of Capricorn dominating is the controlling school master.

Imbalance in the Gemini direction results in the dissemination of untested knowledge. Picture a curriculum founded upon a person's late-night brainstorming. The ideas may have been stimulating at the time, but should we teach our children these ephemeral thoughts?

127

Capricorn insists on integrity and solidity. It ensures that what is learned (education) or communicated (media) is reliable and useful. Gemini may provide information to inform Capricorn of how it can be updated. Together, this quincunx can be dependable (Capricorn) and exciting (Gemini)—ideal for classroom learning or in media broadcasts. Cardinal earth and mutable air create informational structures.

Taurus quincunx Libra

Fixed earth quincunx cardinal air. Both of these signs are ruled by Venus, the goddess of beauty. Taurus relates to the senses, the body, and the beauty of the physical world. Libra is conceptual, addressing aesthetics and the airy world of social norms and civility. The meeting point is *art*. Integration is found through materializing (Taurus) ideals of beauty (Libra). Creating a masterpiece would be an endpoint. The shadow is pretention—the garbage (sometimes literally), which is sold in the name of sophistication. Selling smears of paint for obscene prices as "high art" captures the gist. Materialism (Taurus) for social appearance (Libra) is also a pitfall here.

An issue that arises is that perfection is only an abstract concept. Once an ideal is made tangible, could it ever truly be perfect? Considering that no one has ever drawn a perfect circle, how could one create a flawless piece of art? Also, as soon as a concept is concretized, it is subject to the laws of aging and decay. The physical world (Taurus) is impermanent, while Libra's aesthetic sensibilities are above (air) such inconveniences.

Taurus enjoys simplicity and can find the value in anything. It is comfortable with the natural world, exactly as it is. If Taurus dominates this pairing, then raw materials outweigh Libra's aesthetic ideals. Art is sloppy and lacks any social value. For example, dilapidated clay pots are "nice" to family members but not big sellers at the market. Libra has a refined palate and high standards. Its excess is illustrated in a perfectionist violin-maker who finds the tiniest flaw in an otherwise perfect instrument and destroys it. He is never satisfied, and rarely benefits others with his talent. Too much Libra here results in snobbishness—the priority of achieving an ideal negates any redeeming value of what is constructed.

This interchange is managed by respecting the limits of the physical world and adorning it with the limitless, creative possibilities from the air. Together, sublime art is the potential. Fixed earth and cardinal air beautify our surroundings.

Virgo quincunx Aquarius

Mutable earth quincunx fixed air. These neutral signs deal with the application (Virgo) of the universal mind (Aquarius). How can we create actual workable machines and devices that reflect the awesome intelligence of nature? The integration is found in **technology**. The shadow is the proliferation of gadgets that make modern life dependent on machines. Humanness and meaning are thereby compromised.

This combination asks us to take the time and apply the effort (Virgo) to make some brilliant idea (Aquarius) manifest. Only in the last several decades have humans begun to accelerate this pace of technological development, as seen in the computer and electronics industry. Nevertheless, we've been developing basic technologies for a long time—the bow and arrow, indoor plumbing, or the abacus.

Too much emphasis on Virgo results in a plodding pace. There is a reluctance to modernize techniques, paradigms, or materials. The insistence on familiar results stifles new innovations. As a consequence, we all have the same products and variety is lost. On the other hand, airy Aquarius resists the grounding process and the necessary compromises that are required to produce anything at the earth level. Like trying to capture lightning in a bottle, Aquarius is uncooperative about being stripped-down and put in a box. An imbalance in the Aquarius direction is failure—brilliant possibilities remain out of reach and inventors become alienated from their work.

As we develop our collective intelligence, we are better able to work with Aquarius and make subtle refinements (Virgo) with our technologies. Ideally, these advances improve the quality of life

129

on the planet and also provide tangible evidence (Virgo) that we are moving forward (Aquarius). The resolution of this quincunx also equips us with the means (Virgo) to then reach out towards the cosmos (Aquarius) through telescopes, space exploration, or making contact elsewhere in the universe. There is probably no limit to what is possible with this combination, and the prospects are thrilling to consider. Mutable earth gives a variety of form to the intelligence of fixed air.

Charged quincunx Neutral

These quincunxes pair fire with earth and water with air. As discussed in previous sections, there is a delicate balancing act required with charged and neutral signs. Finding a point of equilibrium is the only way to manage this dynamic well. Too much or too little activation from the charged sign throws it out of balance.

Aries quincunx Virgo

Cardinal fire quincunx mutable earth: The integration here is *maturity*. Aries enjoys its autonomy, but life demands the attendance to responsibilities (Virgo). Aries can meet these challenges of self-development by being productive in some type of craft or service. The shadow is bossing others around with many suggestions of how they can shape up.

At first glance, attaining maturity may not seem like an advanced evolutionary lesson. However, our media shows us an endless parade of immature behaviors from the most seemingly accomplished people! It takes a steadfast commitment to self-development (Virgo) to act (Aries) as a healthy adult.

Virgo wants to curb Aries impulsive selfishness in order to live with integrity. In its excitement to take a big bite out of life (excessive charge), Aries can swagger away from practical considerations. Its flaws then become exaggerated for all to see.

If Virgo holds down the Aries charge, there can be wallowing in disappointment and self-criticism. The failure to rise up and handle responsibilities usually brings consequences. The kid who

130

refuses to do his homework or eat his vegetables gets punished and is sent to his room. This quincunx challenges us to simply grow up. Cardinal fire is tamed by mutable earth.

Leo quincunx Capricorn

Fixed fire quincunx cardinal earth. This connection deals with illuminating (Leo) our authority (Capricorn) in the world. It is powerful, almost regal in flavor—a likable manager, colorfully in charge. The integration of this aspect is found in **dominion**, exercising sovereignty and influence in our life. The shadow is all too common among our celebrities—the promotion of the cult of personality. Being the executive of a magazine (Capricorn) named after yourself, with your picture on every issue (Leo), would be one example.

The rising charge of Leo may swell with self-promotion and lack the earthy know-how and industriousness to back up its bluster. Leo then appears like a fool unprepared for his role. On the other hand, if we have too little charge to meet our public demands (Capricorn), Leo's unlit flame leads to powerlessness. The inability to rise to the challenge renders Leo a spineless "scaredy-cat."

Not many bosses, executives, or even high-paid athletes stay in touch with the wonder and enthusiasm (Leo), which motivated them to achieve (Capricorn) in the first place. Those who can exercise authority and still come across as accessible and warm have integrated this quincunx well. Cardinal earth organizes the impact of fixed fire.

Sagittarius quincunx Taurus

Mutable fire quincunx fixed earth. The integration is developing **gumption**—boldness of enterprise that is strategic and practical. Sagittarius has grand designs for exploration and adventure. Taurus is prudent, steady, and wants personal and financial security. Developing a life plan (Sagittarius) intended to bolster self-worth and our bank account (Taurus) is the lesson. The shadow is the shyster—the people who send emails from Africa promising to

131

pour millions in your bank account or those who run "Ponzi schemes."

A charged-up Sagittarius may be overly-optimistic as it schemes to get ahead. It may be seduced by the "can't miss" investment and pick up the phone to "act now." This strategy leads to folly as pragmatics (Taurus) are ignored. Absent an adequate Sagittarian charge, we may be resigned to our lot in life without protest, gradually sliding into inertia (Taurus) and deadening repetition. The comfort of a dependable paycheck becomes chilling as life loses its meaning.

Responding well to this pairing, we develop a mission (Sagittarius) to make money or attain security (Taurus). There is healthy excitement about practical investments. Fixed earth and mutable fire develop a profitable program.

Cancer quincunx Aquarius

Cardinal water quincunx fixed air. The integration is found in the Greek word *agape*—having love and altruistic feelings for all Cancer pertains to the personal heart, while Aquarius relates to the collective. This combination asks us to emotionally attune to humanity and its evolution. The shadow is losing oneself in causes. Imagine someone eternally camped out in front of the White House holding a protest sign. In the efforts to save the entire planet, we can lose a meaningful connection to our personal relations and even ourself.

The personal emotional needs of Cancer may become excessively charged and an obstacle, rather than a support, to collective advancement. Self-absorption can hold a group or community's process hostage to personal demands. When Cancer becomes activated, its needs become urgent and insatiable. Expecting the world to meet these requirements is a recipe for misery.

Without a Cancer emotional investment in collective evolution, the "why bother?" syndrome emerges. "One person is not going to change the world, so it doesn't matter what I do," is the justification. We become a bystander in our own life. Without "being the change you want to see in the world," the heart becomes

132

cold (Aquarius), and apathy sets in. Success here equates to feeling the impetus to connect with humanity. Fixed air holds the expansive possibilities for cardinal water to love.

Scorpio quincunx Gemini

Fixed water quincunx mutable air. Giving voice to and learning about (Gemini) psychological material in the unconscious (Scorpio) is part of the evolutionary opportunity here. The integration is *honesty*, both in how we address this material, and how we communicate about it to others. Gemini is curious and Scorpio territory is the proverbial Underworld, so choosing to learn about the psyche in search of answers is the program. This combination can manifest as talk therapy, psychology journals, or simply as asking friends probing questions—any discussion (Gemini) of loaded material (Scorpio) would qualify. The shadow is scathing honesty which is heartless and abusive—communication (Gemini) which hurts others (Scorpio).

An excessive Scorpio charge overrides reason and may dramatize or intensify exchanges in ways that undercut an open dialogue. Scorpio may use intimidation, taunts, or other strategies to consume Gemini in its clutches like a wild-eyed witch with a naïve teenager.

If the Scorpio charge is insufficient to provoke deep processes, Gemini minimizes or even pokes fun at the sensitive psychological material. Talking in circles and never really getting to the bottom of an issue leaves those involved perplexed and unsatisfied. Gemini's reason can neutralize the emotions, leaving Scorpio feeling rejected, lonely, or misunderstood.

Managed adeptly, this quincunx is resolved by the ability to move necessary processes along. This combination is like the psychopomp who travels between worlds and communicates without judgment. With honesty, we can learn to give attention, voice, emotion, and, ultimately, passage to what has been buried. This helps to release psychological material. Mutable air disperses fixed water.

133

Pisces quincunx Libra

Mutable water quincunx cardinal air. How do we humanly connect (Libra) in Spirit (Pisces)? How do we embrace each others' souls? With this aspect we connect the scattered pieces of Spirit together through relating. The integration lies with the Sanskrit word **Namaste**, the common greeting that honors the light of divinity in each other. The shadow is taking on the role of martyr or doormat and letting others trample over us. Allowing the house to be trashed by a rowdy group of teenagers just to be a "nice guy" is the gist.

When the Pisces urge to merge grows dominant, we become dreamy about the glorious potentials of our beloved. Pierced by Cupid's arrow, we're intoxicated by love, swooning with fantastic visions and removed from the true realities of interdependence. This is a recipe for letdown and disillusionment.

Without a Pisces charge, the magic of connecting vanishes. Rules, etiquette, and diplomacy are adhered to in the name of creating civility. A state of complacency covers the longing for a more transcendent love, which is seen as impractical and fanciful. Maintaining and feeding a loving spiritual bond with others is the gift available here. Cardinal air socializes mutable water.

An Interconnected System

Each of the 12 stages plays essential roles in evolution. With the inclusion of the quincunx, each of the 12 stages has a relationship with all 11 of the others. Proximity dictates the first link, as each is connected to the preceding and subsequent signs by way of the unfolding plot of the great evolutionary cycle. With the sextile (2), square (2), trine (2), quincunx (2) and opposition (1), every sign is in aspect to the remaining nine signs.

From this viewpoint, each stage/sign has 10 "faces." The two respective neighboring signs don't form aspects to, and therefore don't provide one of the "faces" of, the stage in question.

As a summary of the last 3 chapters, let's look at the 10 faces of each stage/sign. Listed first is the evolutionary task of the stage. Next comes the tension provided by the opposite sign. Harmony is provided by the two signs that trine a given sign, while the two signs in square provide the challenge. Peripheral support is available with the two signs in sextile. And advanced growth is provided by the two signs in quincunx. These 10 "faces" illuminate the 10 evolutionary lessons offered by each of the 12 stages.

Aries

Evolutionary Task: *autonomy*; bridging mysticism (Pisces) and resources (Taurus).

Tension: *behavior* (opposed Libra).

Harmony: *valor* (trine Leo); *conquest* (trine Sagittarius).

Challenge: *protection* (square Cancer); *leadership* (square Capricorn).

Peripheral Support: *agility* (sextile Gemini); *representation* (sextile Aquarius).

Advanced Growth: *passion* (quincunx Scorpio); *maturity* (quincunx Virgo).

Taurus

Evolutionary Task: *resources*; bridging autonomy (Aries) and mind (Gemini).

Tension: *endurance* (opposed Scorpio).

Harmony: *productivity* (trine Virgo); *success* (trine Capricorn).

Challenge: *abundance* (square Leo); *nature* (square Aquarius).

Peripheral Support: **nourishment** (sextile Cancer); **serenity** (sextile Pisces).

Advanced Growth: **gumption** (quincunx Sagittarius); **art** (quincunx Libra).

Gemini

Evolutionary Task: **mind**, bridging resources (Taurus) and heart (Cancer).

Tension: **learning** (opposed Sagittarius).

Harmony: **communication** (trine Libra); **genius** (trine Aquarius).

Challenge: **science** (square Virgo); **understanding** (square Pisces).

Peripheral Support: **agility** (sextile Aries); **fun** (sextile Leo).

Advanced Growth: **education, media** (quincunx Capricorn); **honesty** (quincunx Scorpio).

Cancer

Evolutionary Task: **heart** bridging mind (Gemini) and character (Leo).

Tension: **importance** (opposed Capricorn).

Harmony: **bonding** (trine Scorpio); **empathy** (trine Pisces).

Challenge: **protection** (square Aries); **romantic love** (square Libra).

Peripheral Support: **nourishment** (sextile Taurus); **health care** (sextile Virgo).

Advanced Growth: *self-discovery* (quincunx Sagittarius); *agape* (quincunx Aquarius).

Leo

Evolutionary Task: *character*, bridging heart (Cancer) and competence (Virgo).

Tension: *participation* (opposed Aquarius).

Harmony: *valor* (trine Aries); *grandeur* (trine Sagittarius).

Challenge: *trust* (square Scorpio); *abundance* (square Taurus).

Peripheral Support: *engagement* (sextile Libra); *fun* (sextile Gemini).

Advanced Growth: *spiritual awakening* (quincunx Pisces); *dominion* (quincunx Capricorn).

Virgo

Evolutionary Task: *competence*, bridging character (Leo) and relationship (Libra).

Tension: *improvement* (opposed Pisces).

Harmony: *productivity* (trine Taurus); *industry* (trine Capricorn).

Challenge: *science* (square Gemini); *foresight* (square Sagittarius).

Peripheral Support: *health care* (sextile Cancer); *therapy* (sextile Scorpio).

Advanced Growth: *technology* (quincunx Aquarius); *maturity* (quincunx Aries).

137

Libra

Evolutionary Task: *relationship*, bridging competence (Virgo) and power (Scorpio).

Tension: *behavior* (opposed Aries).

Harmony: *communication* (trine Gemini); *culture* (trine Aquarius).

Challenge: *romantic love* (square Cancer); *civilization* (square Capricorn).

Peripheral Support: *engagement* (sextile Leo); *politics* (sextile Sagittarius).

Advanced Growth: *Namaste* (quincunx Pisces); *art* (quincunx Taurus).

Scorpio

Evolutionary Task: *power*, bridging relationship (Libra) and direction (Sagittarius).

Tension: *endurance* (opposed Scorpio).

Harmony: *bonding* (trine Cancer); *sacred union* (trine Pisces).

Challenge: *trust* (square Leo); *wisdom* (square Aquarius).

Peripheral Support: *command* (sextile Capricorn); *therapy* (sextile Virgo).

Advanced Growth: *passion* (quincunx Aries); *honesty* (quincunx Gemini).

Sagittarius

Evolutionary Task: **direction**, bridging power (Scorpio) and vocation (Capricorn).

Tension: **learning** (opposed Gemini).

Harmony: **grandeur** (trine Leo); **conquest** (trine Aries).

Challenge: **foresight** (square Virgo); **religion** (square Pisces).

Peripheral Support: **politics** (sextile Libra); **congregation** (sextile Aquarius).

Advanced Growth: **gumption** (quincunx Taurus); **self-discovery** (quincunx Cancer).

Capricorn

Evolutionary Task: **vocation**, bridging direction (Sagittarius) and systems (Aquarius).

Tension: **importance** (opposed Cancer).

Harmony: **success** (trine Taurus); **industry** (trine Virgo).

Challenge: **leadership** (square Aries); **civilization** (square Libra).

Peripheral Support: **command** (sextile Scorpio); **charity** (sextile Pisces).

Advanced Growth: **dominion** (quincunx Leo); **education, media** (quincunx Gemini).

139

Aquarius

Evolutionary Task: *systems*; bridging vocation (Capricorn) and mysticism (Pisces).

Tension: *participation* (opposed Leo).

Harmony: *culture* (trine Libra); *genius* (trine Gemini).

Challenge: *nature* (square Taurus); *wisdom* (square Scorpio).

Peripheral Support: *congregation* (sextile Sagittarius); *representation* (sextile Aries).

Advanced Growth: *technology* (quincunx Virgo); *agape* (quincunx Cancer).

Pisces

Evolutionary Task: *mysticism*; bridging systems (Aquarius) and autonomy (Aries).

Tension: *improvement* (opposed Virgo).

Harmony: *empathy* (trine Cancer); *sacred union* (trine Scorpio).

Challenge: *religion* (square Sagittarius); *understanding* (square Gemini).

Peripheral Support: *serenity* (sextile Taurus); *charity* (sextile Capricorn).

Advanced Growth: *spiritual awakening* (quincunx Leo); *Namaste* (quincunx Libra).

Progressive Evolution

Chapter 7

The Evolution of Consciousness

In the following chapters, we'll explore how the elements structure and catalyze the development of consciousness in the grand story of progressive evolution. Many of the spiritual ideas presented in the first half of the book are organized here into a basic model of evolution. The merging of the transpersonal perspective with astrology can be very fruitful, but it does require us to look at the familiar astrology material with fresh eyes.

It's important to clarify how I will be using certain terms here, as they can have a wide range of meanings. These terms, as well as many others, are also listed in the glossary at the end of the book. *Ego* is the sense of a separate, autonomous self. Its goals are survival and the maintenance of a familiar identity. *Awareness*, as previously discussed with the light of fire, is used to name the intangible field that envelops all life. The *unconscious*, at both the personal and collective levels, holds the memories and impact of experience and relates to the water element. *Consciousness* is awareness within the separate self—the merging of fire with water. *Relative* reality encompasses our mundane, everyday experience as perceived through the separate self. The *transpersonal* level of reality refers to the soul and its connection to Spirit.

The variable most relevant to spiritual growth is the development of consciousness. When we become more conscious, we are able to understand, embrace, and approach life from a broader

143

perspective. Just as we develop from infant to adolescent to adult, there is a similar evolutionary process through which a soul advances. The end point has names such as enlightenment or self-realization—a completion of the soul's curriculum and expansion beyond the confines of the personal self/ego.

When we're unconscious, we fail to recognize our role in *creating* our experiences. The apparent separation between self and world, and self and other, sets up a dynamic in which we believe that we must deal with a barrage of stimuli that are coming at us from outside ourself. Some of this stimulation is desired and welcomed, while some of it is perceived as threatening and defended against. This common approach to life tends to perpetuate suffering. We place value judgments on everyone and everything around us, continually evaluating our experience, resisting it, and strategizing to improve it. This is the natural way an ego moves through life, trying to survive and be happy.

The tricky part is that the relative perspective is valid and relevant at the personal level. As we plainly experience, we have separate bodies and separate minds! Keeping consciousness solely identified at this level, however, prevents us from realizing the *transpersonal* level of reality. The perspective at the transpersonal level is quite different. At this level, the soul is our primary identity, and our human experience is understood to be exactly what we need for our spiritual growth. The effect of this view on our everyday life is that the terms "good" and "bad," lose their meaning. Resistance is replaced with a profound openness to everyone and anything that happens to arise in the present.

Spirit is continually trying to catalyze greater awareness, providing one (often) covert opportunity after the next despite our ego's nearly constant resistance. Identifying with the ego leaves us caught in what many spiritual teachers have called the "ego dream." How is it a dream? Life is a series of self-created experiences—the separate self creates a story of the self, of our friends and family, and of humanity and the world as a whole.

If we expect to be let down, we often create it. If we have a story that the world is unfair, we will find evidence to support it. If we believe that relationship happiness is not for us, then we tend to live in such a way as to confirm this belief. If we expect the shoe to drop, then here it comes. On the other hand, if we believe the world is benevolent, then we'll be able to see the kindness of a stranger or the subtle beauty in nature. The world serves as a giant externalization of the psyche. It reflects our beliefs back to us. The ego's dream that it is the center of the universe is actually true, though not quite in the way it thinks!

Is it possible to free ourself from the drama and suffering of the ego dream? Indeed, yes. We can learn to see beyond the machinations of the ego, the externalization of our personal stories, and awaken to something new. We can let go of our attachment to our personal preferences and find our home in the present moment. Life can be experienced with complete openness, a radical acceptance of how reality is unfolding.

This arising of transpersonal awareness can be very scary to the ego and its tight hold on its version of reality. It is a radical shift in identity that, while not a literal death, can seem as such to the ego. Liberation from the ego dream allows us to recognize the self in everything. We become what we always were—Spirit.

The idea here is not to view the ego as negative or to try to destroy it. Action along these lines is itself generated by, and further fuels, the ego. Instead, the leverage point for this shift in identity lies in not being caught in identifying *as* the ego and not being seduced by its beliefs. Since we will still be embodied and continue to have a particular biography, our task is to bridge the transpersonal to the personal, to simultaneously inhabit both levels of reality.

Enter Astrology

There is some debate as to how the ego is located and understood within astrology. Some see the Sun as the indicator of ego, as it's the central manager of our life force. Others point to the Moon since the ego focuses on survival and operates in a reactive way. The view proposed here looks toward both luminaries as being involved with the ego and its transcendence.

The Moon deals with how experiences are absorbed and consolidated. Most of this material is stored unconsciously. There is a parallel in how the Moon in the sky weaves in and out of various degrees of light and how the personal self has different degrees of awareness. We gradually get to know the contents stored in the deep "lunar well" through our life experiences as we continuously bring components of our past experiences into to the present.

Replaying familiar themes in this way presents ongoing opportunity if we are interested in spiritual growth. We dredge up ancient memories that tether us to an earlier, and less evolved, version of ourself. Becoming aware of the themes and patterns allows us to release what we no longer need to carry. As the conditioning of prior experience recedes, we become increasingly centered in the present moment.

The Sun is our presence and awareness, the energy of the now. Serving as the life force, the Sun is how we *consciously* approach the world. Underneath, the Moon's unconscious memories have great influence on our current consciousness—hence we experience the ego dream. Prior to loosening the ego's grip, the Sun radiates out through it. We mistakenly believe the Sun is about ego because it's so influenced by it. The process of loosening the ego, though, gradually liberates the Sun, allowing it to shine independent of the filter of the contracted ego-self. At this point, we can clearly see that the Sun is distinct from the ego but had been wearing it like a disguise. Just as fire evaporates water, the freed energy of the Sun is then available to quicken the remainder of the loosening process.

The ego has its roots in the Moon. Therefore, the extent to which the Moon's issues are resolved has a huge influence on how much the ego controls the life force in the present (Sun). When we resolve the past, we gain access to greater awareness (Sun) in the present, and the resulting power of conscious choice replaces reactive habit. Like the physical Sun that shines its light everywhere and provides warmth without limitation, we can expand into connection with life in an open and generous way.

Resolving the Moon

Emotion is energy in motion. When we experience an emotional charge, something is asking for more movement. Just as the Moon in the sky is a rock, we too have hardened emotional patterns in the soul. Emotional release can loosen the solidified energy, enabling us to move beyond the residue of past experience that wasn't processed through at the time it occurred. When we do process through this material, what is left is learning—the insight, wisdom, or greater depth we achieve through our experiences. It's not that we forget what happened to us, but rather that we are able to let go of our attachment to it.

Life can be very frustrating as we so often repeat familiar soul dramas without a sense of closure. One result is that we develop highly sophisticated coping mechanisms which then also become part of the dynamic. Vitality and creativity fade away when so much of our energy is spent in maintaining a defensive stance toward life. We all value freedom, but most of us are like prisoners held captive by the past.

The resolution to this state of suffering is actually quite simple, though not necessarily easy. What's required is to *feel* the impact of prior experiences—to bring in the energy (Sun) that initiates some internal motion. With the introduction of awareness in the present moment, the solidified past can be energized out of its hardened state. This process can be highly destabilizing, which is why it is so chronically avoided by the ego. Light can appear quite threatening to those who are used to being in the dark. The familiar is comforting on one level, even if its content is painful.

Being willing to feel our repressed emotions allows the solidi-fied lunar material to start to dissolve. Most people feel better—clearer, lighter, relieved—after a good cry or a non-violent venting of anger. The transformative effect is the longer term pay-off for this kind of healing: anger turns to motivation and directness, sadness becomes compassion, and fear may shift into strength and courage. Our greatest pains can actually become the foundation of our power. What a profound reward for being willing to interrupt

147

our habitual defensive reactions and actually engage with the emotions of our inner world.

Choosing the Past

One way to achieve closure with our emotional material is to *choose* our past. Since ego naturally moves toward pleasure and away from pain, we enact some type of resistance when we think something bad or unacceptable has happened. With increased awareness of the benefits of moving energy, we can actually choose to fully accept everything in our past. Easier said than done, though the resulting freedom and power make it well worth it. Some metaphysical understanding can help encourage the process.

Recall that the archetype of Uranus/Aquarius serves as the grand metaphysical container, a behind-the-scenes coordinator of our spiritual growth. It connects everything together for the purpose of spiritual awakening. When we are open to seeing that life does things *for* us, rather than *to* us, our stories can become gentler. Instead of identifying as victims in a cruel or random universe, we understand that, no matter the external appearance of events, life's continual intention is in provoking us to wake up to the next level of our evolution. The severity of these challenges only increases with our resistance to them.

Now, it's certainly true that horrible things happen all the time. Let's consider the following scenario: A woman is sexually abused and then represses the memory. Due to this repression, she experiences chronic apathy and low-grade depression. Anti-depressants are prescribed and she is able to have a more productive life. Most people would consider this a success, as the woman was able to "move on" with her life. However, is there emotional closure? The impact of the abuse remains, though it's been medicated and pushed down into the unconscious.

Let's now consider that the woman is abused a second time. Most people would understandably label this as an awful turn of events. On the personality level, this assessment is all too true. On a spiritual level, though, it may be the ticket to freedom. The buried emotions from prior abuse are certain to become activated. Instead

148

of being unconscious and unintegrated, this woman has the opportunity to get in touch with the array of emotions involved in being abused—rage, grief, terror, etc. There can now be some *movement* of the repressed material and a cathartic process of emotional release. True resolution and peace now become possible. The woman may not need antidepressants anymore.

The second incident of abuse may further spiritual growth, or it may deepen the wounding. It's our response that is key in determining its impact. When we welcome experiences as our evolutionary curriculum, we can align with them. We can also look back and consciously accept—actually *choose*—the rejected events in our biographies when we see all the growth that they have catalyzed. Who wouldn't choose to experience the events that have led to the most spiritual growth?

The End of Separation

To view everything as necessary and meaningful, no matter how unpleasant or even horrific, is to move beyond the ego and its judgments. The knowledge that all souls have been through endless dramas that are largely stored in the unconscious allows us to approach life with the curiosity of an archaeologist. We learn the contours and content of our soul by noticing what situations provoke a charge in us.

These charges are the threads that point us toward the lingering issues within our soul. They come in many guises: the confrontational spouse, the disrespectful neighbor, the absentee parent. There are an abundance of "teachers" out there for us to learn from. Upon activation of an emotional charge, we can trust that there is something unresolved to attend to. With a willingness to explore these charges, submerged lunar material can be contacted and released.

When we move beyond seeing things from the relative perspective as good/bad, there is no blame. There is only appreciation and compassion for the whole huge process of the growth of consciousness. Sure, some people have it rougher than others, but those who experience great difficulty have greater treasure available with successful growth.

Being able to choose our past leads to closure as well as diminishing future charges that would have otherwise arisen. The victim of sexual abuse described earlier may hear that a child has been similarly abused. Instead of getting angry, she may be able to feel love and care for both the victim *and* the perpetrator. The only way to assist the evolution of consciousness is to have compassion for everyone struggling and acting unconsciously. If not, then there is resistance to the realities of life and an insistence on everyone acting in ways that we find acceptable. This is impossible to ask of the world and a surefire recipe for perpetual suffering.

When we give up on the idea that it's preferable for events to unfold in ego-friendly ways, there is no use for seeing things in relative terms. Events are seen as necessary and people are seen as works in progress. All of us are enrolled in a giant school of spiritual learning. We all make mistakes as we go, and that's part of the process of developing consciousness. It's only "bad" if we make it so.

The Moon sees to our survival—a most important function! However, staying in survival mode inhibits mature growth. If we remain unconscious and unresolved, then the Moon functions as a regressive pull to the past. In this way it can be considered negative (pulling energy down), but in no way is the astrological Moon something to treat with disdain. Actually, what's needed is quite the opposite. When we embrace the Moon, we feel love and compassion for ourselves and everyone else.

A Spiritual View of the Luminaries

The two main levels of our reality—the relative and the transpersonal—have different perspectives on astrology and its various components. Seeing this difference of perspective as it applies to the Sun and Moon, the two central energies in the system, can assist us in understanding the dynamics of our evolutionary growth. Though there may be a preference for simplicity, being able

150

to integrate the nuance of two perspectives can be very supportive to our continued development.

The usual way the Sun and Moon are understood is from the relative level. The Sun is considered masculine, and the Moon is considered feminine. Other ways the luminaries are traditionally divided include: rational/emotional, active/receptive, yang/yin, hot/cold, ego/id, independence/relatedness, and God/Goddess. From our position on Earth, it does appear that the luminaries are equal. They are about the same size in the sky, and we have the light of the day (Sun) and the light of the night (Moon)—they make an obvious and complementary pair.

The field of psychological astrology has made great contributions to the endeavor of personal growth. It has done so, in part, by refining the meaning of many components of the astrological system and by advocating for the balancing of the polarities that these meanings create. For instance, Mars is better understood by seeing it in the context of its relationship with Venus. And the expansiveness of Jupiter makes more sense when we think of it forming a natural dyad with the contraction of Saturn. Regarding the luminaries, psychological astrologer Liz Greene offers her views in *Relating*, page 36.

> *In general, the sun is a symbol of consciousness and the moon of the unconscious in a man's horoscope; and in a woman's the moon symbolises consciousness and the sun the unconscious.*

Greene is unquestionably a brilliant astrologer. And yet, the polarity of gender—as well as every other polarity—only applies at the relative level. If we are to move to the transpersonal, we must transcend this type of duality.

To help shift us to a transpersonal perspective of the roles of the luminaries, we can consider some astronomical facts. Though we are used to calling the Moon a "luminary," this is inaccurate. It is bright in our night sky but has no source of light of its own. It merely *reflects the light of the Sun.* The Moon on its own exists in utter darkness. In contrast, the Sun's light illuminates the entire solar system. It also serves as energetic center that sustains all life.

151

While the two bodies appear to be the same size from Earth, they are extremely unequal in this regard as well. The Sun's diameter is actually 400 times larger than the Moon's. But since it is also about 400 times farther away from us than the Moon, the two appear to be about the same size. In terms of volume, the difference is staggering—the Sun occupies roughly as much space as 64 million Moons. The Sun is the massive gravitational center of our entire solar system. The Moon, circling our small planet, obviously has no such role.

Though classified as a "planet" in astrology, we know that the Sun is actually a *star*, which connects it to the wider cosmos. Stars join together in their own clusters, systems, and galaxies. The Moon, like everything else within our solar system, does not have that reach.

From the transpersonal view, we can see the Moon as the vehicle of the separate self, the ego, while the Sun brings us to the broader field of transpersonal awareness. This process is universal for humans, whether we are male or female. Viewing the luminaries in this genderless way may allow us to completely identify with both of them instead of primarily with just one.

Existing in the relative world, the Moon is preoccupied with polarities: past/future, good/bad, and male/female. With the Sun, we can extend into the transpersonal, evolving from our "small" ego-self, to our "bigger" self. Eckhart Tolle's words in *The Power of Now* illustrate this relationship between the luminaries:

> *Past and future obviously have no reality on their own. Just as the moon has no light of its own, but can only reflect the light of the sun, so are past and future only pale reflections of the light, power, and reality of the eternal present.*

Seeing the Sun in this spiritual way assists in understanding the lunar cycle. At the New Moon, the luminaries are together—the individualized consciousness (Moon) is merged with Spirit (Sun), illustrating a divine partnership. The Moon moves away to gather experience and then eventually returns. This is analogous to how

152

individuals separate, incarnate, and then return to the oneness of Spirit.

The Moon has a secure position in the solar system because of the Sun. The Moon *depends* on the Sun to hold it (and the Earth) in place through gravity, but *the Sun doesn't need the Moon.* The light of awareness and universal vitality does not need individual consciousness for it to exist, but individuals are enveloped in the broader sustenance of Spirit. Stated simply, we only exist as a part of Spirit—Spirit exists independently of the human project. For evolutionary growth to proceed, the luminaries function as partners—awareness and presence (Sun) are integrated into the separate self (Moon). Just as the Moon reflects the light of the Sun, the separate self is a reflection of Spirit's magnificence.

Pairings such as yin/yang and male/female represent complementary and equal energies, with neither member of the pairing being superior to the other. This is a potent truth at the relative level, and the luminaries can, of course, be viewed from this level. From the transpersonal perspective, however, the luminaries function as the central players in the process of liberating ourself from polarities altogether. In *viewing* the luminaries in this way, we open the door to *using* them for our evolution into the transpersonal. For more information on understanding the luminaries in a spiritual way, see my book, *Between Past & Presence: A Spiritual View of the Moon & Sun.*

Spiritual Fire

From the common vantage point of separation, all four elements have different functions that are equal in importance. From the transpersonal view, however, fire has special status. Representing *energy*, fire is the basic component of the entire universe. Fire is associated with Spirit, and everything originates in its energetic creativity. It is the constant from which the other elements emerge. Let's review the two main properties of fire—light and heat—both of which have spiritual implications.

The association of light with awareness is straightforward. When light shines on something, it brings it into awareness. Any-

153

thing in the dark is hidden, and therefore eludes our awareness. We commonly say that understanding is achieved when something "comes to light." A primary goal of spiritual practice is increasing awareness and attaining enlightenment. Science informs us that the speed of light is constant in the universe. The spiritual parallel of this fact is that awareness is also universally constant.

Fire is also associated with heat. It is eternally crackling, refusing to stay still. Science has named the condition of a cessation of all energetic movement as *absolute zero*. But this is only a theoretical temperature, as energy never does fully stop. It can't do so since it's interconnected with all energy, just as no part of an actual flame could disconnect itself from the rest of a fire.

Everything is buzzing at a certain temperature—the amount of heat determines the level of excitement in the molecules of the substance. When heat reaches a particular level, it sustains life. Heat is associated with *vitality*—the universe is alive as a vast energetic field. Science describes the law of the *conservation of energy*. The totality of energy in the universe is neither growing nor diminishing. Fire is eternal, a condition which no other element can claim.

It might appear that the element of air (space) is constant, but it turns out this isn't so. Einstein's special theory of relativity informs us that space must be seen in its relation to time—space and time are inherently linked as *spacetime*. Astrologically, Saturn is the energy that organizes space and time to play their part within our familiar, relative reality. Fire is transpersonal, while the other three elements are most relevant in the world of separation.

Chapter 8

Elemental Levels

As we've explored, the four levels of human reality make natural correlations with the astrology elements: the physical links to earth, the emotional to water, the mental to air, and the soul to fire. We've also discussed how these levels function differently, each having its own scope and role within the process of evolution. Here, we'll discuss these four realms in a new way, as the central structure of the grand process of progressive evolution, the development of consciousness. As we'll see, each element manifests in a unique way at each respective level.

Earth: The Physical Level

The first level of reality is the physical. Physics and chemistry are the disciplines that study it. The physical world appears simple. Everything tangible has a particular color, size, weight, and use. There isn't great debate about what to do with a chair, or about the function of a hammer. Due to this apparent simplicity, we learn to have a basic trust in the world. We feel confident that we won't drop off the edge of the earth or float up into the sky when we walk down the street. As children, we learn to interact with the physical world by building block towers or mixing paint colors. We see consistent patterns with these experiments. As we grow older, we quickly learn that we can effectively manipulate the physical realm.

155

The existence of houses, automobiles, and the other myriad products of industry is convincing evidence that we humans can utilize the physical with great mastery.

Although it seems so familiar and straightforward, the physical world is actually extremely complex. The emergence of quantum physics in the early 20th Century initiated a revolution in our understanding. Paralleling the way that a spiritual view of life complements but doesn't replace our more mundane, day-to-day existence, quantum physics complements classical physics without replacing its simple Newtonian laws.

Viewed at the quantum level, the physical world's solidity vanishes, and it reveals its true identity to be energy! This condition has led physicist and psychologist Arnold Mindell to characterize physics as a "house without a foundation." Quantum physics also offers us the principle of *nonlocality*. This principle describes another astounding fact about our "ordinary" physical world: there are connections and communications between particles that are not bound by time and space.

Werner Heisenberg is famous for offering his "uncertainly principle," which states that we cannot know both the location and speed of the (apparent) particles which compose our physical world. If we pinpoint a particle's speed, we can't identify its location, and vice versa. In fact, at the quantum level, things only have a *tendency* to exist; nothing has certainty. There are *probability fields* which may become activated. To top it all off, the *wave-particle duality* asserts that all matter exhibits both wave-like and particle-like properties.

In sum, the physical realm and its abundance of forms turns out not to be solid. Furthermore, it's not even predictable. It's endlessly interconnected in a complexity that goes beyond what we can perceive. How interesting! Although paradoxical, we can see the physical world as both durable and also as basically nothing and uncertain.

Elements at the Earth Level

In this strange world of uncertainty, how might we think of the four elements? We may have to think strangely! Does science

156

give us any evidence of earth, water, air, and fire within physical material? We know that a basic building block at this level is the atom. Atoms join together to form molecular structures. The atom has *neutral* and *charged* components to its energy.

The positive charge of protons correlates with fire, and the negative charge of electrons correlates to water. Neutrons are correlated with both the air and earth elements. This setup reflects the neutral planets Mercury and Venus, both of which have air and earth components. The charged planets (using modern rulership) only rule one sign each.

In the atomic structure, the electron orbits around the nucleus just like the Moon orbits around the Earth. Both the electron and the Moon are associated with the charged element water. At the molecular level electrons are exchanged between atoms to form bonds. This process is similar to how people bond together at the biological level to build relationships that become the sum of the various parts.

Although electrons are particles, they also may be construed as *waves*. In *Quantum Mind,* Arnold Mindell correlates the particle/wave dichotomy with content/process or left/right brain perspectives. When electrons are seen as particles, they are material. When seen as waves, they are energy and involved with process. When the flow of process is interrupted by analysis, electrons miraculously appear as particles. This event is called the "collapse of the wave function," and its stunning significance lies in reflecting how our state of consciousness can determine how the world shows up for us.

Water: The Emotional Level

Life emerges onto the scene at the biological water level. Here, organisms are attuned to nature and participate in the great web of life. There are various levels of consciousness, from people and animals down to the simplicity of plants. We may think of consciousness as an attunement with nature, a *relationship* with life and its rhythms, cycles, and weather. A Venus Flytrap knows when to shut on its prey; trees sprout new leaves in the spring and shed

157

them in the autumn. Inanimate objects obviously have none of these abilities. The Gaia hypothesis asserts that the Earth itself is a living organism. With its abundance of water, this idea would make sense.

Just like at the physical level, everything is interconnected here at the biological level. This is the biosphere and the great food chain that all living things are a part of. Members of the biosphere provide support for each other's survival, both directly and indirectly. Trees and animals exchange oxygen and carbon dioxide. And all plants and animals eventually become food for other parts of the food chain, whether that be grazers, predators, scavengers, or the bacteria and fungi that provide the essential function of decomposition. Among members of many animal species there is often fierce competition for mates and resources. The total picture involves incredibly complex networks of both interdependent sustenance and competitive survival of the fittest.

The biological level as a whole is characterized by vibrancy and vitality. All the colors and textures in nature's palette are on display. Rain forests, rich with life-nurturing water, contain incredibly dense and diverse populations of plants and animals. Deserts, with their scarcity of water, are comparatively barren.

As we've discussed before, water relates to emotion. The feeling function ensures that we are connected to and invested in how life unfolds. Emotions drive us to intimately bond with others and to produce and care for offspring. A central function of the biological level is reproduction, which for humans and many animals is facilitated by liquid genital secretions. The human fetus is surrounded by a watery environment, and milk is our food during infancy. Most types of emotional activation also involve movement of fluids—tears with sadness; adrenaline with anger; perspiration with fear; endorphins with love or joy.

This level is where the separate self experiences all of the bumps and bruises, the growth and breakthroughs that are part of evolutionary development. When we navigate this level well, there is the sensation of being in *flow*. We send out and receive *waves* of energy just by having consciousness. The poetic metaphor that we

158

are sailing down rivers back to the sea may be more real than we imagined! The water level is a vast exchange of consciousness.

Elements at the Water Level

At this level, the elements show up as the literal earth, water, air, and fire that we interact with daily. Our feet stand upon the earth. We drink and bathe in water, exist in spacious air, and are warmed by fire.

The elements are involved in a grand system of interdependency. Everything tangible has earth. We know that water makes up a large part of all living things. Space is all around, and energy, or fire, pervades it all. All four elements are intertwined, forever joined both in us and around us. The same situation occurs on our planet. The Earth itself is composed of land surrounded by water. It has an atmosphere (air) and heat (fire). Furthermore, this earthy/watery sphere is located in spacious air, revolving around a great big ball of fire.

Here is a quote from the IMAX film *Blue Planet*.

> *[The Earth's] natural systems slowly recycle the air, water and even the rock. In one cycle, heat from the sun evaporates water from the ocean to form clouds. Winds drive the clouds over land. Rain from the clouds falls back to the earth and then runs down to the sea, where the cycle begins once more. Heat stored in the clouds can drive them upwards into towering thunderheads. Inside them, powerful electric charges are building.*

There is a lovely spiritual parallel to this summary of Earth's climate process:

> *[The Earth's] natural systems slowly recycle the air, water and even the rock.*
The elements are systemically interconnected and recycled as part of us.

159

In one cycle, heat from the sun evaporates water from the ocean to form clouds.
The fire from our souls influences the development of an auto-nomous consciousness that separates from the underlying unity.

Winds drive the clouds over land.
Developing the intellect gives us perspective on our evolutionary condition.

Rain from the clouds falls back to the earth and then runs down to the sea, where the cycle begins once more.
What we learn may be applied to the way that life is lived before becoming absorbed back to the collective consciousness, only to be born once more.

Heat stored in the clouds can drive them upwards into towering thunderheads.
The spiritual growth we achieve resonates in the glory of nature.

Inside them, powerful electric charges are building.
The elements build toward another incarnation, using the building blocks of their basic charges.

Air: The Mental Level

There are three personal levels to our existence—physical (earth), biological (water), and mental (air). The earth is our found-ation; the water is our center; and the air level is our heights. Air is the level of mind. With the advancements and technologies of the so-called information age, the air level has risen in importance. It has become natural that people tend to identify with their thoughts. Around the time that the exploration of the frontiers of the mind began to accelerate, Descartes proclaimed, "I think therefore I am." This view encapsulates the modern mindset.

The fields dedicated to studying the air level vary by their focus, and every discipline makes use of the mind in some way. The mental level is where we strive to comprehend existence and integrate knowledge. The thirst for information is seemingly un-quenchable. Humans have ventured into the most specialized areas

160

of study in a wide array of disciplines, and yet there is still so much to learn. From computer technology to building rockets to understanding quantum physics, there is unlimited information to grasp.

Air is neutral and rational. Knowledge is *supposed to be* objective and impartial, facts being elevated over opinions or commentary. However we can't avoid injecting ourselves into everything we experience. Some people are more attuned to neutrality and are able to approach this level logically, while others have more of a charged approached which tends to be more psychological. Ultimately, we all have both of these faculties as the brain's split into the hemispheres illustrates.

There is a parallel between air at the physical and mental levels. Out in space, air is cool, detached, clear, and objective. The closer it gets to Earth, however, the more air becomes associated with the wind in our atmosphere. Wind is actually the result of hydrostatic pressure (water) and temperature (fire), the fluctuations of the charged elements. The analogy here is that information becomes increasingly subjective the closer it hits home. When the subject is removed, air is rightfully understood for its objectivity.

Air is involved with transmitting information. Having cognitive functioning that is based on a *brain and nervous system* establishes membership in the air level. Plants and more primitive animal life remain solely at the water level.

Communication is another component of the air level and similarly draws the line between life at the water and air levels. Communication lubricates social interactions as well as serving as the medium of information exchange. When we speak, airwaves are filled with our voices. Radio and other communication technologies refer to being "on the air," when transmitting sound. The air level hosts sound—it has an auditory orientation. The speed of sound is very fast, echoing the same buzzing going on in our heads.

Air also deals with *socialization*, and this is another way to separate the air level from the water. In order to connect intelligently with others, some form of brain is necessary to process information and make decisions. The organization of complex social behavior in the forms of communities and societies becomes

161

possible here. The expansion into collectivity through networking is a function of the air element.

Humor lives within the province of air. The more sophisticated the mind becomes, the greater the capacity to play within the realms of language and ideas. We notice that some animals, such as chimpanzees and dolphins, have great humor potential, while animals with simpler neurological systems, such as a mouse, are not intentionally comedic. As for us humans, the more we develop the brain, the more access we have to its wondrous potential for satire, slapstick, and other improvisations.

Elements at the Air Level

At the air level, the elements are intangible concepts, descriptions, or ideas. They are relevant in understanding ourselves as well as the larger world. The air level is *symbolic*. In traditional astrological thought, the elements have only been understood here in terms of their psychological and archetypal meanings instead of in a multi-leveled way. The following is a summary of this information and was also given in Chapter 1.

Earth is stable and structured. It relates to our physical bodies and practical issues. We label earthy people "solid"; someone reliable may be called "a rock" or "unmovable." They are "down to earth", the "salt of the earth", "grounded," and have good "common sense." Earth types may simplify matters to the bare essentials and others might label them "thick-headed." They tend to be task-oriented, materialistic, dependable, and effective. Functioning primarily in consensus reality, they operate within established structures and paradigms.

Water is emotional, vulnerable, loving, and attuned to needs. Watery people may "go with the flow." Some may be prone to "gush," and others are "flooded" with intense emotions. We consider watery people "deep" and those without this element, "shallow." They tend to "absorb" life and can be quite sensitive to their environment. They remind us about the frailty of the human condition, how each of us has a tender heart inside. Watery people are natural nurturers, though they are also prone to hurting others if they lose their center. At the extreme, watery people can be frantic, emotionally demanding, or extremely insecure.

Air is rational and reasonable, communicative, intellectual, and aesthetically-minded. We may call airy people "brainy," "cool," "ungrounded," "space cadets," or, most famously, "air heads." Some airy people "need their space," and can be aloof, superficial, or detached. These people can also be friendly, fascinating, or even brilliant. They like complexity, sophistication, nuance, and variety. They tend to move around physically or socially—always enthralled by what they might learn or experience.

Fire is the part of us that is untamed and passionate, wanting to take a big bite out of life or spread good cheer. We may call fiery people "warm," "hot," "burning with desire," or, sometimes, "hot-headed." Fiery people can be impulsive, seek center stage, or display their colors brightly. They have ample supplies of energy and motivation to pursue their aims. They are daring, sensation-seekers, and can be aggressive or dangerous.

To further understand the elements at this level, we can look at the astrological signs, as their nature is psychological and archetypal. The air level is personal, so it does include a spectrum of expression contingent upon the degree of proficiency we have with the archetype. Here we'll look at the range from optimal to mismanaged uses.

Earth

Optimal Taurus: peaceful, secure, artistic, natural, strong, gentle.
Mismanaged Taurus: stubborn, greedy, uncomfortable, indolent, gluttonous.

Optimal Virgo: precise, adept, humble, capable, satisfied, helpful.
Mismanaged Virgo: obsessive, anxious, lost in details, repressed, worn out.

Optimal Capricorn: dignified, ethical, reliable, powerful, enduring.
Mismanaged Capricorn: controlling, uncaring, relentless, afraid, power hungry.

Water

Optimal Cancer: empathic, heartfelt, emotionally intelligent, devoted, thoughtful.
Mismanaged Cancer: defensive, lonely, crabby, prickly, upset, overprotective.

Optimal Scorpio: strong, purposeful, intense, compelling, determined, honest.
Mismanaged Scorpio: hurt, vengeful, brooding, harsh, manipulative, abusive.

Optimal Pisces: contemplative, mystical, psychic, aware, poetic, fluid, inspiring.
Mismanaged Pisces: confused, absent, escapist, dreamy, lost, weak.

Air

Optimal Gemini: witty, curious, flexible, articulate, jack-of-all-trades, fascinating.
Mismanaged Gemini: disorganized, rushed, over-intellectualizing, tangential, immature.

Optimal Libra: graceful, sophisticated, charming, fair, aesthetically-minded, amiable.
Mismanaged Libra: slick, co-dependent, overly pleasing, phony, snobbish.

Optimal Aquarius: innovative, brilliant, virtuoso, humanitarian, unique, social, free.
Mismanaged Aquarius: unstable, rebellious, eccentric, detached, invisible, erratic.

Fire

Optimal Aries: brave, bold, decisive, heroic, athletic, passionate.
Mismanaged Aries: impulsive, violent, anti-social, brash, macho, forceful.

Optimal Leo: noble, colorful, charismatic, entertaining, present, creative.
Mismanaged Leo: childish, boasting, egocentric, entitled, demanding, naive.

Optimal Sagittarius: purposeful, wise, confident, adventuresome, erudite, intrepid.
Mismanaged Sagittarius: bombastic, lackadaisical, dogmatic, imprudent, arrogant.

Fire: The Soul Level

The fire level is associated with the soul. Theology is geared toward studying the soul, while mysticism aims to directly experience it.

Fire energizes the physical ground, fuels the entire range of emotion and life forms, and is embedded in the intellect. At these three levels fire can be discussed using language. However, at its own level, the transpersonal, there are no words that can express the direct experience of fire. As soon as words are put on it, the experience is unavoidably pulled into the mental level and thereby distorted. When spiritual experience is analyzed, fire vanishes into the thin air of thoughts.

Fire is the creative spark of life that burns eternally. Its role for us while we're in the state of separation is to *fuel evolutionary momentum toward spiritual realization.* The link from the personal to the transpersonal is the soul.

The soul is a part of Spirit that ventures off to fulfill a specific spiritual mission. The soul remains connected to the oneness and strives to return back to it. The soul is like a flame that is part of the broader fire of Spirit. And the way that we connect to Spirit is through fire.

> *Unless the eye catch fire, God will not be seen.*
> *Unless the ear catch fire, God will not be heard.*
> *Unless the tongue catch fire, God will not be named.*
> *Unless the heart catch fire, God will not be loved.*
> *Unless the mind catch fire, God will not be known.*

William Blake

Although the soul seems elusive to our normal perception, we can develop greater awareness of it. The key is to move beyond being caught in, and identified with, the chatter of the mind. We can then experience the light (awareness) and heat (presence) of fire.

When we become absorbed *in the present moment* there is often an unmistakable quality of freedom and lightness. Being present may sound simple, but we tend to be chronically distracted by thoughts, feelings, or sensations. When we are present, we connect consciousness (water) with the soul (fire).

By connecting with the soul, we are able to receive fire's creative inspiration. The most obvious routes are through spiritual practice: meditation, yoga, vision quests, etc. However, since fire is pervasive, we can become aware of it at any time and during any activity! With the right attunement, everything can be meaningful for our spiritual growth. The soul level *inspires (in-Spirit) us with its creativity.*

Elements at the Fire Level

At the soul/fire level, the elements exist as *evolutionary lessons.* They take on broader themes that have to do with *learning*, rather than describing a person's attributes. At the personality level, fire is assertive and daring, while at the spiritual level it offers the opportunity to develop courage and trust in our free will. These two levels are often conflated in astrological literature. The way to make a clear distinction is to consider psychological style vs. the spiritual

166

lessons being addressed. Again, we can look at the 12 astrology signs (or themes) to understand the soul lessons pertinent to the fire level. This summary overlaps with the descriptions of the 12 stages given in Chapter 3, but is worth repeating in this context.

Earth

The spiritual lessons of the earth element have to do with *showing up in the realm of incarnation to perform tasks*. There is an intention to work within consensus reality as a potent force. Souls with an earth emphasis advance by manifesting their intentions tangibly.

Taurus is the most self-oriented of the earth signs. It deals with *the attainment of self-worth* and feeling comfortable and secure in the body. Souls working with the Taurus archetype (not only as the Sun sign) may have spiritual histories of conflict, estrangement, abuse, or other experiences which could damage a soul's connection to itself. The task is to reconnect with our inner resources, which can then be expressed outward as tangible expressions of beauty and strength through a hands-on resourcefulness.

Virgo is more interpersonal in its orientation. The spiritual lesson here is to *master a craft which can assist the development of ourself and others*. Achieving this mastery requires focus and dedication. The next step is to share our skills with others which then feeds their growth. Souls working with Virgo may have refused to focus their energy in the past, or they may have resisted working with others to solve problems.

Capricorn has a collective focus. It involves the *achievement of stature* and then the guiding of evolution from a position of authority. The curriculum here entails learning to direct, manage, or influence societal matters. Developing a healthy sense of importance allows us to assume responsibilities with maturity. Souls working with Capricorn may be new to this level of prominence. Collective evolution depends on particular individuals shouldering significant weight so that we can all make it up the proverbial mountain.

Water

Water lessons involve *the development of emotional maturation.* There is an intention to get in touch with feeling, to *strengthen the bonds* that make evolution worthwhile. The willingness to invest in people—ourself, others, the collective—allows us to join in our shared interconnectedness.

Cancer concerns the heart. Its lesson is about *becoming emotionally intelligent and aware of our basic humanness.* This is accomplished through introspection, investing in family, and learning to love ourself. Having learned well, we can then use Cancer energy to prod others out of their unconsciousness. Souls accentuated with Cancer may have acted with immaturity in the soul history, and now is the time to correct this. By so doing, there is an acceptance of the self, which models to others how to emotionally develop.

Scorpio is learning to *intimately bond and emotionally share with others.* The arenas here include sexuality, merging resources, and exchanging deep truths with others. Souls working with the Scorpio archetype may have histories where this level of interpersonal penetration was unattainable or was fraught with problems. Managing the intense dynamics of merging yields soul wisdom which may then be applied to broader issues of collective evolution. Issues of power, survival, and darkness can then be addressed from a place of strength.

Pisces lessons involve connecting the heart with Spirit—*developing love and compassion for everyone and everything.* Pisces aims to enliven our shared emotional connectedness through serving humanity from a selfless place. Souls with a strong Pisces attunement may have been previously unaware that there is a collective consciousness. This realization in their current life assists them in broadening the spiritual vision. With this development, there are countless ways to contribute and inspire others to feel our inherent interconnectivity.

Air

The evolutionary lesson of the air element is *to learn how to create civilization*. Air gives us extraordinary mental capacities that allow us to modernize our lives and plan appropriate societal development. The creation of healthy civilization enables us to move our collective focus away from mere survival and towards the unlimited possibilities represented by the sky.

Gemini is learning to *develop the intellect and communicate knowledge*. Civilizing the world starts with individuals gathering information. The more we become (truly) educated, the greater the chances we can solve the challenges that inevitably arise. Souls enrolled with considerable Gemini are especially equipped to enter learning arenas. They first serve their own growth and can then play a significant role in teaching others. Their soul history may include lethargy, lack of curiosity, or the inability to engage their mind. Now the job is to become enthralled by learning and contribute to its expansion.

Libra takes learning and communication to an interpersonal context. It involves the lesson of *forming equitable relationships based on civility and mutual benefit*. Whether through friendships, marriage, or in business contexts, entering interpersonal agreements that help organize civilization is the program. Diplomacy and fairness further evolution by creating peaceful civility. Souls with a Libra attunement benefit personally from excelling at the interpersonal arts, and they may assume roles where this is valuable to others. This process helps to heal prior spiritual experiences where things may have been unjust in some way.

Aquarius is finding ways to *align with the collective intelligence and connect the global world family*. The realization that a macro-intelligence envelops us all is still quite radical. Nevertheless, it's crucial to be assertive in implementing this view on the collective level if we are to progress as a species. Those with an Aquarian orientation are here to lead us into the future. They benefit by thinking "outside the box" and believing in their ideas and visions about what's possible for our collective future. We all benefit from a wiser, more loving, more sustainable culture initiated by Aquarian paradigm shifts.

Fire

The spiritual lesson of fire involves *the animation of the soul to enliven the world*. Although fire is transpersonal, it becomes relevant as a catalyst for evolution in personal ways through incarnation. The fiery creative force rouses us to participate in evolution. Fire instigates energetic movement, creativity, and renewal. Its awareness and presence is showcased through our actions.

Aries is learning to *align the individual will with soul intent*. Aries is developing the courage to forge ahead in a focused and effective way, which requires the willingness to assert what the soul knows as its truth. Prior soul experiences may have lacked this warrior spirit as the path of less resistance was taken. Now, personal growth is furthered by displays of strength and boldness. Any group of people requires leaders of this caliber.

Leo is learning to *be radiantly present, noble, and self-aware*. This sign has the responsibility of displaying the pure creativity of Spirit in all of its color and jubilance. Realizing that this program is ultimately not about the ego is the higher intention. Those working on developing Leo may have soul histories where they didn't or couldn't express themselves. Now they have the necessary charisma and attractiveness that makes others take notice. Through some talent they inspire others to similarly radiate their unique gifts. Spirit is best animated on this planet when everyone participates.

Sagittarius is learning to *move with purpose from a position of spiritual understanding*. This sign aims to develop a mission which serves as a compass for the whole life. Through higher education, travel, and accumulating a wide array of experience, we broaden our horizons. One result of this process is the forming of cross-cultural connections based on realizing our shared humanity. As the first collective sign, Sagittarius informs us that we are all in this together. Those accentuated with Sagittarius may have a soul legacy where the wisdom of our shared spirituality was lacking. Now, with the attainment of this lofty goal, they serve as our inspirational coaches

170

who cheer for evolutionary advancement and rally for us to give it all we've got.

	Earth	Water	Air	Fire
Fire Level	Learning Earth Lessons	Learning Water Lessons	Learning Air Lessons	Learning Fire Lessons
Air Level	Earthy	Watery	Airy	Fiery
Water Level	Matter	Liquid	Space	Energy
Earth Level	Neutrons	Electrons	Neutrons	Protons

Summarizing Elemental Levels
Figure 13

Chapter 9

Liberation & Manifestation

In this chapter, the four levels introduced are organized in a broad philosophical structure of evolutionary growth. The sequential movement from earth to water to air to fire connects matter back to Spirit. The evolutionary picture also includes a manifesting channel, by which unified Spirit is brought down into the material world as individual souls.

This ascending/descending movement is described in many philosophical, spiritual, and religious traditions. It is found in ancient Greek texts, within many currents of Eastern philosophy, and in the major Western religions. Significant figures who have commented on and expanded this philosophy include Plotinus, Marsilio Ficino, Meister Eckhart, René Guénon, Frithjof Schuon, Sri Aurobindo, Ananda Coomaraswamy, Helena Blavatsky, Huston Smith, Alan Watts, and Chögyam Trungpa Rinpoche.

The term "Perennial Philosophy" was first used by Agostino Steuco in the 16th Century, before Gottfried Leibniz more prominently built upon the idea in the latter part of the 17th Century. Aldous Huxley helped to popularize the term for a 20th Century audience. He wrote, "Rudiments of the Perennial Philosophy may be found among the traditionary lore of primitive peoples in every region of the world, and in its fully developed forms it has a place in every one of the higher religions."

The intention here is to bring this sweeping understanding of evolution into the field of astrology. The *elemental levels* are an eloquent and simple way to understand this philosophy.

The process of Spirit splitting into separateness and then eventually returning to oneness has been the subject of great debate for millennia. Every religion or spiritual teaching sympathetic to this philosophy dresses it with particular practices, biases, characters, and methods. We ascend and connect with God through Jesus or meditation or asceticism or "working on our issues" —you name it. There is no shortage of prescriptions.

Some versions of the philosophy are basic and general, while others present a high degree of specificity and complexity as to how evolution proceeds. Transpersonal philosopher Ken Wilber has meticulously examined the different versions of this philosophy and has offered an "integral" view. He sees a common thread of evolutionary progression through five broad stages: matter, life, mind, soul, and finally Spirit. This outline seamlessly connects with the four astrology elements and Spirit underlying it all. Wilber's extensive work is highly recommended for those interested in further study.

Liberation

The process of evolution has unfolded over many eons. The farther back we go in Earth's history, the slower the changes occurred. The emergence of complex life was a series of subtle adjustments to the environment over great stretches of time. The evolutionary process accelerated into greater levels of complexity. The technological breakthroughs of the last century illustrate that this acceleration continues to quicken. Perhaps we are at a point when the pace of evolution is ready to make an even more dramatic increase.

Evolutionary acceleration matches what we notice in nature. Earth is stationary. Water flows, but is relatively slow. Sound travels quickly through air, and light is extremely fast. Evolution proceeded slowly in the beginning stages and now seems to be happening quicker than some of us can keep up with.

174

Back towards the beginning, we can imagine a time when this planet (earth) was devoid of life. Then, primitive life forms emerged from the primordial soup (water) as autonomous beings. These early life forms gradually developed skills and learned to communicate (air). Somewhere, at some time, there was a remarkable moment when our early ancestors first made fire.

This procession corresponds to the evolutionary movement from body (physical) to heart (emotional) to mind (mental) to soul (spiritual). Each level builds upon the previous, while also moving beyond it. Therefore, evolutionary movement from level to level assumes a pyramid form (see graphic below). The pyramid has been a captivating symbol for many cultures. It's seen most famously in Egyptian and Mayan cultures, but its resonance is far broader as an archetype in our collective consciousness.

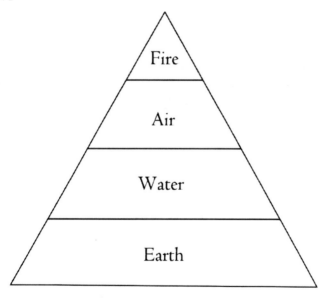

The Liberating Pyramid
Figure 14

The liberating channel begins with the earth element, the great foundation that serves as a platform for evolution. Like the bottom of a pyramid, everything stems from this widest and most

175

mundane level. The water level is where life appears. Fittingly, membership at this level requires water for sustenance. The next movement is the development and utilization of mental functioning, which requires some form of nervous system. The air level accordingly has a smaller membership than does the water level.

We use the ingenuity of our minds not only practically, as in harnessing fire, but also for broader metaphysical and existential questing. At some point in evolution we developed the concept of spirituality; we began to understand that our souls are part of something bigger. We then invented various practices aimed at experiencing Spirit directly. Those of us who seek to attain spiritual realization are a subset of the wider mental level. The zenith of the pyramid would be the illumination of Spirit, or enlightenment (fire). Like the tendency of heat to rise, our souls seek to elevate and return.

Since our individual souls are eternally linked to Spirit, we can think of Spirit as a fifth level. However, understanding Spirit as a "level" is not quite right, as it actually envelops all the other levels. Oneness eludes systems of classification and division. Nevertheless, from the standpoint of the intellect positioned in the relative world, we can situate Spirit as an all-encompassing level.

At this collective moment on the evolutionary ladder, the freedom and brilliance of the mind has captured our imaginations. The evolutionary motion launched many eons ago is enjoying a thrilling ride through the air even as its movement continues toward a fiery communion. In fact, we may be at the cusp of collectively upgrading our consciousness to this mystical and mysterious level.

Ideally, the air level leads to the fire level. We can learn how to focus awareness and resolve the issues which take us away from being present. The intellect is responsible for creating educational systems, functional civilization, and has enabled ventures into air and space. Now we are being challenged to move further to incorporate the transpersonal and implement wiser ways of living on this planet. It certainly seems that if we do not move beyond the immediacy of personal desires (which lead to pollution, resource depletion, climate catastrophes, etc.), we are prone to destroying the

Earth foundation which hosts us. There has never before been such a pressing need for our collective evolution.

Manifestation

There is another pyramid representing the manifestation process, but this one is upside-down. The pyramid's base is the vast oneness of Spirit. Everything originates from this unified source. As the manifesting channel moves down the elemental levels, there is a narrowing process which eventually leads to membership on the earth level.

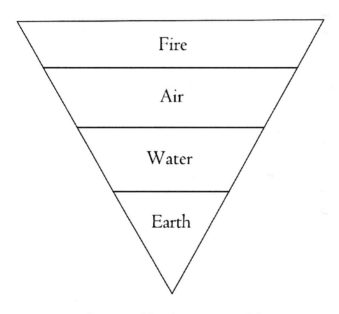

The Manifesting Pyramid

Figure 15

The fire level crackles with the creativity of an endless field of possibilities that transcends reason and human limitations. Souls connect to Spirit at the fire level. We are individual flames of a larger fire. As seen in bringing two candles together and then apart, fire easily separates but is able to reunite into one flame. The soul

177

can be separate and simultaneously maintain connection to the larger fire source.

From the fiery oneness, souls seek to incarnate in order to fulfill specific missions. At the fire level there are agreements among souls, spirit guides who assist the process of growth, and other transpersonal activity. A great book which details the process of souls incarnating is *Journey of Souls* by Michael Newton. Mystics, shamans, and sages tell us of a busy realm of spiritual activity occurring beyond our usual awareness.

The next level of the manifesting channel is the descent into more rational comprehension of the spiritual mission. It is impossible for a soul that has lived for many lifetimes to resolve its past experiences and karma in a single lifetime. Particular evolutionary work is accepted and agreed upon for each incarnation. At the air level, the multitude of creative possibilities is narrowed into a specific plan. The astrology chart depicts this plan's details and dynamics. As the astrology chart is relevant for this particular solar system, there is a narrowing from the endless reach of fire to the eventual incarnation on Earth.

Moving farther, the soul reaches the water level; life. The general intentions of the air level now become specified to the unique conditions which surround the incarnating soul. During the gestation period, the soul forms a specific body. The water level allows it to become familiar with the physical world before birth. Our autonomy is initiated at birth. The umbilical cord is cut, and the earth level is engaged as we take our first breath. From the start, our life circumstances fuel our spiritual development through the classrooms of body, heart, mind, and soul as we then begin moving upward through the liberating channel.

Inspiration into Action

The liberating and manifesting channels have additional relevance aside from incarnation and spiritual development. They apply to any transformation between energy and form. For instance, when wood burns, its matter is changed to energy along the liberating channel. The conversion of calories (energy, fire) into physical movement is an example of manifestation.

One of the central roles of these channels is bringing inspiration into action. The origination of the word "inspiration" is "in Spirit." When inspired, we become charged to bring a creative vision (fire) into form. This process involves refining (air) this creativity into a concrete plan. The next step is to embody (water) the plan, to connect to it with our heart. The final step is to then put the plan into motion, to take action and participate on the earth level.

Whether we are conscious of it or not, our minds are often filled with inspiration which seeks to manifest. The "a ha!" moment is something everyone is familiar with. Very creative people widely acknowledge that the process has much to do with getting the self—the ego—out of the way to allow inspiration to enter.

At the water level, the ego is running the show. It is strongly attached to a particular personal story that gives it an identity and a familiar orientation to life. This attachment can often derail our connecting to inspiration since the ego may be skeptical of new directions. A popular spiritual metaphor is that when our cups are too full (water) nothing new can enter. We must empty the self to be receptive and allow Spirit to *emerge* through us.

Interlocking Pyramids

Together the liberating and manifesting channels portray an endless dance of separating and reuniting with Spirit. These channels are interdependent and continually in motion. Although we are evolving in the liberating channel, we are always manifesting the creative impulses of Spirit. When we overlay the liberating and manifesting channels, the image is one of interlocking pyramids.

179

Ascending to the point of the liberating pyramid in our evolutionary progression, we find that the narrowest and most exclusive position (enlightenment) becomes the infinite reach of Spirit—the broad base of the manifesting pyramid. In the other direction we see that the manifesting pyramid forms a singular point at the earth level; the fullness of Spirit travels down into denser levels and narrows into nothing. Recall that the physical world has this paradox of being simultaneously durable from one view, while being essentially non-existent from another. From the relative perspective of the liberating channel, the earth level is the broad, sturdy container in which everything grows!

The interlocking pyramids resemble the Star of David found in Judaism. The Jewish faith is the oldest monotheistic tradition and served as the foundation for Christianity. Therefore, a great majority of people in the Western world can claim a direct lineage back to this symbol. As will be discussed later, many Eastern spiritual symbols and iconography can also be related to the astrological system.

Our Orientation

To summarize our human situation within the channels: The first three levels form the personal consciousness: physical/earth, emotional/water, and mental/air. Transcending our bodies, emotions and minds is the soul/fire level, which is beyond our usual consciousness. Recall from page 159 the IMAX movie: *[The Earth's] natural systems slowly recycle the air, water and even the rock.* We see how air, water and earth, which correlate to the personal levels, are recycled. Fire is the spiritual web of energy in which the other elements arise.

The neutral levels serve as necessary structures for the processes of the charged levels. Consensus reality is formed by the sensate (earth) and conceptual (air) levels. In between these levels is the water level, our inherent biological connection to all life.

Water is our center, our heart—it connects and deepens other levels. The air/mental level becomes increasingly more psychological for people that are emotionally attuned. And sensory input from the earth/physical level affects us more strongly when the feeling level is online. Higher levels of transpersonal consciousness at the fire/soul become personally relevant through the deepening that consciousness (water) brings.

Within this model of four elemental levels, consciousness mostly inhabits the middle two (water and air). The human condition is typified by our biological (water) and cognitive (air) functioning. The earth level is not experiential, and the fire level usually seems beyond our everyday consciousness.

Consciousness is always marinating in some emotional stew. Like the waves of an ocean, it ebbs and flows in emotional intensity and poignancy. Even when we view life in a detached and cerebral way, our tender heart still pumps its rich lifeblood beneath our awareness. We are innately and always vulnerable, imperfect creatures who are trying to satisfy our needs in a relatively short lifespan. Like all animals, we eat, sleep, and mate. There's no escaping our primal nature, no matter how smart we think we are.

Learning is fully accomplished when it's integrated into our behavior and the emotional quality of our consciousness. When we know our issues but continue to repeat our familiar struggles, we have evidence that we have not yet integrated the lessons. Water is the level of *processing* and integration into the flow of the life force.

We are all wounded in some way. If a soul incarnates, we can be sure there is more learning, healing, and integrating to do.

181

Evolutionary growth has much to do with the reconciliation and healing of the Moon, which is paired with our biology and the water level.

While the fire level is less accessible than the water, we are still always connected to it. The evolutionary project involves progressing to the *clarity* of soul awareness and realization. It is not where we are usually oriented as we face the necessary lessons in evolving to its promise. Water (unconscious) is where we are personally stationed, and the fire level is where the soul connects with Spirit. The physical (earth) and mental (air) levels act as stabilizers that connect to consensus reality.

What we experience as consciousness is the dynamic product of the interaction between our unconscious self (physical, lunar, water) with the broader field of awareness and vitality (metaphysical, solar, fire), which lights it up. The relationship between the water (heart) and fire (soul) levels is the connection between the personal and the transpersonal parts of the self. Gary Zukav eloquently captures this situation in *The Seat of the Soul*:

> *Feelings, as we shall see, are the means through which we can discern the parts of itself that the soul seeks to heal, and through which we come to see the action of the soul in physical matter. The road to your soul is through your heart.*

Personal to Transpersonal

The great challenge at this point in our collective evolution is shifting consciousness from solely identifying as a separate, personal ego, in the relative world to incorporating the transpersonal level. Although life is multidimensional, our typical consciousness is anchored to the familiar dimensions of our everyday world. Upon raising consciousness to the transpersonal, simply being in the timeless "now" defines our primary experience. Since transpersonal experience can be as elusive as it is necessary, some more commentary on how it relates to astrology may be useful.

This movement from the personal to the transpersonal is seen with the progression from Saturn to the outer planets (Uranus,

182

Neptune, Pluto). In transpersonal levels of consciousness, we become free of the personal story of a "me" in terms of that being our primary identity. We have greater access to the broader field of awareness which contains us. In fact, we realize that we actually *are* this field of awareness. We exist as a part of nature—without judgment or resistance. Instead of continually strategizing to meet personal needs, we experience the perfection of life in its ebb and flow. By accepting these natural rhythms, we are better able to collaborate with whatever unfolds.

A shift to the transpersonal level does not permanently dissolve the personal—both can be experienced simultaneously. This dual access is seen astrologically by way of the Earth's position within both Saturn's and the outer planet's orbits. Saturn is closer to us, so our more immediate experience is one of relative separateness, without which there'd be no manifesting channel, no autonomy and individuality.

There is another essential point to make about life within the separating influence of Saturn: the four elements assume individual identities. We experience the elements separately and honor each element for the qualities it has. Consequently, *all of the qualities of the elements become equally important.* It is true that earth can be transcended and that everything is essentially energy (fire), but this is true only from the transpersonal view. We must be able to hold paradoxical truths to honor both of these realities.

The Universality of Symbolism

Bridging the air level to the fire includes the world of symbolism. Symbols are comprehended by the mind (air) and pertain to the transpersonal (fire). They are designed to orient consciousness toward phenomena which have universal themes.

Just as the Star of David perfectly illustrates the liberating and manifesting channels, many other spiritual symbols can be linked to astrology. The astrological system is non-denominational. It simply describes and illustrates our connection to reality without an ideological agenda. With its far-reaching and universal scope,

183

astrology may be seen as the template for many other spiritual systems.

One of the most widespread of all religious symbols is the Christian Cross.

The defining feature of the cross is the intersection of a horizontal and a vertical line. The first represents our personal human world with its lateral relationships; the second represents our vertical connection to the divine. The horizontal line is analogous to cyclical evolution, while the vertical goes with progressive evolution. Additionally, the intersecting lines point to the four directions, which have relevance in several ways in the astrological system.

Although this version of the cross has proliferated with the rise of Christianity, it has many variations which precede the religion. Some believe that these earlier crosses symbolized sacred fire or the Sun. In fact, the Sun Cross is a symbol used by Christian Gnostics. It references not only the Sun, but also the four directions. Native Americans also make extensive use of the four directions with the Medicine Wheel.

The Sun Cross has an obvious resemblance to an astrology chart. The 4 directions define the angles of a chart and are related to the seasonal changes marked by the solstices and equinoxes. This symbol, along with similar versions of it, was not only used by the Gnostics. Evidence of it has been found in Paleolithic caves, in Mesopotamia, within the Prehistoric religion of Bronze Age Europe, as well as among many indigenous and pagan peoples. It is now used in astrology and astronomy to represent the Earth.

Another popular symbol primarily found in modern Christianity, but also employed elsewhere and predating Christianity, is the Ichthys, the symbol of the fish.

The rise of Christianity occurred at the beginning of the Pisces Age, the astrology sign associated with the Fishes. The teachings of Jesus are very Piscean, as seen with the Golden Rule, the advocacy of compassion, healing, and transcendence. The Ichthys is related to another symbol, the Vesica Pisces, which literally means the "bladder of a fish."

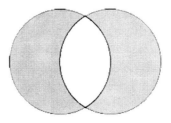

This symbol is the intersection of two circles. It has a mystical meaning within Sacred Geometry. The illustration depicts the movement from oneness into separation. The Vesica Pisces is the intersection formed by this split. In order for Spirit to give birth to everything in the manifest world, the underlying unity must divide.

185

The astrology sign Pisces can be thought of as the womb from which all things derive. The Vesica Pisces resembles the yoni (female genitals), which similarly gives birth.

Many spiritual symbols have circular parts. As reviewed in the first part of this book, astrology is defined by cycles. One of the most prevalent cyclical symbols is the Ouroboros, which is found in Hongshan and Hindu cultures before even Ancient Egypt, Phoenicia, and Greece, where it was named the Ouroboros. It is used in Gnostic, Hermetic, Theosophist, and Alchemical contexts. It has been found in both Aztec and Toltec ruins and also appears in many mythologies and in Freemasonry.

The image of a snake or dragon eating its own tail represents the unending cyclical flow of life, how nature constantly recreates itself. This symbol represents the idea of primordial unity which endures throughout the process of change. Besides the obvious correlation to the cyclical movement in astrology, there is a similarity in the Lunar Nodes being based on mythology pertaining to a Dragon's Tail (South Node) and Head (North Node). In order to reach a state of spiritual integration, we must reconcile the polarity indicated by the Lunar Nodes in the astrology chart.

Another popular symbol configured in a circle is the Yin-Yang, which comes from Chinese philosophy and Taoism.

This symbol portrays duality within a unified whole. It is about the reconciliation of opposites within the context of unity. It suggests how members of a pairing inform, complement, and are indispensable to each other. Notice how there is black in the white area and white in the black, indicating how opposites actually have commonalities. In astrology, all of this is found in the opposition aspect. Opposite signs not only provide the tension of polarity, they also have a similarity. This symbol not only illustrates the crux of aspect theory pertaining to the opposition, it represents the dance of opposites within the cyclical flow of nature.

In Buddhism, the primary symbol is the Dharmacakra or "Wheel of Dharma."

Again we can see the cyclical theme, here represented by a chariot wheel. This symbol suggests "the turning of the wheel", which has multiple meanings relating to the cyclical nature of life. The most common version of the Dharmacakra, which has eight spokes, resembles the Sun Cross with additional spokes at the midpoints of the four directions. The eight-part structure is widely used in astrology to describe the lunar phases. Additionally, there is the popular 8th harmonic aspects of the semisquare and sesquisquare. There is also a 12-spoke version, which correlates most precisely with astrology's natural order of 12 phases.

A main symbol found in Hinduism is the Lotus Flower.

There are several variations on the Lotus Flower, but they all illustrate the familiar circular shape and unfolding petals. The petals symbolize the expansion of the soul stemming from a unified center. As with the Dharmacakra, the astrological correlation here is the circular gestalt with individual parts along the periphery, which parallels the astrology cycle and its attendant phases.

Many spiritual symbols have celestial phenomena front and center. Most famously is the Star and Crescent, which is usually associated with Islam. This symbol, however, shows up in a variety of contexts from the Mediterranean to Asia to India and from the Byzantine to Hellenistic to Ottoman cultures.

This symbol immediately takes the viewer up to the heavens. The crescent shape is, of course, the Moon, and the star is representative of the broader star fields which envelops us. The astrological associations are quite obvious. Echoing the Moon's

188

prominence in this symbol, many cultures use a lunar-based calendar.

Another symbol used in Islam is the Rub el Hizb, which is associated with Islam's holy book, the Quran. It is found on many emblems and flags.

The Rub el Hizb is configured as two overlapping squares which form an eight-pointed star. In the center of the Rub el Hizb is a circle. Once again we notice star and circle symbology. Furthermore, the circle in the middle is surrounded by extensions in various directions—a pattern noticed in some of the other symbols. This configuration gives the feeling of motion around a center point, exactly what we have on the astrology wheel.

The most identified symbol of Wicca (neo-Paganism) is the pentagram, or five-pointed star.

This star brings to mind the quintile, the aspect most associated with transpersonal ingenuity and transcendence. Wiccans associate the five points with the four elements and Spirit, which

189

holds them all together. Indeed, nature-based religions, including the varieties of Paganism and neo-Paganism, are filled with astrology-related themes—the four directions, the four elements, stars and planets, levels of reality, and, often, reincarnation. Astrology has been closely associated with nature-based religions, and it's often categorized as part of them. However, the universality of astrology gives it a far broader reach.

Chapter 10

The Spiral Stairway

The first part of this book addressed cyclical evolution—how the movement around the zodiac describes an evolutionary program. We explored the various ways in which the stages of the system relate to each other to convey an assortment of spiritual lessons. The second part of this book looked at progressive evolution—the return of souls back to Spirit as consciousness learns to liberate itself. There is also an opposite manifesting movement from oneness into the realms of separation.

Cyclical and progressive evolution combine to form an exquisite spiral stairway. The steps of this stairway are the 12 stages of cyclical evolution, while the vertical trajectory results from the evolution of consciousness. Here again we see the familiar neutral organization of a system along with our charged responses to it.

One of the major points of this book is that our quality of consciousness is the primary factor in determining how our chart manifests. This view denies the relevancy of naming the planets as benefic, malefic, or "poorly placed." These designations only apply to terrain that is flat. With an understanding that consciousness evolves and meets the various parts of the system progressively, our relationship to astrology changes dramatically. As we learn our lessons, we address the evolutionary themes of the cyclical layout in more advanced ways.

191

The spiral is a fascinating pattern. At the biological level we see examples of the spiral throughout nature—the structure of DNA, the formation of various shells, plants, and animals, the layout of stars in galaxies. The mathematical elegance of spirals is a great example of nature's intelligence being matched by its beauty.

The Spiritual Path

The most obvious question is, "Where does the spiral stairway lead?" Does it take us to nothingness, a release from the cycles of life and death? Could it lead to a blissful existence in some heavenly garden? There are many perspectives, and who among us still spiritually unfinished can say?

One challenge with the proverbial "spiritual path" is that it has a built-in paradox. From one perspective, we move through life addressing our lessons and developing consciousness—around and up the stairway we go. From another perspective, there is no path, just the present moment in all of its fullness. All we have to do is just be—to sit in the eternal now without resistance. The "path" is not so much a road that stretches out ahead; it's everywhere, and in everything!

This seeming contradiction is reconciled by seeing that the spiral stairway is climbed from the position of the separate self (Moon), which is primarily stationed at the water level. In our soul growth we must therefore address our necessary lessons in the familiar relative world. With this orientation, it's appropriate to climb the spiral stairway as a spiritual path.

At the same time, we also have the solar faculty of awareness and vitality, which connects us with the broader transpersonal field. When the Moon reaches a certain level of resolution, consciousness becomes less anchored to the relative world. The Sun brings us to a wider reality which can be brought into the personal self as an awakened mind. A spiritual path becomes irrelevant for the "enlightened." Where would you need to go? The spiral stairway is there for those in need of climbing it. Having incarnated on this planet is a reliable indication of this necessity.

As mentioned previously, many spiritual authorities have offered views on this evolutionary process. The common denominator is a developmental process towards more advanced states of consciousness, despite some differences about the details. All models of spiritual growth fit within the broad schematic of the four elemental levels described in this book.

Although the process is the same for us, there is no universal script as to the particulars. One person may realize his soul intentions through retreat and devoted spiritual practice. Another may need to assume a powerful role as a leader, while someone else's soul requires a focus on interpersonal relationships as the primary area of integration. There are 12 different stages to address in cyclical evolution, and all of us have a different attunement to each of them. The natal astrology chart conveys the unique parameters of any person's path. The wonderful gift of understanding our astrology charts is that it indicates our optimal path up the stairway.

Climbing the Stairway

During the early developmental years, the water level is the primary realm where consciousness is situated. An infant's consciousness is centered on body and emotion—a preoccupation with touch, safety, and food. We gradually achieve a sense of autonomy and ego structure, which readies us for the long journey of awareness ahead. The agreement to incarnate appears to be that we must start out unconsciously.

In the formative years, we address the air level in school. There is an expectation to learn enough facts and know-how to take part in consensus reality and be able to contribute a skill to society. After completing high school, we are considered to be adults. The measurement of successful development is the ability to be self-sufficient, which some proficiency with the air level provides.

For most of us, spiritual development is absent from our education. Contemplative practices are not taught in the typical K-12 school curriculum. The dominant paradigm is fact-driven (air). There's also the question of the appropriateness of bringing

193

anything "spiritual" into the public domain, especially when spiritual and religious are not distinguished from each other. Spiritual issues are handled privately in families and/or in organized religious settings. In these contexts, there also tends to be a focus on teachings (air) instead of experience (fire). There is little available in mainstream Western culture to support an engagement with the fire level.

Collectively, we are still very ignorant of the fire level. Most people identify completely with the drama of the separate self without even knowing that there could be more. For them, conventional measurements of achievement such as money or status determine success. The dominant culture reinforces this situation. What usually makes the news or the gossip rounds is sensational—stories indicative of *not evolving* (scandal, conflict, crisis, etc.)

When we are young, the lessons of cyclical evolution are largely mismanaged. If we don't cultivate awareness, then the mismanagement of the lessons repeats in various ways until we do.

One way astrology can provide guidance is by way of transits and progressions, which signal when certain lessons are active. Some of these are specific to individual charts, while others are universal. Among the universal transits we all experience at approximately the same age, the Saturn cycle stands out as particularly helpful in understanding the rhythm of our human chronology. Although age doesn't necessarily correlate with the extent of spiritual maturation, the unfolding stages of life tend to be connected to the inherent functioning of the body-mind system.

Saturn takes twenty-nine years to circle the Sun. In its first cycle around our chart, it visits all of our planets and houses in the form of some trials and tribulations of growing up. A big part of this process is learning about our unconscious habits and tendencies. As we approach thirty, we enter true adulthood. The tests of the Saturn Return provides clarity, a winnowing process enabling and encouraging us to focus on what is most essential in our life. Ideally, we establish the direction and orientation for the middle chapter of our life.

An overarching theme of our second Saturn cycle has to do with our relationship to psychological and spiritual evolution. A

194

wide range of attitudes is possible—from active engagement with our lessons to rigid attachment to and defense of our ego identity and its view, opinion, and habits. Dramatic steps in our evolution are available—we are empowered to make great strides during our "prime."

As we near sixty at the second Saturn Return, external activity for many of us begins to decline, which may free us for a more contemplative lifestyle. No longer preoccupied with "making it" or raising children, the elder years can be an ideal time to cultivate awareness. Any wisdom gathered thus far provides a foundation for further development. Sadly, many do not realize this opportunity and succumb to a gradual decline. The third Saturn cycle can be marked by despair with the foreboding specter of death lurking ahead. The ego is alarmed by its impending fate and may renew and even amplify its defensive measures.

The Saturn cycle portrays three very different phases of life. The first is the movement from unconsciousness. The second is of empowerment, the implementation of awareness into the prime of life. The third is managing the process of releasing the separate self and developing gratitude for the journey.

Managing the Lessons

The lessons of cyclical evolution are handled differently in the three Saturn phases. Let's look at a couple examples.

If we have Aries square Capricorn featured in the chart, developing *leadership* is the potential, with tyranny being the shadow. In the formative years, we may be drawn to themes of power, regardless of our gender. There may be a glorification of leaders, athletes or military personnel or, on the other hand, perhaps a marked distaste for such figures. Either way, there is likely to be a charge around the exercising of authority.

Peer groups dynamics and interactions with adults provide opportunities to learn toughness and decisiveness. There is likely to be conflict about dominance issues and who gets to be the boss.

The challenging experiences in the formative years can greatly influence the expression of the central themes in the second

195

Saturn cycle. In this case, there may be greater knowledge about what makes a leader effective. The energy of the natal aspect will synchronously connect in the world to create appropriate tests in leadership positions. Success in such roles is strongly linked to the quality and extent of our awareness.

Ideally, we teach what we have learned. During the third Saturn cycle, leadership mentoring is appropriate. Showing patience for those less adept with this lesson can further our own self-acceptance for having been less seasoned at one point. We can review, accept, and ultimately feel gratitude for the process we went through.

By the end of the second Saturn cycle, a continued absence of clear exercising of authority would likely lead to an exaggeration of the shadow—tyrannical behavior. The geezer who shakes his cane and yells at the kids to get off his yard is full of many years of mismanaged energy. Everywhere he looks he sees failure: in the government, a family member, or with his favorite sports team. And he has a limitless supply of venomous criticism for all of it. He has failed to express his own leadership and has projected that frustration outward. His world has turned into an endless room of mirrors which infuriates him from every angle.

As a second example, let's suppose that our chart contains a sextile aspect between Pisces and Taurus. The potential here is to develop *serenity*, while the shadow is sloth. During the first Saturn cycle, there might be introversion or shyness, a general deference to others stemming from a desire to maintain peace. If this pattern strengthens, we may limit our participation in life, for the tendency is to take the "easier" path.

During the next phase of life, there may be more emphasis on cultivating inner peace. Whereas a child may use retreat in a reactive way, an adult is more able to consciously choose to use quiet moments to connect with inspiration. The serenity available may support personal, interpersonal, or professional endeavors. This aspect can provide a spiritual center. Without actively engaging this center, however, we may end up attempting to find solace in television or any other passive activity and thereby deepen a pattern of lethargy.

In the third Saturn cycle, there is the potential for deep spiritual peace, a calm and compassionate disposition that may be soothing for others. Meditative skills may be strong, and these contribute to a sense of well-being. In contrast, this aspect may manifest in the sloth direction as even further diminished activity and quiet dissatisfaction. A senior on this end of the spectrum may feel resignation and prefer to sleep or numb out in some way.

In sum, everyone climbs their own spiral stairway. The lessons of cyclical evolution are laid out differently in every astrology chart. Addressing these lessons consciously requires effort and remembering how we mismanaged them when we were young. It is up to us to increase awareness (fire) of our habitual patterns (Moon) and then to direct behavior consciously. Astrology can be of enormous assistance in moving from the air to the fire level. It is our task to use its information well to continue making strides in climbing the spiral stairway.

Bridging Worlds

There is a focus on liberation in most spiritual models, and rightfully so. Shouldn't we learn how to move beyond the ego and reach greater soul realization? On the other hand, there are those who advocate living in the "real world" of our most immediate surroundings as the best way to truly be "spiritual." These two approaches are aligned respectively with the yang (air, fire) and yin (earth, water) elements. Depending on our particular attunement to the elements, there is often a preference for either liberation or manifestation. These two different approaches can easily polarize, but progressing to the fire level and *consciously* bringing that awareness into the parameters of everyday life is to bridge worlds. Being in the world but not of it is the ideal being championed in this book. This integration is the true masterwork.

Almost everyone currently alive has Neptune sextile Pluto in the natal chart. (Note that Pluto is transpersonal, though it concerns the interface of the transpersonal with the psychology and emotional status of the separate self). The Neptune/Pluto sextile concerns the integration of the transcendent (Neptune) with the psychological (Pluto) and gives us a context to learn how to balance the two channels. Ancient wisdom traditions rooted in mystical experience (Neptune, liberation) long predate the opening of psychological insight which has flourished in recent decades, especially since the Uranus/Pluto conjunction of the 1960s. Indeed, spiritual practices which include the emotional and psychological realms (manifestation) are becoming more widespread. Now at the Uranus/Pluto square, our task is to further this integrative process and *honor all levels of reality simultaneously.*

It is indeed true that we are developing upwards, not downwards. We move from the personal to the transpersonal and increasingly broaden our awareness. At the same time, *the manifesting channel is just as relevant*, as Spirit is continually emerging through us. In fact, an overemphasis on liberation results in what has been termed the "spiritual bypass" in which painful experience is denied or glossed over in favor of emotional suppression and glib optimism.

Ascending (air, fire) spirituality is attractive for those who, consciously or not, may want to evade the unpleasantness of painful experiences. Joining with lofty spiritual teachings and having peak experiences can be truly affirming and exalting. Many spiritual paths, however, do not adequately address the psychological, emotional, and somatic (water, earth) realms. This oversight is a common criticism of the New Age movement, though this tendency for bypass can be found in many paths.

We are just as involved with the manifesting channel as we are the liberating. Although less immediate than our everyday reality, transpersonal realms inform our experience while also enveloping us. Inspiration and creativity come from Spirit for us to deliver into the world. Spirit is continually whispering to us in the guises of synchronicities, spirit guides, or our dreams. Ignorance of such guidance does not diminish its reality or relevance.

Fixation on the yin elements to the exclusion of metaphysical exploration is also quite common, as this stance aligns with our mainstream paradigm of reality. Modern psychology and many body-centered modalities rightfully address water and earth but neglect the spiritual dimension.

198

Though most charts carry a particular elemental emphasis (by way of the planetary placements), we all have all four of them in our charts, just as we all have bodies, hearts, minds, and souls. Sometimes we make excuses by claiming that since an element is weak in our chart, we are "off the hook" concerning that element's function. This attitude is misguided and a recipe for imbalance and the resulting consequences. If there is an element with less emphasis, it may actually require more effort and focus to properly integrate it. The key is to engage with all four elements no matter what our inherent attunement is. Being aware of some predictable patterns generated by elemental deficiencies can be helpful.

Elemental Deficiencies

The most common situation of elemental imbalance occurs when one element is less represented than the other three. In some cases, there are no planets in any of the signs of one of the elements. Some people are particularly strong in two elements and weak in the other two. And others carry an elemental balance. Regardless of our elemental composition, we must learn to engage all four. Let's first look at the situation in which one element is absent or at least less prominent than the others.

Without the grounding energy of earth, there may be a tendency to fly off into mental speculation. We may be out of touch with our body and averse to creating structure. There is likely to be plenty of thrill-seeking, a zest for unbounded experience, and an endless advocacy of open-ended possibilities. A challenge here is that with our head in the clouds, the bills may not get paid. If discipline and resolve are attended to, this combination can manifest as inspirational and effective. If not, then life is full of unlived potentials. Implementing earthy organization and attention to mundane matters is crucial for worldly advancement. Some form of body awareness technique, such as yoga, tai chi, or a mindful approach to athletics could be helpful. Charge dominates this combination, with air being the only neutral element. Air creates the space for processes (fire, water) to spread and wander. This is a passionate combination, especially about ideas.

199

When air is missing or minimal, there tends to be a lack of objectivity, perspective, and reason. There is heavy grounding— earth and water anchor fire, which creates a sense of urgency, strong opinions, and drive. Accomplishment of some kind is of prime importance, though being high-strung is the pitfall. Money or belongings may have an increased focus, and it could be difficult to see the larger picture. The lack of objectivity may lead to overly-charged thinking. Some form of mindfulness practice would be helpful in terms of learning not to get caught up in dramatic intensity. Those of us lacking in the air element would also benefit from watching video of ourself or recording thoughts on a voice recorder. Upon review of this material and the self-awareness it can foster, more detachment and objectivity can emerge.

With fire in low supply, there may be a lack of enthusiasm, energy, or spark for life. The tendency is to be grounded, detached, and, at the extreme, depressed. Neutrality dominates and is charged by water; emotions, rather than inspiration, runs the show. Life may easily turn into a series of tasks instead of an enjoyable adventure. Ideas are easily grounded into form—this combination may be a wiz at mundane tasks. There is a scientific or analytical bent motivated by satisfying underlying needs for competence or industriousness. Missing the whimsical influence of fire, this combination is the most reliable and steadfast. Efforts in the direction of recreation help the imbalance. Having a hobby, being able to break away to travel, and exercise can each serve to break up routine and get the energy moving. Checking in as to what is *really* motivating behavior is useful. Finding a cause to believe in and to help generate some passion creates greater balance. Success is probable here, but aligning with what is truly valued or important is the challenge.

With a lack of water, there is a tendency to avoid emotional and interpersonal process. The presence of both yang elements fuels an outward focus, and earth expects results. We might steamroll others and lack receptivity to their needs. The neutrality emphasizes pragmatics, while the yang elements want a broad reach. There may be a drive to make a social or global impact instead of investing in personal matters. There is toughness in this dry combination. It has a "We can do it!" attitude. A helpful question to then ask is,

200

"Why do you want to?" Greater integration is found through receptiveness. Listening and empathy skills are helpful to develop. Having children or supporting others' vulnerability in some way may assist in settling into the heart. Spending time in actual water may be calming.

Having an elemental imbalance can make us completely useless in the related function. However, with successful evolutionary momentum, the bolstering of the missing element enables the others to maximize their potency. If we lack earth we can focus on discipline and still attain success. If we lack air we can develop reason and be well-informed. If we lack fire we can cultivate enthusiasm and become inspirational. Those who lack water who learn to deepen can make a meaningful impact. Taking measures to develop these inferior functions pays off substantially. Lacking an element is not a sentence to incompleteness. It's an invitation to stretch ourself toward wholeness.

About Time

While "enrolled" in this Earth school, we are subject to life within the consensus reality of time, which is a part of the relative world. Correlated with Saturn, time sets up a neutral organization. As we watch the clock tick ahead in lockstep precision, we have the sensation of past, present, and future.

Uranus is the neutral energy aligned with the transpersonal perspective. As the nervous system of the cosmic mind, it is aware of everything, and is beyond our usual perception of linear time. One consequence of its multidimensional functioning is that the karma we accrue doesn't neatly return to us in a cause and effect manner. Rather, karmic resonances reside outside the rhythm of our everyday experience. Uranus plays the part of keeping these metaphysical records of prior karma, which are delivered to us in consensus reality by Saturn, the so-called "Lord of karma."

Some view Saturn as a malefic energy that delivers punishment. However, the idea of karma asserts that we simply experience the result of prior behaviors. Since we all are emerging from unconsciousness, it makes sense that we all make mistakes. The consequences we face for acting unconsciously are valuable lessons. Consequences also certainly include reward, maturation, or any other "positive" result of healthy behavior.

The "karmic load" we carry resides at the transpersonal level. Although everything is bound to return to us in some way, the fact that issues are processed in transpersonal dimensions could mean that they return in various forms, many of which would evade our conscious understanding. However, astrology does provide a framework to understand this mysterious process of reconciling karma. It lets us know which karma is most relevant to our experience while in the state of incarnation. Astrology helps us bridge worlds.

Transits, progressions, and other techniques inform us when karmic themes are especially highlighted. Time allows us to precisely track the motion of the planets around our charts. Although we can never be certain as to how events will precisely unfold, we can have certainty of the *thematic* nature of our experience at any given time. Since astrology pertains to all levels of experience, some specific events may manifest more biographically than others. We may work out some karma in ways that are less event-oriented, such as in dreams or through an emotional experience. Astrology can help us navigate and see how the karmic wheels operate for our unique circumstance.

Fate and Free Will

One of the most enduring and enigmatic issues in human life is that of fate vs. free will. The question boils down to how much freedom we actually have. The perspective in this book embraces the reality of free will, but asserts that its activation relies on our claiming our freedom by progressing through the liberating channel. When we attain greater awareness, we are able to make conscious choices. In contrast, if we remain unconscious we fail to recognize our responsibility for the repeating lessons that confront us. We spin our wheels, imprisoned by our habitual reactions.

The universe sets up the structure (neutral) to life, which has a sense of being fated. We can't change our DNA, the time in history in which we're born, or our parents. We have no control over our astrology chart or what transits are occurring at any given time. And we have no say about the organization of the physical (earth) or nonphysical worlds (air). The organization of spiritual lessons of cyclical evolution is beyond our consent.

Within these parameters, we can approach life anyway we see fit. Management of the charged elements determines how we navigate the structures we find ourselves in. We have impulses and preferences which drive our choices. It appears that we are continually exercising free will. One moment we choose to take a walk, another moment it's time for a snack. However, we are driven by unconscious needs and ego attachments until we develop awareness of the specific dynamics of our unconscious.

Without progressing through the liberating channel, we are prone, perhaps fated, to meet our karmic lessons (described by the Lunar Nodes) and respond to them in familiar (Moon) ways. Since the broader field of spiritual awareness is not integrated, there is little creativity as to how we respond to life's challenges. We may feel that we must *deal with life* instead of create it. By progressing to the fire level, the separate self becomes a vehicle for Spirit's creativity to spread into the world. The answer to the question of fate vs. free will is not "black and white." As we evolve, we become increasingly able to experience the freedom that comes with the ability to make conscious choices rooted in the present moment.

The Self-Destruct Mechanism

What if we don't engage the liberating channel? What happens if, collectively, we remain unconscious?

As we go through life, many of us encounter experiences that we deem to be unacceptable and unforgivable. Abuse, murder, and genocide, for example, seem reprehensible and absolutely wrong. There are many things that a soul *distances* itself from. In astrology, Pluto is associated with all the painful or taboo topics that we lock in the proverbial closet. Not wanting to address and feel the severity of hurt or pain lurking in this territory is understandable. However, this avoidance leads to a fragmented condition in the soul. In order to attain wholeness, it must be addressed.

As we've explored, the Moon also relates to unconscious material, but there is a dramatic difference between the Lunar and Plutonic terrain. When our growth brings the Moon into awareness, we recognize its emotional themes; it feels familiar. Pluto's content, in contrast, is considered so distasteful that it's been banished to the farthest reaches of the solar system. We claim desperately, both to ourself and to others, that it doesn't belong to us. To engage with Plutonian material, we need to unflinchingly immerse ourselves in our darkness. Often this healing process is catalyzed by stressful interpersonal events or by larger global issues such as war or catastrophe. Plutonian material has an unmistakably intense charge. It tends to be quite overwhelming, which is why we often feel compelled to resist it so strongly.

Progressing to the fire level requires us to be open to all of life. If we choose to reject or condemn the Plutonian realm, we end up trapping ourselves in the Saturnian container of the relative world. To open the door to transpersonal oneness, we first need to accept the unacceptable, to let go of our resistance and make peace with what has been most traumatic for us. This usually requires feeling what was too painful to feel at the initial time of impact.

When we don't address our dark and painful Pluto material, we add to the collective shadow. The common strategies of deflecting or projecting lead to our larger crises such as degrading human life or the planet. The dishonor and decadence we see on the global scale originates in the unhealed recesses of individual psyches.

Pluto's gift is in catalyzing breakthroughs in consciousness. However, when these breakthroughs are resisted, the energy can build to the point of triggering some kind of annihilation. Although our personal basin of denied pain will not destroy the planet, the collectively repressed Pluto eventually will. It's only a matter of time until a catastrophic turn of events compromises our survival. It may take the form of ruining our relationship with the planet, unleashing devastating warheads, or some other way of creating hell on Earth.

However it may unfold, Pluto serves as a self-destruct mechanism if we fail to grow.

Climbing the spiral stairway can lead us to heaven on earth. Staying in the darkness of unconsciousness can create a living nightmare. Either way, Pluto triggers the process of recycling. With a commitment to healing, our greatest wounds turn into a foundation of strength and courage, supporting healthy and bold action in the world. The "crap" which was previously avoided transforms into the fertilizer which feeds new growth and creativity.

If the evolution of consciousness does not proceed, then Pluto instigates recycling through eventual annihilation on this planet. If we were to perish due to living unconsciously, then Pluto provides the necessary transformation to hit the restart button. No matter how upsetting, it would actually be freeing for us to recycle in some way if our collective shadow got the better of us. The Pluto self-destruct mechanism is actually a benevolent way for Spirit to assure us some form of release. Eventually we would rise again like the proverbial phoenix from the ashes.

The Spiritual Landscape

Throughout this book, we have traversed the underlying spiritual landscape of astrology with the elements as our guides. To summarize our explorations:

The planets, signs, and houses all have elemental associations. We can also think of the levels of reality (body, heart, mind, and soul) as being aligned with their respective elements. The elements can also be understood as operating *within* each of these levels. Earth and water compose the physical world, while air and fire make up the nonphysical. Earth and air are associated with left brain (content) channels, while water and fire (process) pertain to the right brain. Both cyclical and progressive evolutionary motion is understood through the interplay of the elements.

Each of the four elements plays a miraculous role. All the light and heat we experience is fire. The Sun is the center of our system and gives forth radiance which sustains everything, repeating the theme that everything comes from Spirit. Our Sun is like a nucleus, while the solar system is like a cell in a far larger body. The Sun joins with other stars to form a tapestry of energy, a dazzling light display. As fire relates to vitality, we see that the entire universe is alive.

Not only is the universe alive, it's intelligent. Space (air) is an endless metaphysical container holding all movement within its expanse. This container is bristling with endless connections—a nervous system of epic proportions. Everything is plugged into this phenomenal brain. From the movements of the planets, to the movement of an electron, the intelligence which pervades all of life is breathtaking in scope, astonishing in complexity.

Water adds the depth of consciousness. It allows autonomous life to flourish. From the position of consciousness, everything deepens in subjective ways necessary for soul growth. As consciousness extends out into the wider world, all processes contribute to a collective consciousness. We learn to navigate the ocean of life, saturated with significance.

Earth is the great foundation. The physical realm provides the broad container in which life sprouts. We tread on matter, never really doubting its solidity. Miraculously, physics tells us that there's hardly anything to it. Although it appears that we are humans having spiritual experiences, the fleeting quality to earth illustrates the converse. We are blessed to incarnate in the physical realm for our evolution.

The elements combine to form one world. Spirit is unified but also separates to initiate and maintain the glorious evolutionary process. Just as we breathe in and out, the universe eternally moves from creative potential to density and back again, continually manifesting and liberating. As with the hemispheres of our brain, there is a split into charged (process) and neutral (content) designations, and the interplay between them triggers evolution in a huge variety of ways.

The experiential, passionate qualities of the charged elements position them as the primary agents of an evolving, spiritual existence. The charged elements make us feel alive and propel our soul mission. Their subjectivity requires the balancing influence of the neutral elements. Air and earth are the silent partners that make

206

this evolutionary project actually work. Without the neutral elements, and the structure and dependability they provide, life would be indistinguishable from a dream. The spiritual landscape we reside in has both this consensus reality, as well as the unique dynamics of a very subjective soul condition. The full embracing of incarnation leads us to strive to reach greater spiritual wholeness and to contribute to our collective evolution.

From the radiant oneness of Spirit, we enter the realms of separation. Each of us has a unique attunement to nature's elements and can learn to use them all with skill. As we evolve, we gain perspective on and wisdom about the fascinating evolutionary journey we're on. By integrating awareness into the unconscious, we learn to make conscious choices in the eternal present. We move toward greater spiritual realization as we climb the spiral stairway and eventually return home.

Appendix

Complex Aspect Configurations

This Appendix is for those interested in further study of the evolutionary purpose of various complex aspects, which involve more than two signs. For instance, what is the lesson offered by the Yod, T-Square, or other configurations?

There are obviously more variables to consider, but we can examine the patterns in the same way individual aspects were discussed. Some of the evolutionary lessons depicted by these aspects become quite advanced! The amount of information revealed by all the possible complex aspects would easily fill its own book. For now, we'll limit the in-depth exploration to the Grand Trine, the T-Square, and the Yod. A few other interesting patterns will be introduced, though a thorough discussion of them will await another time.

An Evolutionary Technique

With three signs involved in an aspect configuration, a triangle is formed. We can name the triangle's three points as A, B, and C. The lines AB, AC, and BC connect these points and form the sides of the triangle. This evolutionary technique assumes that line AB has relevance to point C since C is connected to both A and B.

209

The three points of a triangle are the basic evolutionary programs of the various signs (*autonomy, resources, mind,* etc)., while the lines (AB, AC, BC) are the product of integrating two signs, as explained in chapters 4-6.

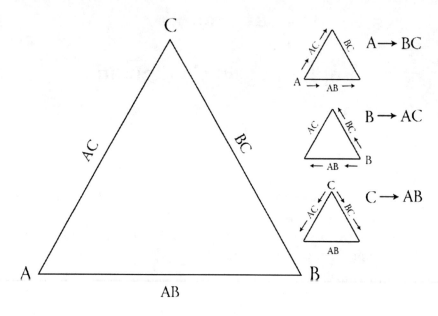

An Evolutionary Technique

Figure 16

One example we looked at was *autonomy* (Aries) and *vocation* (Capricorn) producing **leadership**. The situation gets more complex when we consider that the line of the triangle that is **leadership** has a relationship with the point on the triangle which is *not* Aries or Capricorn. If the configuration were a T-Square, for example, then either Libra or Cancer would complete this particular triangle. **Leadership** (Aries/Capricorn) connects to *relationship* (Libra) through the two connecting lines of **behavior** (Aries/Libra) and **civilization** (Libra/Capricorn). In the other T-Square, **leadership** (Aries/Capricorn) connects to *heart* (Cancer) through **protection** (Aries/Cancer) and **importance** (Cancer/Capricorn).

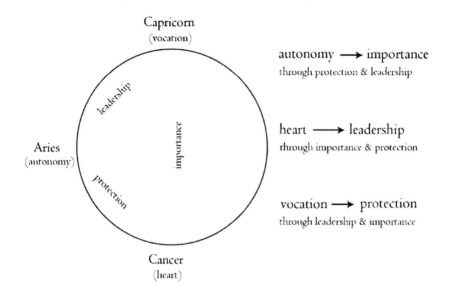

Capricorn
(vocation)

Aries
(autonomy)

Cancer
(heart)

leadership

importance

protection

autonomy ⟶ importance
through protection & leadership

heart ⟶ leadership
through importance & protection

vocation ⟶ protection
through leadership & importance

Example of the Evolutionary Technique

Figure 17

The meanings generated by the various complex aspects are multifaceted and require some contemplation to fully understand them. What may result is a new and deep appreciation for the amazing intelligence of astrology.

So how *is* it that **leadership** connects to *heart* through **protection** and **importance?** It is like a riddle to chew on. Leaders who come from a heart-centered place protect what is most important. The evolutionary opportunity here is to learn to stay connected to our roots while serving in the world. We must, as always, also be aware of the darker possibilities, as there is no guarantee that these lessons will be managed consciously. Let's do a couple more examples of these triangles using a Grand Trine and then a Yod.

A Grand Trine connects the three signs of one of the elements. For this example, we'll use air. Libra/Aquarius (**culture**) joins with Gemini (*mind*), through the other two trines of

Gemini/Aquarius (*genius*) and Gemini/Libra (**communication**). So, *mind* impacts **culture** through **genius** and **communication**. A great example of the expression of this trine is found in William Shakespeare, who influenced culture through his mind by being a genius and communicating his intellect to others. The other parts of this Grand Trine will be reviewed later.

To form a Yod, two quincunxes converge at a shared point. For example, Virgo and Cancer both form quincunxes to Aquarius. Therefore, *systems* (Aquarius) connect with **health care** (Virgo/Cancer) through **technology** (Virgo/Aquarius) and **agape** (Cancer/Aquarius). The spiritual intelligence of Aquarian systemic functioning becomes actualized in the realm of health care by the development of technologies and the universal love for all (agape).

Let's review all the other Grand Trine, T-Square, and Yod combinations.

The Grand Trine

A Grand Trine is a flowing system in which energy easily moves between the personal, the social, and the collective. The sum of the energy is greater than the parts. The element involved is greatly accentuated, both in terms of its potential strengths as well as its follies.

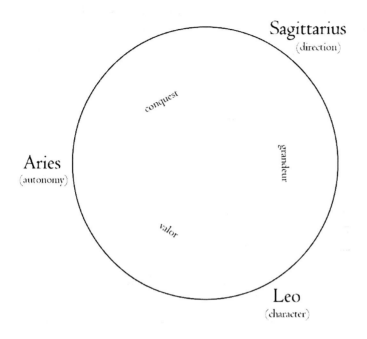

Sagittarius
(direction)

conquest

grandeur

Aries
(autonomy)

valor

Leo
(character)

The Grand Trine
Figure 18

The Fire Grand Trine connects Aries/Leo (*valor*) to Leo/ Sagittarius (*grandeur*) to Aries/Sagittarius (*conquest*). The flavor here is one of great vitality and having the ability to inspire others to accomplish some worldly purpose. Fire builds momentum around the triangle, each leg of it reinforcing the others. The sense that anything is possible becomes contagious. Fire's charge ignites the will to move forward. The evolutionary purpose of this configuration is similar to that of fire itself—*excitation.* As the first element in the zodiac, fire activates and enlivens. The shadow is found with explosion, which occurs when ignition is not done consciously. Acceleration without brakes would equate to brashness connecting to grandiosity leading to destruction. This Grand Trine can result in a grand mess!

Using the evolutionary technique described above, we can see the following: *Autonomy* (Aries) connects to ***grandeur*** (Leo/

213

Sagittarius) through *conquest* (Aries/Sagittarius) and *valor* (Aries/ Leo). *Character* (Leo) connects to *conquest* through *grandeur* and *valor*, and *direction* (Sagittarius) connects to *valor* through *grandeur* and *conquest*. These lessons pertain to the realization of a sense of majesty by acting in dignified and purposeful ways.

Next comes the Earth Grand Trine bridging *productivity* (Taurus/Virgo), *industry* (Virgo/Capricorn), and *success* (Taurus/Capricorn). This aspect illustrates the flow of natural resources into the development of products that contribute to both individual success and a robust economy. The practicality of the earth element is reinforced by each leg of the triangle, promoting *utility*. The shadow of earth manifests as wastefulness, workaholism, and materialism, all stemming from trying to maximize utility. Neutrality can become stuck in routine without questioning it.

Resources (Taurus) connect to *industry* (Virgo/Capricorn) through *productivity* and *success*. *Competence* (Virgo) connects to *success* (Taurus/Capricorn) through *productivity* and *industry*. *Vocation* (Capricorn) connects to *productivity* (Taurus/Virgo) through *success* and *industry*. The earth lessons illustrate how determined business savvy brings about economic growth.

The Air Grand Trine links *communication* (Gemini/ Libra), *culture* (Libra/Aquarius), and *genius* (Gemini/Aquarius). Ideas move swiftly from the self to others to the creation of a social milieu. The flowing quality to the trine allows the speedy air element to establish its evolutionary purpose—*connection*. The shadow is found in lying, conformity, and erratic mental conditions. We can just as easily have chaotic thinking patterns connect to others through lying and establish a culture of conformity to such thoughts. The neutral quality here may manifest as not doing anything about such a dynamic (no charge).

As mentioned above, *mind* (Gemini) connects with *culture* through *communication* and *genius*. *Relationship* (Libra) connects to *genius* through *communication* and *culture*. *Systems* (Aquarius) connect with *communication* through *culture* and *genius*. The air Grand Trine portrays the flow of mental and social energy, which informs the development of advanced society.

The Water Grand Trine joins *bonding* (Cancer/Scorpio), *sacred union* (Scorpio/Pisces), and *empathy* (Cancer/Pisces). Emotions are often irrational and unruly. Among humans enrolled in this "evolutionary school," few of us bond together without some amount of conflict. When done well, bonding, sacred union, and having empathy flow together. We attain wisdom about what's really involved when we emotionally interact with others. And we find the evolutionary lesson of water—*depth*. The shadow here is drowning, as abuse, misery, and victimization may also easily join together when consciousness is lacking. The charged quality to water could reinforce itself in a downward spiral of subjectivity and heightened reactions.

Heart (Cancer) connects to *sacred union* through *bonding* and *empathy*. *Power* (Scorpio) connects to *empathy* through *sacred union* and *bonding*. *Mysticism* (Pisces) connects to *bonding* through *empathy* and *sacred union*. The water Grand Trine illustrates how emotional energy spreads from personal to social to universal in order to nourish life.

The T-Square

The T-Square features three signs: two in opposition, with the third forming a square to each. This aspect is highly frictional, as there is a tremendous amount of energy working at cross purposes. The potential shadow possibilities are in equal measure to the evolutionary opportunities.

The two signs in opposition are involved in their balancing act, trying to resolve a fundamental evolutionary issue. Unlike the Grand Trine, where there is equality throughout the aspect, the T-Square primarily focuses on the opposition and secondarily on the squares. The opposition is more fundamental, while the square is more advanced. Working the opposition well is like strengthening the backbone of the complex configuration.

215

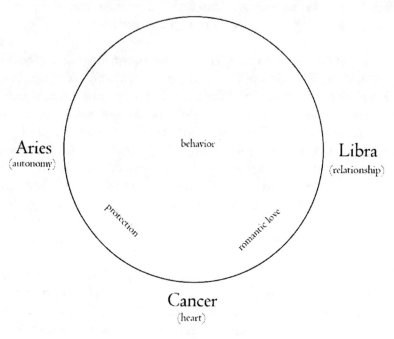

The T-Square

Figure 19

The sign in the position of squaring the opposition complicates the dynamic. It occupies the central position, either creating exciting new ways to build from the tension or introducing a destructive component. Whether or not it's operating consciously is, as always, the determining factor. If it is, then the root issue of the opposition is boosted towards its resolution and giant evolutionary steps are made possible.

There is an evolutionary lesson to the two squares that compose the T-Square. By looking at the integration, supportive ways to resolve the conflicts emerge. The sign that would turn the T-Square into a Grand Cross also gives clues to the resolution. Although not a part of the configuration, its qualities are supportive. In the following descriptions of the T-Squares, the sign listed in the middle is in the central position of squaring the opposition.

The Cardinal T-Squares

Aries/Cancer/Libra: Aries/Libra addresses issues of *beha-vior*—how does family and our *heart* (Cancer) impact behavior? Cancer adds an emotional element to the self-other dynamic, bringing another charge to negotiate. Ideally, the self-other dynamic deepens—there is greater authenticity in the exchange. Cancer stimulates Aries to assert itself into the relationship, while it also helps Libra recognize if its needs are being met. Family (Cancer) responsibilities pressure Aries/Libra to work out the needs of the self in relationship—there are mouths to feed, in-laws to please, and a mortgage to pay. How does the self preserve its autonomy while also finding time to invest in the relationship?

By *protecting* (Aries/Cancer) what is truly important and feeling refreshed by the bonds of *romantic love* (Cancer/Libra), this aspect can be resolved. *Behavior* (Aries/Libra) is informed by *heart* (Cancer). The shadow is overprotecting our autonomy and having romantic dissatisfaction create an unsettled home. If there are children, they would be raised in a hotbed of tension. Without *behavior through heart*, there is strife and fragmentation. Support is found with Capricorn. Having gainful employment not only provides a necessary balancing outlet to family concerns, the finan-cial stability it secures helps to negotiate the competing demands of self/family/other.

Heart (Cancer) connects to *behavior* through *romantic love* and *protection*. *Autonomy* (Aries) connects to *romantic love* through *behavior* and *protection*. *Relationship* (Libra) connects to *protection* through *romantic love* and *behavior*.

Aries/Capricorn/Libra: *Behavior* is being pressured by *vo-cation* (Capricorn). It takes long hours to work with Capricorn, and focus requires that distractions be shut out. How do we keep both the self and relationship healthy while ambition is pursued? Capri-corn adds the component of realism. Its neutrality reminds us to keep focusing on tasks without yielding to distractions. It can bring sturdiness to the self (Aries), as well as longevity to relationship

217

(Libra). Managed well, the self/other dynamic is brought into the public eye.

Through exercising *leadership* (Aries/Capricorn) and taking part in *civilization* (Libra/Capricorn), the autonomous self can join powerfully with a partner and together, become a public force. This aspect deals with *behavior through vocation*. The shadow is being caught up in career pursuits. If Aries/Capricorn turns tyrannical, how is a partner going to feel? If Libra/Capricorn becomes preoccupied with social status, the individual is lost. A relationship can follow a script of complacency. Living within a "country club" marriage may muffle the fire of the individual. There is then the possibility of acting out (Aries). If this T-Square is managed poorly, there is a public airing of "dirty laundry," a soiling of reputation through scandal and the inevitable gossip. Support is found through Cancer—leading from the heart. If the bonds that tie the individual to the relationship are strong, the emergence into being public is better handled. In fact, others will be moved by the model of integrity being displayed.

Vocation (Capricorn) connects to *behavior* through *leadership* and *civilization*. *Autonomy* (Aries) connects to *civilization* through *behavior* and *leadership*. *Relationship* (Libra) connects to *leadership* through *civilization* and *behavior*.

Cancer/Aries/Capricorn: The Cancer/Capricorn polarity is striving for *importance*—how does the actions of the self (Aries) influence this process? With this aspect, it is completely up to the individual to decide how to manage the competing demands of vocation and family. There are family (Cancer) and societal (Capricorn) expectations that impinge on our free will. Being a charged sign, Aries may react to this conditioning and assert, "It's my life!" There is potential for rebellion. On the other hand, with a low charge, we can easily be sculpted by these external expectations and relinquish our power.

Through exercising *leadership* (Aries/Capricorn) and *protecting* (Aries/Cancer) what is truly important, we come to make decisions deliberatively. Managed well, we choose a vocation that both ignites our personal fire (Aries) and responsibly supports

218

our family. *Importance through autonomy* is thereby achieved. The shadow possibilities are being tyrannical about our chosen career or overprotecting family influences. Both of these outcomes lead to the individual behaving in a reactive, rather than proactive, fashion. Support is found with Libra—being able to approach issues diplomatically and with consideration of all sides.

Autonomy (Aries) connects to *importance* through *protection* and *leadership*. *Heart* (Cancer) connects to *leadership* through *importance* and *protection*. *Vocation* (Capricorn) connects to *protection* through *importance* and *leadership*.

Cancer/Libra/Capricorn: The axis of *importance* is being impacted by *relationship*. Libra concerns the attainment of a pleasing status quo and is willing to schmooze in order to keep things nice. This aspect deals with the pressures from social relations into realms of family and vocation. Being in relationship can lead to nesting (Cancer) and improve our social status (Capricorn). Libra's neutralizing tendency can also make us prone to fall into routines in these areas and just go along with expectations. An example of this scenario is the compliant husband who repeatedly agrees to host the dinner party even though he'd rather watch the ballgame.

The tools available to negotiate this friction are *romantic love* (Cancer/Libra) and taking part in *civilization* (Libra/Capricorn). If the emotional bonds of relationship are strong, then there's rootedness in love. It's a joy to find *importance through relationship* and branch out into the wider world. Without this emotional foundation, the institution of relationship turns into a prison. The personal will is deadened by conventionality, appearances, and responsibilities. Support is found with the autonomy and empowered decision-making of Aries.

Relationship (Libra) connects to *importance* through *romantic love* and *civilization*. *Heart* (Cancer) connects to *civilization* through *romantic love* and *importance*. *Vocation* (Capricorn) connects to *romantic love* through *civilization* and *importance*.

The cardinal T-Squares challenge us to put what is most central in life first. By balancing the needs of self, family, relationship, and career, we are able to see to our core responsibilities.

The Fixed T-Squares

Taurus/Leo/Scorpio: The axis of *endurance* is squared by *character*. How can we use the personality (Leo) to attain resources (Taurus) and engage in meaningful intimacy (Scorpio)? This T-Square deals with the issue of securing reward and abundance, having a life worth living. Leo's appetite for life pressures Taurus to have the resources, financial and otherwise, to do as it pleases. It also applies pressure to the dynamics of intimacy (Scorpio) to allow for recreational pursuits. Leo may say, "What's in it for me?" The other question, though, is whether the personality is *only* going to seek reward? Ideally, Leo commits to the self/other dynamic.

By developing *abundance* (Taurus/Leo) and *trust* (Leo/ Scorpio) we are able to live large (Leo) and enjoy a fulfilling life. Through accomplishing these evolutionary tasks, we come to feel both secure in the self (Taurus) and deeply connected to others (Scorpio). Attaining *endurance through character* is living with nobility through thick and thin. Without *abundance* and *trust,* Leo is prone to behave narcissistically. With a heightened Leo charge, the shadow potential of this T-Square is to maximize money and pleasure (Taurus) and use people (Scorpio) for egoic reasons. With no arousal of a Leo charge, joy diminishes and life endures without much spark. Support is found through Aquarius. When the personality sees that it's a part of groups and broader systems (astrology for example), this collective involvement puts Leo pursuits in perspective.

Character (Leo) connects to *endurance* through *trust* and *abundance*. *Resources* (Taurus) connect to *trust* through *endurance* and *abundance*. *Power* (Scorpio) connects with *abundance* through *trust* and *endurance*.

220

Taurus/Aquarius/Scorpio: *Systems* square the polarity of **endurance**. How can systems or collective membership strengthen us? This T-Square deals with how progressive evolution (Aquarius), this energetic life container we are enveloped in, applies pressure to how we endure. Indicative of the fixed modality, the issues relevant for our spiritual growth continually challenge us. The spiritual intelligence (Aquarius) demands us to be firm (Taurus) and intimately involved in process (Scorpio). As a neutral sign, Aquarius has no sentiment about the impact of difficult life lessons on our sense of stability (Taurus) or the pain frequently involved with interpersonal work (Scorpio).

The universe uses **nature** (Taurus/Aquarius) and **wisdom** (Scorpio/Aquarius) to instigate progress (Aquarius). The collective mind (Aquarius) permeates matter (Taurus) and is alive like a wise magician in our deepest soul work (Scorpio). When there is cooperation with this intelligence, **endurance through systems** is achieved, and we are able to evolve. The shadow is being stuck (fixed modality) in the limitations of our more basic animal nature (Taurus) and endlessly repeating unhealthy patterns (Scorpio). Support is found through Leo—a radiant life force which carries out evolutionary intentions.

Systems (Aquarius) connect to **endurance** through **wisdom** and **nature**. *Resources* (Taurus) connect to **wisdom** through **endurance** and **nature**. *Power* (Scorpio) connects to **nature** through **wisdom** and **endurance**.

Leo/Taurus/Aquarius: *Resources* square the axis of **participation**. Do we have the resources of confidence and determination (Taurus) to participate in the collective milieu (Aquarius) with a unique character (Leo)? If Taurus resists, it consolidates power and bolsters itself materially. Life is then focused solely on the physical world, and participation is limited to that arena. The other possibility lies in using the body (Taurus) as a temporary spiritual vessel necessary to participate in evolution.

Some tools available in this pursuit are **nature** (Taurus/Aquarius) and **abundance** (Taurus/Leo). The awareness that nature is a synthesis of mind and matter empowers us to connect with it in a multitude of ways. An abundance of resources helps us find allies and mutual support in the personal realm. Ultimately, we can learn *participation through resources*, by being solid in the self (Taurus) and connected to life (Leo/Aquarius). The shadow is participating from a place of stubbornness—everything has to be set up on our terms. Support is found with Scorpio and its ability to negotiate intimacy and dive into the cauldron of spiritual processes.

Resources (Taurus) connect to *participation* through *abundance* and *nature*. *Character* (Leo) connects with *nature* through *participation* and *abundance*. *Systems* (Aquarius) connect with *abundance* through *participation* and *nature*.

Leo/Scorpio/Aquarius: How does *power* impact *participation?* This configuration deals with the influx of mainly unconscious psychological material (Scorpio) into how the personality (Leo) functions in the world (Aquarius). There are pressures to bond or merge, to share resources and have intimate experiences. Connecting passionately—including sexually—helps bring our unconscious psychological material to the surface. The resolution of this T-Square is the successful management of our shadow tendencies in the broader world.

At the unconscious end of the spectrum, there is the potential to release everything in the personal *Pandora's Box* into social exchange. All of the unsavory remnants of prior wounding are let loose for others to see. This unintentional exposure can be a boon to growth if it encourages us to put some needed attention on these issues. Ideally, *wisdom* (Scorpio/Aquarius) and *trust* (Scorpio/Leo) assist in committing to this healing process. The shadow possibilities of unconsciousness and mistrust aggravate the wounding indicative of Scorpio and create a maddening spiral of interpersonal entanglements. Ultimately, *participation through power* enables us to heal the soul by deeply connecting with all that life brings us. Holding our ground (Taurus) and developing calmness and security in the self provides the supportive anchor to deal with the intense processes of this T-Square.

Power (Scorpio) connects to *participation* through *trust* and *wisdom*. *Character* (Leo) connects to *wisdom* through *trust* and ***participation***. *Systems* (Aquarius) connect to ***trust*** through ***wisdom*** and ***participation***.

The fixed T-Squares invite a deepening into enriching areas of life. Resources, character, power, and systems can be negotiated to bring a sustained investment in joyful growth.

The Mutable T-Squares

Gemini/Virgo/Sagittarius: How is *competence* used for ***learning***? How skilled, precise, and ready are we to figure out the world and our place in it? How can we apply the self in ways that promote knowledge? Becoming knowledgeable in a craft opens the mind to the intricacies of how things work. However, becoming too specialized in one area will lead to a narrow perspective.

Skill development (Virgo) can inform us about how the world works. With a hands-on approach, we learn through doing. We are informed by ***science***, as well as the strategic planning found in ***foresight***, which guide our pursuits. Managed well, ***learning through competence*** is established. The shadow to navigate is limitation and extreme skepticism. Virgo can limit the reach of Gemini/Sagittarius in terms of what is considered to be most useful, practical, or efficient, which may strangle the endless possibilities of the mutable signs. Pisces provides the counterpoint to this aspect, reminding us to be inspired and attain the broadest perspective through the development of consciousness.

Competence (Virgo) connects to ***learning*** through ***science*** and ***foresight***. *Mind* (Gemini) connects to ***foresight*** through ***science*** and ***learning***. *Direction* (Sagittarius) connects to ***science*** through ***learning*** and ***foresight***.

Gemini/Pisces/Sagittarius: How can *mysticism* impact the ***learning*** process? In short, how can we know God? Will there be confusion, impotence, or disorientation? Or is it possible to actually gain knowledge of and direct experience with the workings of Spirit? This aspect asks us to check what we think we know with some form of contemplative practice. The challenge is establishing and maintaining fluency with very different modes of processing and understanding.

The authentic wisdom teachings from *religion* and a balanced *understanding* of the phenomena which compose this world are assets in this venture. Respecting both left and right brain modes of perception can be a difficult task. Sifting through what is informative and what is superfluous is similarly arduous. Support is found in Virgo's discernment and its discipline, which can maintain a daily spiritual practice. *Learning through mysticism* is then made possible. The shadow is reaching erroneous spiritual conclusions based on misguided or unclear ventures in consciousness.

Mysticism (Pisces) connects to *learning* through *understanding* and *religion*. *Mind* (Gemini) connects to *religion* through *understanding* and *learning*. *Direction* (Sagittarius) connects to *understanding* through *learning* and *religion*.

Virgo/Gemini/Pisces: How can *mind* impact *improvement?* How do thoughts influence the developmental process? What type of information supports growth, and what kind may actually stifle it? This T-Square challenges the burgeoning intellect to be well-rounded. The openness of Gemini certainly has its time and place, but if the mind stays youthful and questioning, it is prone to also stay immature. The integration is to use constructive information to assist in our spiritual development.

The tools available here are *science* and *understanding*. Science informs us of how the world works in our familiar dimensions, while a balanced understanding teaches us that there could be more to it. All of this input enables us to find *improvement through mind*. Our perceptual and intellectual faculties have endless complexity, which can enable us to grapple with this strange situation of bridging multiple worlds. The shadow is to never draw conclusions. Gemini endlessly accrues information but is clueless with taking further steps. Improvement requires decisiveness, and Sagittarius provides the missing leg. By developing direction, being able to see the broader picture, and arriving at a meaningful life purpose, we are able to utilize the powers of the mind most advantageously.

224

Mind (Gemini) connects to ***improvement*** through ***science*** and ***understanding****. Competence* (Virgo) connects to ***understanding*** through ***improvement*** and ***science****. Mysticism* (Pisces) connects to ***science*** through ***improvement*** and ***understanding****.*

Virgo/Sagittarius/Pisces: How can *direction* impact ***improvement****?* How does an overarching life philosophy impact development? Which beliefs get in the way, and which can be supportive? Our world view is often instilled at a very young age. True to Sagittarius being a charged sign, we usually become very attached to these constructs. This aspect asks for an expansion of the belief system in order to maximize the breadth of spiritual seeking. Without this expansion, the entire configuration hardens into dogmatic prescriptions. Ideology doesn't always match the way things actually are. The program here is to amend our beliefs so they align with reality.

We can use ***religion*** and ***foresight*** as tools on the journey. Religion provides a foundation, as its accumulated spiritual philosophies can be instructive. Also, the gifts of foresight enable us to plan our life's trajectory according to such principles. With these tools, we can pursue ***improvement through direction*** by living in accord with our moral compass. In order to avoid the shadow of missionary zeal, Gemini is the prescription. Through continually learning and having a "beginner's mind," the compass is recalibrated and renewed.

Direction (Sagittarius) connects to ***improvement*** through ***foresight*** and ***religion****. Competence* (Virgo) connects to ***religion*** through ***improvement*** and ***foresight****. Mysticism* connects to ***foresight*** through ***improvement*** and ***religion****.*

The mutable T-Squares address the dynamics among mind, competence, direction, and mysticism—how we make sense of our existential circumstance. Through reconciling these aspects, we comprehend and experience our true spiritual nature.

The Yod

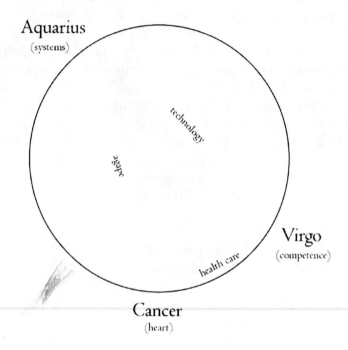

The Yod

Figure 20

The Yod has been called the "finger of God." It is an aspectual configuration composed of three planets—two in sextile to each other, and both of those quincunx the third. The two planets in sextile are in a harmonious connection, and together they pressure the third to grow in novel ways. The quincunx is an aspect of negotiation or adjustment, so this combination is inherently unbalanced. By making a concerted effort to integrate the singular sign at the point of the triangle with the supportive team, a powerful energetic system becomes functional. As the Yod is composed of quincunxes, these energetic systems pertain to advanced evolutionary programs.

A yod will either involve one neutral and two charged signs or, alternatively, two neutral and one charged sign. The interplay between neutral and charged works the same way as in other aspects (square, opposition, etc.) except that there are now three variables at play instead of two. The rising of intensity of the charged elements and the accompanying balance by the neutral creates a lively, though unstable, system.

Aries quincunx Virgo/Scorpio

Virgo/Scorpio aims to develop mastery or to accomplish something urgent. It could be in the form of *therapy*, or in more mundane situations such as working with others to build sandbag barriers for an impending flood. Whatever the task, the consequences of failure loom large. The doctor tells you that if you don't lose some weight or quit smoking, the end could be near. Pointing towards Aries, this aspect focuses the responsibility of action on personal behavior and *autonomy*—to act as if our life depends on it, because it just might.

It takes *maturity* and *passion* to meet the challenges and succeed. Done well, it promotes personal empowerment (Aries) and the strength to live healthfully (Virgo) and with conviction (Scorpio). A poor integration of Virgo with Scorpio would fuel reckless behavior (Aries), with the results bringing shame, guilt (Virgo), or catastrophe (Scorpio). Virgo/Scorpio can get lost in process, strategy, and tinkering. There comes a time when you must get off the therapist's couch or finish recovering from an operation and assertively seize control of life. Identifying as injured, wounded, or handicapped could further entrench a debilitated state. Exercising the strength of will (Aries) enables us to meet the challenges that life offers.

Autonomy (Aries) connects to *therapy* through *maturity* and *passion*. *Competence* (Virgo) connects to *passion* through *maturity* and *therapy*. *Power* (Scorpio) connects to *maturity* through *passion* and *therapy*.

Taurus quincunx Libra/Sagittarius

Libra/Sagittarius pertains to *politics*—creating laws based on a moral code, joining together in joint purpose, and forming philosophical or policy consensus. As seen in political arenas, there is a lot of hot (Sagittarius) air (Libra) in this combination. Sooner or later the debate needs to be put to rest, and that's what this yod concerns. Taurus brings stability, a focus on the mundane world, *resources*, and our everyday experience. Grounding laws into the fabric of how things really are is potentially dicey. Whatever is too theoretical, or based merely on hopeful assumptions, gets the reality treatment with Taurus. With *gumption*, politics become earthed through the strategic implementation of principles. *Art* brings ideals into tangible form. In this case, the social principles of Libra are concretized. Taurus/Libra also has correlations to the money involved in seeing policy become manifest—the allocation of resources.

Successful integration results in creating a functioning status quo (Taurus) that reflects morality and the highest ideals. We can also apply what actually works in the real world (Taurus) to future policy-making discussions. The shadow version occurs if Taurus rigidifies principles that were not well-founded. This creates inertia and social compliance—having the laws of the land reflect errant principles. People then behave in agreeable ways (Libra) to maintain equilibrium, until passions and opinions (Sagittarius) become intensified.

Resources (Taurus) connect to *politics* through *gumption* and *art*. *Relationship* (Libra) connects with *gumption* through *art* and *politics*. *Direction* (Sagittarius) connects with *art* through *gumption* and *politics*.

Gemini quincunx Scorpio/Capricorn

Scorpio/Capricorn concerns the consolidation of power—the bolstering of institutions to be instruments of social change. This combination is about the wisdom and experience gained through tradition and preservation. The *command* felt in the stur-

228

diness of an ancient cathedral is a good metaphor. Both Scorpio and Capricorn can be secretive and prone to becoming underhanded and controlling. Gemini injects openness and new ideas— the freedom of information about how government and other social institutions are run. Journalists and other questioners (Gemini) are welcome. In fact, all input is helpful. *Education* informs the youth as they learn about history and governance. Pupils learn *honesty* as they mature, leading to the ethical use of command.

The shadow can manifest as mind control and propaganda as the dominant power structure (Capricorn/Scorpio) controls information (Gemini). Think of Orwell's *1984* or the Nazi Party for a real-life example. Intellectual oppression is only changed by an intense Scorpio charge, the ferocity of which catalyzes people to join in toppling the empire (Capricorn) to free the mind.

Mind (Gemini) connects to *command* through *honesty* and *education. Power* (Scorpio) connects to *education* through *honesty* and *command. Vocation* (Capricorn) connects to *honesty* through *education* and *command.*

Cancer quincunx Sagittarius/Aquarius

Sagittarius/Aquarius forms a holistic philosophy, unrestrained quests, world togetherness, the integration of religions, or a spiritual mission for the collective. Imagine a mass *congregation* in the same boat. Would we be able to get along? Many people have marvelous dreams of world peace and harmony, of realizing the proverbial melting pot. However this idealistic vision often discounts the realistic human element. There are personal emotional needs, family concerns, and issues of love and bonding (Cancer) when people join. This yod involves the process of sampling what the world family offers and then using *self-discovery* to see what emotionally resonates. When there is *agape* we are moved to find ways to connect to everyone. Functioning well, Sagittarius/ Aquarius expands the definition of home and stretches the heart to include new ways of being. This yod challenges us to discover what

229

prevents us from loving everybody and to then find a way to open beyond this limitation.

The shadow results in lots of clutter and chaos. Picture various kinds of people speaking many languages all living in one house trying to prepare a meal that would appeal to everyone. Cancer can retreat to being territorial and protective, which opens the doors to misunderstandings and others feeling hurt or offended. Ultimately, when we personally connect with others (Cancer) we can change our views (Sagittarius) and reach greater unity (Aquarius). Attitudes are changed in the heart. When families reflect greater ethnic and cultural diversity, the ideal of the melting pot can become a reality.

Heart (Cancer) connects to **congregation** through **self-discovery** and **agape**. *Direction* (Sagittarius) connects to **agape** through **congregation** and **self-discovery**. *Systems* (Aquarius) connect to **self-discovery** through **congregation** and **agape**.

Leo quincunx Capricorn/Pisces

Capricorn/Pisces wants to infuse social structures with benevolence, to create tangible expressions of altruism and love. **Charity** needs individuals to embody and radiate such noble intentions. Leo gives warmth and a human touch, putting smiles on faces in the name of giving. Live-Aid, Band-Aid, and other large-scale performances designed to assist the needy are examples of what is possible here. Certain personalities (Leo) become ambassadors of altruism, such as Princess Diana or Bono. Through **dominion** and **spiritual awakening**, individuals are organized and sufficiently aware to take it upon themselves to contribute in such a way. When this yod is functioning well, it could be like a theatrical performance that contains a mature and inspiring message.

Leo enjoys attention, so the shadow is when individuals (Leo) use the transpersonal (Pisces) for status or gain (Capricorn). This is one form of "spiritual materialism." Leo must also guard against making Capricorn/Pisces trivial. Picture the beauty contestant chewing her gum and claiming she'll end world hunger "Ya know, and things like that," if she becomes Miss America. The

230

potential here, though, is magnanimous—truly animating and structuring the most compassionate of intentions.

Character (Leo) connects to **charity** through **dominion** and **spiritual awakening**. *Vocation* (Capricorn) connects to **spiritual awakening** through **dominion** and **charity**. *Mysticism* (Pisces) connects to **dominion** through **spiritual awakening** and **charity**.

Virgo quincunx Aquarius/Aries

Aquarius/Aries concerns freedom and self-alignment—the **representation** of a truth or larger communal construct in our behavior. This combination is at risk of being impulsive, rebellious, and insensitive toward others. Virgo adds a dose of humility and responsibility. This yod deals with channeling our free will (Aries) into projects (Virgo) which are consistent with our soul intentions (Aquarius). This task is handled through **maturity** and the availability of **technology** for such endeavors. There are many ways to direct our energy, and the lesson here is to be not only responsible to the self but also accountable to others. Later on, we can become a skillful mentor or instructor who teaches self-improvement to others.

Virgo can feel like a downer to the high-octane Aries/ Aquarius sextile. If it gets inadequately integrated, it could manifest as nit-picking, continually advising how to do things better. Without maturity, the shadow emerges. This combination could spiral down into unproductive practices which sabotage efforts towards improving this planet. Functioning well, individuals take it upon themselves to do their part.

Competence (Virgo) connects with **representation** through **maturity** and **technology**. *Autonomy* (Aries) connects with **technology** through **maturity** and **representation**. *Systems* (Aquarius) connect with **maturity** through **representation** and **technology**.

231

Libra quincunx Pisces/Taurus

Pisces/Taurus is contemplative and still. How often do we find this *serenity* in relationship (Libra)? This yod seeks to bring this tranquil intention into interpersonal contexts. Through *Namaste*, we appreciate the divine in the other. Through *art*, our physical surroundings can reflect our transcendent ideals and provide the optimal setting for us to hold the consciousness of appreciation.

The shadow is overdoing interpersonal etiquette. Libra can put on a charming phoniness when interacting with the benevolent sextile. Picture the fawning, apologetic, overly-effusive sycophant who hangs on every word and is full of unnecessary praise. These relationships may be soothing, but without an inspired Pisces charge they can also easily become dull and boring. The evolutionary challenge is to realize conscious togetherness. Pisces would need to stay sufficiently charged in order to bring a sense of wonder and expansion and to find higher levels of spiritual love through harmony.

Relationship (Libra) connects with *serenity* through *art* and *Namaste*. *Resources* (Taurus) connect with *Namaste* through *serenity* and *art*. *Mysticism* (Pisces) connects to *art* through *serenity* and *Namaste*.

Scorpio quincunx Aries/Gemini

The integration of Aries/Gemini is *agility*—learning the optimal ways to behave and assert ourself. It is a youthful combination reminiscent of the carefree spirit found on school playgrounds. What this pairing lacks is depth. With this yod pointing to Scorpio, learning how to catalyze interpersonal processes is on tap. Scorpionic territory must, however, be approached with sufficient respect. Otherwise, the versatile Aries/Gemini eagerly jumps in to the deep end of the pool and promptly drowns. For instance, Aries/Gemini may be curious about sex and intimacy (Scorpio), only to find that these compelling areas are full of hazards. Picture a lustful 17 year-old who can't wait to lose his virginity and gets involved with a married woman (who happens to have a jealous and burly husband)—careful what you wish for!

By developing some **passion** for venturing into transformative experiences and conducting ourself with **honesty**, Aries/Gemini becomes more learned about the most impactful exchanges that humans trigger in each other. Instead of just youthful agility, Scorpio brings the wisdom to know how our behavior is received by others. The shadow is giving into the temptation to experiment with the taboo in secretive and inappropriate ways. Then, elaborate alibis are created to cover the indiscretions.

Power (Scorpio) connects to **agility** through **passion** and **honesty**. *Autonomy* (Aries) connects with **honesty** through **passion** and **agility**. *Mind* (Gemini) connects to **passion** through **honesty** and **agility**.

Sagittarius quincunx Taurus/Cancer

Taurus/Cancer finds **nourishment** as stability supports love to create a committed home life. It feels like a secure base, which is necessary to form loving attachments. However, we all must leave the nest someday. Sagittarius pertains to higher learning or setting out on our own adventure. This combination is like a young adult leaving for college, or someone who takes a break from their comfortable routine in order to travel. Ideally, Taurus/Cancer provides a nourishing launching pad for broader excursions. Through **self-discovery** and **gumption** we figure out who we are and what we want to achieve in the wider world.

Sagittarius is restless and may upset the secure base in the form of urgency to leave home. On the other hand, with the Sagittarius charge dormant, life becomes a series of unrealized aspirations. The 37-year-old who still lives with his parents and dreams of one day living his true purpose is an example. When a greater range of world experiences (Sagittarius) is gathered, we find our authentic truth and can settle (Taurus/Cancer) into a life that reflects it. The shadow stems from not venturing out to live our purpose. Then we are prone to be the irritable director who tells everyone else how they can live with more bravado.

233

Direction (Sagittarius) connects with **nourishment** through **gumption** and **self-discovery**. *Resources* (Taurus) connect with **self-discovery** through **nourishment** and **gumption**. *Heart* (Cancer) connects with **gumption** through **nourishment** and **self-discovery**.

Capricorn quincunx Gemini/Leo

Gemini/Leo is **fun** and comedic. Its improvisational nature supports the development of personal preferences—what the personality really enjoys. As we mature and solidify these preferences, vocation (Capricorn) becomes a natural outlet which can to radiate our talents. This yod puts pressure on manifesting (Capricorn) good ideas, hammering stimulating intentions into form. Ideally, we can sculpt a career that stems from our natural curiosity and inclinations. It is possible to actually like what we do for a living! Through **education** and **dominion**, we cultivate the knowledge and confidence needed to professionally excel.

The shadow is seen with selling out youthful dreams in order to secure a steady paycheck or increased status found through conformity. Leo's charge can alter this decline by roaring its unique character and toppling the stagnation.

Vocation (Capricorn) connects with **fun** through **dominion** and **education**. *Mind* (Gemini) connects with **dominion** through **fun** and **education**. *Character* (Leo) connects with **education** through **fun** and **dominion**.

Aquarius quincunx Cancer/Virgo

Cancer/Virgo deals with the development of **health care**—bringing heart into mutable earth projects in helpful ways. Cancer gets us in touch with the emotional impetus to help, while Virgo finds practical ways to actually do this. These signs are personal and social in scope, but the quincunxes to Aquarius bring a transpersonal component. The desire to assist others in need of support is greatly enhanced by bringing the intelligence of Spirit (Aquarius) into manifestation. The unlimited possibilities of Aquarius are

234

grounded and made personally relevant through *agape* and *technology*, which provide the love and methods to deliver the best care.

If Aquarius remains elusive, then it's difficult to figure out how to modernize. Medical practitioners bring strange ideas and weird techniques into form. Although these methods may initially be fraught with errors, they can help us figure out more effective practices. The shadow is administering care which is unsafe or even debilitating. Ultimately, the resolution of this Yod equips us with the means to incrementally ground the Aquarian intelligence in loving ways.

Systems (Aquarius) connect with **health care** through **technology** and **agape**. *Heart* (Cancer) connects with **technology** through **health care** and **agape**. *Competence* (Virgo) connects with **agape** through **technology** and **health care**.

Pisces quincunx Leo/Libra

The Leo/Libra sextile illustrates how sharing supports connection. Expressing ourself to another who truly receives us creates *engagement*. These two signs also have a flair for artistry. Leo enjoys its natural creative talents and showiness, while Libra has an eye toward refining art to meet a cultural ideal. These social signs are brought to the metaphysical through this yod. Pisces adds an element of psychedelic or mystical allure, and we are taken to glorious heights. Having a peak experience at the movies, theater, or art gallery is exactly the point. Art as spiritual practice, rather than mere entertainment, is the integration of these three signs. When we advance in our *spiritual awakening* and are able to see divinity in everything (*Namaste*), this promise is reached.

If Pisces is poorly integrated, art becomes sloppy or pretentiously vague. Consider some modern art which strives to capture a transcendent message but just misses the mark. Audiences are left scratching their heads instead of having their consciousness raised. Leo/Libra may be overly concerned with presentation or style, which could sabotage the expansive and flowing quality of Pisces. The shadow is using spirituality to create a alluring, albeit phony,

235

social image. Managed well, culture can give us a peak into other worlds.

Mysticism (Pisces) connects to **engagement** through *Namaste* and *spiritual awakening*. *Character* (Leo) connects to *Namaste* through **engagement** and **spiritual awakening**. *Relationship* (Libra) connects to **spiritual awakening** through **engagement** and *Namaste*.

Other Complex Configurations

If we consider the ways that three or more signs can be connected, we generate a multitude of possibilities—all sorts of triangles, rectangles, stars, and other shapes. In this final section, some of the known configurations will be mentioned. A few other obscure ones will also be introduced.

A Kite is a formation consisting of a Grand Trine with a fourth planet added. This fourth planet makes an opposition to one of the planets in the Grand Trine, and sextiles the other two.

A Mystic Rectangle features two planets in opposition, two sextiles, and two trines.

A Grand Sextile is a hexagram formed by connecting six sextiles.

A Grand Quintile is a five-pointed star. Also, there are configurations using three or four quintiles. Rick Levine calls a triangle composed of two biquintiles and a quintile a "Golden Yod," and four quintiles in aspect a "Golden Bowl." See his book, *Quantum Astrology*, for more info.

There are even more variations using the septiles, octiles, or noviles, and other more obscure aspects. The minor aspects (semisextiles, semisquares, sesquisquares, etc.) make aspect configurations among themselves and also join with major aspects to form complex geometrical shapes. The variations would please any curious Gemini! The more complex the aspect configuration, the more advanced the evolutionary programs are. The evolutionary technique introduced at the beginning of the Appendix would need to be expanded to discuss configurations beyond three sides. To keep these analyses manageable, only configurations in a triangular

236

shape will be discussed. Compared to the Grand Trine, T-Square, and Yod, the following aspect configurations are far less known and understood. In fact, two of the three don't even have names at this point. However, this shouldn't marginalize their importance as they are made from the same aspects as the more famous ones.

We will look at three patterns. 1) A triangle formed by an opposition, trine and sextile. 2) A triangle formed by a square, trine, and quincunx. 3) A triangle formed by a square, sextile, and quincunx.

The Wedge

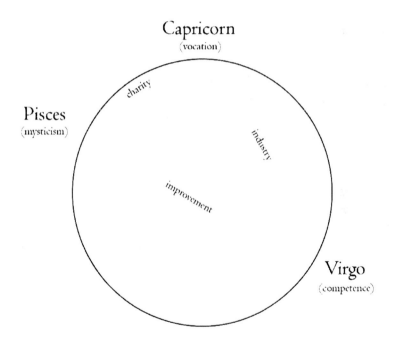

The Wedge

Figure 21

A triangle composed of an opposition, trine, and sextile has been termed a "wedge" in some astrology discourse, so that'll be the name used here. As with the T-Square, the sign making two aspects to an opposition plays the pivotal role in the resolution of the configuration. The opposition forms the backbone to the configuration, while the trine and sextile are more secondary. Therefore, the focus will be on how the additional sign influences the opposition. Unlike the T-Square in which pressure is added to the opposition by a square, the wedge's secondary aspects are supportive.

There are 24 possible wedges. Each of the six oppositions has four signs which make a trine and sextile to it. The following list names the evolutionary connections each wedge depicts, and gives a short statement about its meaning. In-depth discussion of each of the triangles is beyond the introductory scope of this section. The reader is encouraged to reflect on these triangles and reach further insight about their nature.

Aries/Libra & Gemini: *Mind* (Gemini) connects to **behavior** through **agility** and **communication**. *Autonomy* (Aries) connects to **communication** through **agility** and **behavior**. *Relationship* (Libra) connects to **agility** through **communication** and **behavior**. Being versatile, curious, and speaking our ideas assists us with interpersonal sharing.

Aries/Libra & Leo: *Character* (Leo) connects to **behavior** through **valor** and **engagement**. *Autonomy* (Aries) connects to **engagement** through **behavior** and **valor**. *Relationship* (Libra) connects to **valor** through **engagement** and **behavior**. The ability to fully show up in relationship brings greater illumination to interpersonal processes.

Aries/Libra & Sagittarius: *Direction* (Sagittarius) connects to **behavior** through **conquest** and **politics**. *Autonomy* (Aries) connects to **politics** through **conquest** and **behavior**. *Relationship* (Libra) connects to **conquest** through **politics** and **behavior**. Having a life mission impacts the self-other dynamic by joining in shared purpose.

238

Aries/Libra & Aquarius: *Systems* (Aquarius) connect to **behavior** through **representation** and **culture**. *Autonomy* (Aries) connects to **culture** through **behavior** and **representation**. *Relationship* (Libra) connects to **representation** through **culture** and **behavior**. Collectivity becomes personally relevant in our individual relationship with culture.

Taurus/Scorpio & Cancer: *Heart* (Cancer) connects to **endurance** through **nourishment** and **bonding**. *Resources* (Taurus) connect to **bonding** through **nourishment** and **endurance**. *Power* (Scorpio) connects to **nourishment** through **endurance** and **bonding**. Emotional investment deepens our connection to what is sustainable for the self and others.

Taurus/Scorpio & Virgo: *Competence* (Virgo) connects to **endurance** through **productivity** and **therapy**. *Resources* (Taurus) connect to **therapy** through **productivity** and **endurance**. *Power* (Scorpio) connects to **productivity** through **endurance** and **therapy**. Maintaining focus on tasks and personal challenges increases effectiveness.

Taurus/Scorpio & Capricorn: *Vocation* (Capricorn) connects to **endurance** through **success** and **command**. *Resources* (Taurus) connect to **command** through **success** and **endurance**. *Power* (Scorpio) connects to **success** through **command** and **endurance**. Managerial prowess assists in career longevity.

Taurus/Scorpio & Pisces: *Mysticism* (Pisces) connects to **endurance** through **serenity** and **sacred union**. *Resources* (Taurus) connect to **sacred union** through **serenity** and **endurance**. *Power* (Scorpio) connects with **serenity** through **sacred union** and **endurance**. We maintain awareness of the loving embrace of Spirit through cultivating inner peace and sharing in sacred moments.

Gemini/Sagittarius & Aries: *Autonomy* (Aries) connects to **learning** through **agility** and **conquest**. *Mind* (Gemini) connects to **conquest** through **learning** and **agility**. *Direction* (Sagittarius)

239

connects to *agility* through *learning* and *conquest.* Through assertiveness and setting goals, we can get excited about learning.

Gemini/Sagittarius & Leo: *Character* (Leo) connects to *learning* through *fun* and *grandeur. Mind* (Gemini) connects to *grandeur* through *fun* and *learning. Direction* (Sagittarius) connects to *fun* through *grandeur* and *learning.* Animating the learning process with enthusiasm strengthens personal development.

Gemini/Sagittarius & Libra: *Relationship* (Libra) connects to *learning* through *communication* and *politics. Mind* (Gemini) connects to *politics* through *communication* and *learning. Direction* (Sagittarius) connects to *communication* through *politics* and *learning.* Diplomacy advances the exchange of knowledge.

Gemini/Sagittarius & Aquarius: *Systems* (Aquarius) connect to *learning* through *genius* and *congregation. Mind* (Gemini) connects to *congregation* through *learning* and *genius. Direction* (Sagittarius) connects to *genius* through *learning* and *congregation.* The intelligence of nature is universally accessible; it can be brought into the individual and shared with groups.

Cancer/Capricorn & Taurus: *Resources* (Taurus) connect to *importance* through *nourishment* and *success. Heart* (Cancer) connects to *success* through *nourishment* and *importance. Vocation* (Capricorn) connects to *nourishment* through *success* and *importance.* Investing in the self leads to making an impact.

Cancer/Capricorn & Virgo: *Competence* (Virgo) connects to *importance* through *health care* and *industry. Heart* (Cancer) connects to *industry* through *health care* and *importance. Vocation* (Capricorn) connects to *health care* through *importance* and *industry.* Self-care and diligence maximizes efficiency.

Cancer/Capricorn & Scorpio: *Power* (Scorpio) connects to *importance* through *command* and *bonding*. *Heart* (Cancer) connects to *command* through *importance* and *bonding*. *Vocation* (Capricorn) connects to *bonding* through *importance* and *command*. Developing stature is furthered by confidence and sensitivity.

Cancer/Capricorn & Pisces: *Mysticism* (Pisces) connects to *importance* through *empathy* and *charity*. *Heart* (Cancer) connects to *charity* through *empathy* and *importance*. *Vocation* (Capricorn) connects to *empathy* through *charity* and *importance*. Universal love gains potency in the world by those who structure society in accordance with it.

Leo/Aquarius & Aries: *Autonomy* (Aries) connects to *participation* through *valor* and *representation*. *Character* (Leo) connects to *representation* through *valor* and *participation*. *Systems* (Aquarius) connect to *valor* through *representation* and *participation*. The individual can choose what causes to advocate and enliven.

Leo/Aquarius & Gemini: *Mind* (Gemini) connects to *participation* through *fun* and *genius*. *Character* (Leo) connects to *genius* through *fun* and *participation*. *Systems* (Aquarius) connect to *fun* through *genius* and *participation*. The mind is endlessly fascinated by the variety of what life offers.

Leo/Aquarius & Libra: *Relationship* (Libra) connects to *participation* through *culture* and *engagement*. *Character* (Leo) connects to *culture* through *engagement* and *participation*. *Systems* (Aquarius) connect to *engagement* through *culture* and *participation*. Social networking creates the structure to bring people together.

Leo/Aquarius & Sagittarius: *Direction* (Sagittarius) connects with *participation* through *grandeur* and *congregation*. *Character* (Leo) connects with *congregation* through *grandeur* and *partici-*

241

pation. *Systems* (Sagittarius) connect to **grandeur** through **congregation** and **participation.** Energizing a shared purpose provides the meaning to form groups.

Virgo/Pisces & Taurus: *Resources* (Taurus) connects with **improvement** through **serenity** and **productivity.** *Competence* (Virgo) connects with **serenity** through **productivity** and **improvement.** *Mysticism* (Pisces) connects to **productivity** through **serenity** and **improvement.** Being calm assists us in handling the tasks at hand.

Virgo/Pisces & Cancer: *Heart* (Cancer) connects to **improvement** through **health care** and **empathy.** *Competence* (Virgo) connects to **empathy** through **health care** and **improvement.** *Mysticism* (Pisces) connects to **health care** through **empathy** and **improvement.** Love of self and other stimulates healing.

Virgo/Pisces & Scorpio: *Power* (Scorpio) connects to **improvement** through **therapy** and **sacred union.** *Competence* (Virgo) connects to **sacred union** through **therapy** and **improvement.** *Mysticism* (Pisces) connects to **therapy** through **sacred union** and **improvement.** We become stronger through supportive and caring confrontation.

Virgo/Pisces & Capricorn: **Vocation** (Capricorn) connects to **improvement** through **charity** and **industry.** *Competence* (Virgo) connects to **charity** through **industry** and **improvement.** *Mysticism* connects to **industry** through **charity** and **improvement.** Our careers can help heal the planet if we are steadfast with this pursuit.

The Square-Trine-Quincunx Triangle

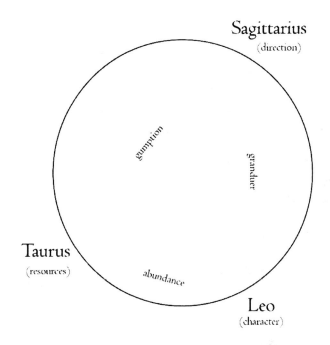

Sagittarius
(direction)

gumption

grandeur

Taurus
(resources)

abundance

Leo
(character)

The Square-Trine-Quinqunx Triangle

Figure 22

There is currently no name for this triangle. In fact, in my research I failed to find any references to it at all. This should not diminish its evolutionary importance as we are dealing with the synthesis of three very important aspects. Due to the marginalization of the quincunx, complex aspect configurations involving the 150-degree aspect have largely not been explored, with the Yod as the exception.

It turns out that this triangle may have major significance. The Grand Trine deals with the same element, which centers its evolutionary themes around that element. The T-Square does the same with the modalities. The Wedge shows some interesting

243

supportive ways in which oppositions can be worked with. With this triangle, the evolutionary lessons bridge both element and modality—there is support and friction in each one. The square brings friction, the trine harmony, while the quincunx reveals advanced lessons. Unlike the other complex aspect configurations, the variety of aspects which inform this triangle (especially the advanced nature of the quincunx) give it the broadest, and most sophisticated scope.

Furthermore, other complex aspect configurations center around one particular part of the formation. The Yod focuses on what the quincunxes point to, and the T-Square and Wedge focus on the opposition. With this triangle, there is no primary focus. Rather, the three legs of the triangle each contribute to a broader evolutionary program.

In all of the research for this book, perhaps the most surprising development was running into this fascinating triangle. I think that someday this configuration will be a significant part of astrology, and it's exciting to begin to understand its evolutionary importance.

There are 24 of these triangles. Six of them are composed of neutral signs, and six are charged. The other 12 have a mix of both neutral and charged signs. The evolutionary connections are listed along with a brief statement of its purpose.

Neutral Square-Trine-Quincunx Triangles

Taurus/Libra/Capricorn: *Resources* (Taurus) connect to **civilization** through **art** and **success**. *Relationship* (Libra) connects to **success** through **art** and **civilization**. *Vocation* (Capricorn) connects to **art** through **success** and **civilization**. This aspect deals with the flow of money—from the personal bank account, to an investment in career, to funding infrastructures. It concerns investing in the development of buildings or architecture in a civilized society. Building a museum captures its essence.

Taurus/Libra/Aquarius: *Resources* (Taurus) connect to **culture** through **art** and **nature**. *Relationship* (Libra) connects to **nature**

244

through *art* and **culture**. *Systems* (Aquarius) connect to **art** through **culture** and **nature**. This triangle involves the manifestation of our highest artistic ideals. The depiction of nature in the most pleasing ways informs high culture and inspires us to live in alignment with this purity. This combination feels like the Renaissance, or the cultural heights of Ancient Greece.

Taurus/Virgo/Aquarius: *Resources* (Taurus) connect to **technology** through **productivity** and **nature**. *Competence* (Virgo) connects to **nature** through **technology** and **productivity**. *Systems* (Aquarius) connect to **productivity** through **technology** and **nature**. The evolutionary program here is the proliferation of technological advances through mass production. Having televisions and computers commonly available as personal possessions allows the broad intelligence of nature to be accessible everywhere. Only within the last few decades have we seen evolution spread in this way.

Gemini/Virgo/Aquarius: *Mind* (Gemini) connects to **technology** through **science** and **genius**. *Competence* (Virgo) connects to **genius** through **science** and **technology**. *Systems* (Aquarius) connect to **science** through **genius** and **technology**. Comprehending quantum physics, rocket science, or even astrology brings the sheer brilliance of Spirit into our everyday world. This triangle challenges us to bridge science with the transpersonal—to reach unfathomable insight into the nature of reality. Perhaps science will become more open to Spirit in our lifetime, and we'll get to watch this evolution unfold!

Gemini/Libra/Capricorn: *Mind* (Gemini) connects to **civilization** through **communication** and **education**. *Relationship* (Libra) connects to **education** through **communication** and **civilization**. *Vocation* (Capricorn) connects to **communication** through **civilization** and **education**. This evolutionary program seeks to create universities or other centers where people join and socialize in contexts of higher learning. This combination provides the setting where people press forward a more sophisticated society.

245

Gemini/Virgo/Capricorn: *Mind* (Gemini) connects to *industry* through *science* and *education*. *Competence* (Virgo) connects to *education* through *science* and *industry*. *Vocation* (Capricorn) connects to *science* through *education* and *industry*. Bringing advanced intellectual discourse into the mainstream is the program here. How can the media and other social and institutional organizations continually challenge us to think? What if television programming were more sophisticated? What if more of it were truly educational?

Charged Square-Trine-Quincunx Triangles

Aries/Leo/Scorpio: *Autonomy* (Aries) connects to *trust* through *valor* and *passion*. *Character* (Leo) connects with *passion* through *valor* and *trust*. *Power* (Scorpio) connects with *valor* through *trust* and *passion*. Have you had much intense, long/lasting, playful intimacy lately? The lesson here is to have the trust or safety with a partner to really rock & roll in the bedroom in the most thrillingly orgasmic way.

Aries/Cancer/Scorpio: *Autonomy* (Aries) connects to *bonding* through *protection* and *passion*. *Heart* (Cancer) connects to *passion* through *protection* and *bonding*. *Power* (Scorpio) connects to *protection* through *bonding* and *passion*. Do you love anyone so much that you would readily die for them? This program is to live for love, and love to live.

Aries/Cancer/Sagittarius: *Autonomy* (Aries) connects to *self-discovery* through *conquest* and *protection*. *Heart* (Cancer) connects to *conquest* through *protection* and *self-discovery*. *Direction* (Sagittarius) connects to *protection* through *conquest* and *self-discovery*. What cause would you lay your life on the line to protect? The lesson here is to touch in with what matters most and courageously defend it in the wider world.

246

Cancer/Sagittarius/Pisces: *Heart* (Cancer) connects to **religion** through **self-discovery** and **empathy**. *Direction* (Sagittarius) connects to **empathy** through **self-discovery** and **religion**. *Mysticism* (Pisces) connects to **self-discovery** through **religion** and **empathy**. The evolutionary task is to connect the heart with spiritual experience—being moved to tears by experiencing the divine.

Leo/Sagittarius/Pisces: *Character* (Leo) connects to **religion** through **grandeur** and **spiritual awakening**. *Direction* (Sagittarius) connects to **spiritual awakening** through **grandeur** and **religion**. *Mysticism* (Pisces) connects to **grandeur** through **spiritual awakening** and **religion**. Are you able to animate Spirit through your radiance? The evolutionary opportunity here is to generously inspire through benevolence and positivity.

Leo/Scorpio/Pisces: *Character* (Leo) connects to **sacred union** through **trust** and **spiritual awakening**. *Power* (Scorpio) connects to **spiritual awakening** through **trust** and **sacred union**. *Mysticism* (Pisces) connects to **trust** through **spiritual awakening** and **sacred union**. Have you mastered the fine points of sacred sexuality? The program here is for our intimate exchanges to promote spiritual growth.

Mixed Square-Trine-Quincunx Triangles

Aries/Leo/Capricorn: *Autonomy* (Aries) connects to **dominion** through **leadership** and **valor**. *Character* (Leo) connects to **leadership** through **dominion** and **valor**. *Vocation* (Capricorn) connects to **valor** through **leadership** and **dominion**. This triangle asks for enlightened self-promotion. Courageously taking charge of our potency in the world is the lesson.

Aries/Virgo/Sagittarius: *Autonomy* (Aries) connects to **foresight** through **conquest** and **maturity**. *Competence* (Virgo) connects to **conquest** through **maturity** and **foresight**. *Direction* connects to **maturity** through **conquest** and **foresight**. We often need persistence and stamina to reach our goals. One form of this theme

247

would be being able to withstand a rigorous training program in order to get the necessary degree or experience.

Aries/Virgo/Capricorn: *Autonomy* (Aries) connects to **industry** through **maturity** and **leadership**. *Competence* (Virgo) connects to **leadership** through **maturity** and **industry**. *Vocation* (Capricorn) connects to **maturity** through **industry** and **leadership**. The evolutionary opportunity here is to climb the corporate ladder. Being willing to gradually work our way up will eventually pay off.

Taurus/Leo/Sagittarius: *Resources* (Taurus) connect to **grandeur** through **abundance** and **gumption**. *Character* (Leo) connects to **gumption** through **abundance** and **grandeur**. *Direction* (Sagittarius) connects to **abundance** through **gumption** and **grandeur**. The lesson is to believe in ourself enough to completely go for it, to live life fully without regret. Being willing to back up this confidence with money or with whatever else is necessary enables us to pursue our goals wholeheartedly.

Taurus/Leo/Capricorn: *Resources* (Taurus) connect to **dominion** through **success** and **abundance**. *Character* (Leo) connects to **success** through **abundance** and **dominion**. *Vocation* (Capricorn) connects to **abundance** through **success** and **dominion**. This program concerns the solidification of our reputation, being known for delivering a substantial vocational contribution. Managing money (Taurus) status (Capricorn) and acclaim (Leo), potentially equals fame.

Taurus/Virgo/Sagittarius: *Resources* (Taurus) connect to **foresight** through **productivity** and **gumption**. *Competence* (Virgo) connects to **gumption** through **productivity** and **foresight**. *Direction* (Sagittarius) connects to **productivity** through **gumption** and **foresight**. This program involves the investment of resources and gradually watching it bear fruit. Setting up a college fund for a child captures the spirit. Having perspective that hard work today leads to bounty tomorrow keeps us working on our development.

248

Gemini/Scorpio/Aquarius: *Mind* (Gemini) connects to *wisdom* through *honesty* and *genius*. *Power* (Scorpio) connects to *genius* through *wisdom* and *honesty*. *Systems* (Aquarius) connect to *honesty* through *wisdom* and *genius*. This program is the complete transformation of the intellect from being rational to incorporating transpersonal experiences. Whereas the air signs are mental, the inclusion of Scorpio adds the depth only gained through process or experience. Connecting to others, and to life itself, from the position of mystery and metaphysical possibility accelerates evolution. Ultimately, integration of this triangle leads to the mind of the shaman.

Gemini/Scorpio/Pisces: *Mind* (Gemini) connects to *sacred union* through *honesty* and *understanding*. *Power* (Scorpio) connects to *understanding* through *honesty* and *sacred union*. *Mysticism* (Pisces) connects to *honesty* through *sacred union* and *understanding*. Part of the evolution available here is to learn how to shift perception from the relative to the transpersonal. Learning how to see everything as interconnected as well as sharing this experience with others brings profundity to interpersonal sharing. Speaking from a place of spiritual truth accelerates intimacy.

Gemini/Libra/Pisces: *Mind* (Gemini) connects to *Namaste* through *understanding* and *communication*. *Relationship* (Libra) connects to *understanding* through *Namaste* and *communication*. *Mysticism* (Pisces) connects to *communication* through *Namaste* and *understanding*. As with the previous triangle, the lesson is to speak to others with the knowledge that they are a mirror of ourself. This triangle has a more social, rather than emotional, scope. Being able to enter the social milieu with this perspective fills human interaction with a mystical bent.

Cancer/Libra/Aquarius: *Heart* (Cancer) connects to *culture* through *romantic love* and *agape*. *Relationship* (Libra) connects to *agape* through *romantic love* and *culture*. *Systems* (Aquarius) connect to *romantic love* through *culture* and *agape*. The opportunity is to make the social culture emotionally satisfying. Ideally, we

249

become moved to connect with groups in heartfelt ways which promote peace and togetherness. Sharing love among friends, allies, or the collective is the goal to strive for.

Cancer/Libra/Pisces: *Heart* (Cancer) connects to **Namaste** through **romantic love** and **empathy**. *Relationship* (Libra) connects to **empathy** through **Namaste** and **romantic love**. *Mysticism* (Pisces) connects to **romantic love** through **Namaste** and **empathy**. This triangle involves some form of ritual or process which heals or bonds people together. Making compassion available in social contexts deepens interactions. This combination provides a soothing or gentle quality to the way that we treat others.

Cancer/Scorpio/Aquarius: *Heart* (Cancer) connects to **wisdom** through **bonding** and **agape**. *Power* (Scorpio) connects to **agape** through **wisdom** and **bonding**. *Systems* (Aquarius) connect to **bonding** through **wisdom** and **agape**. This program involves a confrontation with unconscious material while others witness us. Sharing this process of spiritual growth with a loved one broadens our perspective and creates meaningful intimacy.

The Square-Sextile-Quincunx Triangle

There are 24 of this type of triangle, all of them mixed between charged and neutral signs. The evolutionary connections are listed along with a brief summary of its meaning.

250

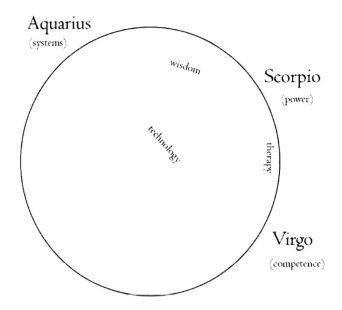

Aquarius
(systems)

wisdom

Scorpio
(power)

technology

therapy

Virgo
(competence)

The Square-Sextile-Quinqunx Triangle
Figure 23

Aries/Gemini/Capricorn: *Autonomy* (Aries) connects to *education* through *agility* and *leadership*. *Mind* (Gemini) connects to *leadership* through *agility* and *education*. *Vocation* (Capricorn) connects to *agility* through *leadership* and *education*. The evolutionary agenda is to excel in school. Not necessarily about competing against others, this triangle asks us to challenge ourself to perform at the highest level.

Aries/Gemini/Virgo: *Autonomy* (Aries) connects to *science* through *maturity* and *agility*. *Mind* (Gemini) connects to *maturity* through *agility* and *science*. *Competence* (Virgo) connects to *agility* through *science* and *maturity*. The learning here involves con-

251

ducting informative experiments. Making a concoction out of the condiments in the refrigerator is how a youngster might go about it.

Aries/Cancer/Aquarius: *Autonomy* (Aries) connects to **agape** through **protection** and **representation**. *Heart* (Cancer) connects to **representation** through **protection** and **agape**. *Systems* (Aquarius) connect to **protection** through **agape** and **representation**. How can an individual protect the best interests of the collective? What can a single person do to help out? Volunteering to help clean up after an environmental disaster is one example of working this triangle.

Aries/Scorpio/Aquarius: *Autonomy* connects to **wisdom** through **representation** and **passion**. *Power* (Scorpio) connects to **representation** through **passion** and **wisdom**. *Systems* (Aquarius) connect to **passion** through **representation** and **wisdom**. This configuration asks us to find a cause worth advocating for. How can an individual play a role in changing the world? Evolution proceeds by attempting just this.

Aries/Cancer/Virgo: *Autonomy* (Aries) connects to **health care** through **maturity** and **protection**. *Heart* (Cancer) connects to **maturity** through **health care** and **protection**. *Competence* (Virgo) connects to **protection** through **health care** and **maturity**. Sometimes it's important to limit external activity in order to take care of personal needs. The growth lies in developing the courage to do important personal work and make necessary improvements.

Aries/Scorpio/Capricorn: *Autonomy* (Aries) connects to **command** through **passion** and **leadership**. *Power* (Scorpio) connects to **leadership** through **passion** and **command**. *Vocation* (Capricorn) connects to **passion** through **command** and **leadership**. This program is about maximizing authority by becoming a seasoned elder. Success here looks like the sure-handed leader who is wise and experienced.

Taurus/Cancer/Aquarius: *Resources* (Taurus) connect to *agape* through *nourishment* and *nature*. *Heart* (Cancer) connects to *nature* through *agape* and *nourishment*. *Systems* (Aquarius) connect to *nourishment* through *nature* and *agape*. The lesson here is to learn how to feed the collective. Advances in agriculture are suggested—learning how to maximize the harvest for everyone's benefit.

Taurus/Cancer/Libra: *Resources* (Taurus) connect to *romantic love* through *nourishment* and *art*. *Heart* (Cancer) connects to *art* through *romantic love* and *nourishment*. *Relationship* (Libra) connects to *nourishment* through *romantic love* and *art*. Being moved by beauty is the lesson. What draws the sensitivity from the inside out for others to see? How can we connect in this sublime moment?

Taurus/Leo/Pisces: *Resources* (Taurus) connect to *spiritual awakening* through *abundance* and *serenity*. *Character* (Leo) connects to *serenity* through *spiritual awakening* and *abundance*. *Mysticism* (Pisces) connects to *abundance* through *spiritual awakening* and *serenity*. The development here is toward a quiet joy—feeling completely safe and at peace in the world. There is a renewal of innocence and an appreciation of the simple pleasures in life. Having spiritual awareness in everyday ways is comforting.

Taurus/Sagittarius/Pisces: *Resources* (Taurus) connect to *religion* through *gumption* and *serenity*. *Direction* (Sagittarius) connects to *serenity* through *religion* and *gumption*. *Mysticism* (Pisces) connects to *gumption* through *serenity* and *religion*. What is the best way to promote Spirit with gentleness? How can we be agents of compassion? Is it possible to be "love snipers" who fire bullets of love at everyone?

Taurus/Sagittarius/Aquarius: *Resources* (Taurus) connect to *congregation* through *gumption* and *nature*. *Direction* (Sagittarius) connects to *nature* through *congregation* and *gumption*. *Systems* (Aquarius) connect to *gumption* through *nature* and *congrega-*

253

tion. This plan involves funding a group, cause, or other humanitarian project to make it a reality. Pooling resources for mutual benefit brings togetherness and common cause.

Taurus/Leo/Libra: *Resources* (Taurus) connect to **engagement** through **abundance** and **art**. *Character* (Leo) connects to **art** through **engagement** and **abundance**. *Relationship* (Libra) connects to **abundance** through **art** and **engagement**. This triangle involves the development of a creative talent or hobby and the sharing of it with others. Anything that puts a smile on someone's face would qualify. Developing the confidence to share and experience good cheer is on tap.

Gemini/Leo/Scorpio: *Mind* (Gemini) connects to **trust** through **fun** and **honesty**. *Character* (Leo) connects to **honesty** through **fun** and **trust**. *Power* (Scorpio) connects to **fun** through **trust** and **honesty**. This learning is about taking verbal risks in the process of getting to know someone, revealing ourself to bring about a deeper connection. Ultimately, an appreciation for the other is life-affirming.

Gemini/Leo/Pisces: *Mind* (Gemini) connects to **spiritual awakening** through **fun** and **understanding**. *Character* (Leo) connects to **understanding** through **fun** and **spiritual awakening**. *Mysticism* (Pisces) connects to **fun** through **spiritual awakening** and **understanding**. Can play be spiritual practice? Is it possible to be carried into transpersonal states of consciousness while having a good time? The plan here is to learn how to awaken while letting go in recreational experiences.

Gemini/Virgo/Scorpio: *Mind* (Gemini) connects to **therapy** through **science** and **honesty**. *Competence* (Virgo) connects **honesty** through **science** and **therapy**. *Power* (Scorpio) connects to **science** through **therapy** and **honesty**. In order to reveal what is going on to others we must speak the truth. Then we can get to the bottom of things and learn about our own, and the larger field of, psychology.

Gemini/Capricorn/Pisces: *Mind* (Gemini) connects to **charity** through **education** and **understanding**. *Vocation* (Capricorn) connects to **understanding** through **education** and **charity**. *Mysticism* (Pisces) connects to **education** through **charity** and **understanding**. The idea here is to teach universal compassion through good deeds. A school program that equips students to contribute to the world in openhearted ways is an example.

Cancer/Virgo/Sagittarius: *Heart* (Cancer) connects to **foresight** through **health care** and **self-discovery**. *Competence* (Virgo) connects to **self-discovery** through **health care** and **foresight**. *Direction* (Sagittarius) connects to **health care** through **foresight** and **self-discovery**. This triangle feels like the humanitarian organization, *Doctors Without Borders*, or any other far-reaching program designed to assist others in foreign nations. Sharing in loving tasks which connect people cross-culturally is the program.

Cancer/Libra/Sagittarius: *Heart* (Cancer) connects to **politics** through **romantic love** and **self-discovery**. *Relationship* (Libra) connects to **self-discovery** through **politics** and **romantic love**. *Direction* (Sagittarius) connects to **romantic love** through **politics** and **self-discovery**. This triangle addresses the social dynamics of the reality that we are all a part of the world family. How can we all get along? What are the common denominators that we can all agree on? Extending ourself to those we may not know bridges the distance.

Leo/Libra/Capricorn: *Character* (Leo) connects to **civilization** through **engagement** and **dominion**. *Relationship* (Libra) connects to **dominion** through **engagement** and **civilization**. *Vocation* (Capricorn) connects to **engagement** through **dominion** and **civilization**. This triangle is like the Academy Awards or any other situation where there is celebration for our contributions. There is a sense of style, acclaim, and worldly appreciation. Ideally, we use this recognition or fame in ways which promote civilization instead of the ego.

255

Leo/Scorpio/Capricorn: *Character* (Leo) connects to **command** through **trust** and **dominion**. *Power* (Scorpio) connects to **dominion** through **trust** and **command**. *Vocation* (Capricorn) connects to **trust** through **dominion** and **command**. Wielding authority responsibly requires us to earn the respect of others. Taking interest and honoring those impacted by our decisions allows them to come aboard.

Virgo/Scorpio/Aquarius: *Competence* (Virgo) connects to **wisdom** through **therapy** and **technology**. *Power* (Scorpio) connects to **technology** through **wisdom** and **therapy**. *Systems* (Aquarius) connect to **therapy** through **technology** and **wisdom**. Figuring out the techniques or methodology to do deep spiritual work is the program here. Developing the skills to be a shaman, hypnotist, or any other agent of awakening catalyzes growth in others as well as in ourself.

Virgo/Sagittarius/Aquarius: *Competence* (Virgo) connects to **congregation** through **foresight** and **technology**. *Direction* (Sagittarius) connects to **technology** through **congregation** and **foresight**. *Systems* (Aquarius) connects to **foresight** through **congregation** and **technology**. Making technological innovations spiritually meaningful and figuring out how to live on this planet in sustainable ways is the program.

Libra/Sagittarius/Pisces: *Relationship* (Libra) connects to **religion** through **politics** and **Namaste**. *Direction* (Sagittarius) connects to **Namaste** through **religion** and **politics**. *Mysticism* (Pisces) connects to **politics** through **Namaste** and **religion**. The growth here is to bridge religious, political, or philosophical differences by seeing and experiencing the oneness which underlies our existence.

Libra/Capricorn/Pisces: *Relationship* (Libra) connects to **charity** through **Namaste** and **civilization**. *Vocation* (Capricorn) connects to **Namaste** through **charity** and **civilization**. *Mysticism* (Pisces) connects to **civilization** through **Namaste** and **charity**. The opportunity is to organize large-scale efforts to assist those in need of help. At the time of this writing, a massive earthquake in Haiti has devastated the country. This triangle involves helping those in need in pragmatic and loving ways.

Glossary

Awakening: The experience of loosening the identification with ego and connecting with *and identifying as* the broader field of awareness.

Awareness: An all-enveloping field which is the context of all the content of our experience.

Charged: Paired with the right brain, primarily involves various degrees of quality.

Consciousness: The mixture of awareness with the unconscious of the separate self.

Cyclical Evolution: The process of learning specific lessons in all realms of human experience which contributes to our spiritual growth.

Devolution: The opposite of evolution, deepening patterns of re-gression.

Duality: Distinguishing between things from the perspective of separation—oneness divided into form.

Ego: The experience of a separate self with its priority of survival. It has the most direct correlation to the astrological Moon.

Ego dream: The condition of meeting the psyche in the external world and failing to recognize it as such, being caught in relative reality.

Enlightenment: The state of complete awakening into Spirit.

Evolution: A process of incremental growth towards a more ad-vanced state of being. Human evolution includes healing as well as growth.

258

Evolutionary Astrology: A branch of astrology which assumes rein-carnation and the growth of the soul as the overarching human story.

Integration: The state of having processed necessary lessons suffi-ciently to produce noticeable and consistent changes in our percep-tions, beliefs, and behavior.

Karma: The law of cause and effect; the natural consequences of our actions; the collection of prior behavioral tendencies to be ad-dressed, reconciled, and integrated.

Left brain: Pertaining to content, order, rationality, precision, reason, logic, temporal distinctions.

Liberation: The evolutionary channel from the physical and per-sonal to the nonphysical and transpersonal in the sequence of earth, water, air, then fire. This channel involves the evolution of con-sciousness towards spiritual awakening.

Manifestation: The evolutionary channel that moves in the reverse direction from the liberation channel. It's most dramatic event oc-curs when a soul incarnates into an individual human.

Neutral: Paired with the left brain, involves various degrees of quantity but not quality.

Nondual: The Oneness that exists outside of time and space and yet also gives rise to both of them.

Personal Story: The narrative each of us has about our separate self. It is usually colored by interpretations and preferences which derive from the ego.

Presence: The energy and state that results from centering con-sciousness in the present moment.

259

Progressive Evolution: The development of consciousness through elemental levels in the process of spiritual growth.

Relative Reality: The common, everyday world filled with separation, value judgments, and egoic attachments.

Right brain: Pertaining to process, creativity, intuition, emotion, inspiration, transcendence.

Samsara: The cycle of birth, death, and rebirth.

Shadow: Any part of ourself that we'd prefer not to see. We repress, deny, or project it onto others. In terms of managing astrological aspects, the involvement of our shadow leads to distorted or regressive expressions and behaviors that contribute to devolution.

Soul: A part of Spirit which separates to fulfill evolutionary work.

Spirit: One of many words used to describe the all-encompassing context of Existence. Other names include God, Goddess, Allah, the Creator, Brahman, the Tao, Oneness, or the Absolute.

Transpersonal: Pertaining to phenomena beyond the personal, including soul and Spirit.

Unconscious: The deep well of accumulated experiences absorbed by the separate self.

Wholeness: The state of accepting and connecting with all of who we are, not just what meets ego preferences.

Bibliography & Further Reading

Adyashanti. *The End of Your World*. Sounds True. Boulder, CO. 2008.

-----. *True Meditation*. Sounds True. Boulder, CO. 2006.

Arroyo, Stephen. *Astrology Karma & Transformation*, 2nd Edition. CRCS Publications. Sebastopol, CA. 1992.

-----. *Astrology, Psychology and the Four Elements*. CRCS Publications. Sebastopol, CA. 1975.

Blavatsky, Helena. *The Secret Doctrine: The Synthesis of Science, Religion and Philosophy*. Reprinted by Adamant Media Corporation. 2005.

Capra, Fritjof. *The Tao of Physics*, 3rd Edition. Shambhala. Boston, MA. 1991.

Coomaraswamy, Rama, ed. *The Essential Ananda K. Coomaraswamy (The Perennial Philosophy Series)*. World Wisdom. Bloomington, IN. 2003.

Cunningham, Donna. *Being a Lunar Type in a Solar World*. Weiser. York Beach, ME. 1982.

Eckhart, Meister. *Selected Writings*. Penguin Books. London, England. 1995.

Fernandez, Maurice. *Astrology and the Evolution of Consciousness, Volume 1*. Evolutionary Astrology, Inc. Land O' Lakes, FL. 2009.

Forrest, Steven. *Yesterday's Sky*. Seven Paws Press. Borrego Springs, CA, 2008.

-----. *The Book of Pluto*. ACS Publications. San Diego, CA. 1994.

-----. *The Night Speaks*. ACS Publications. San Diego, CA. 1993.

Godman, David, ed. *Be As You Are: The Teachings of Sri Ramana Maharshi*. Penguin. 1992.

Green, Jeffrey Wolf. *Pluto: The Evolutionary Journey of the Soul, Volume 1*. Llewellyn Publications. St. Paul, MN. 1985.

Greene, Liz. *Relating*. Weiser. York Beach, ME. 1977

Greene, Liz & Howard Sasportas. *The Luminaries*. Weiser. York Beach, ME. 1992.

Grof, Stanislav. *The Holotropic Mind*. HarperCollins. New York, NY. 1993.

Hand, Robert. *Horoscope Symbols*. Schiffer Publishing. Atglen, PA. 1981.

Herlihy, John, ed. *The Essential Rene Guenon: Metaphysics, Tradition, and the Crisis of Modernity*. World Wisdom. Bloomington, IN. 2009.

Huxley, Aldous. *The Perennial Philosophy*. Harper & Row. New York, NY. 1945.

Katie, Byron. *A Thousand Names for Joy*. Harmony Books, New York, NY. 2007.

-----. *Loving What Is*. Harmony Books. New York, NY. 2002

Katz, Jerry. *One, Essential Writings on Nonduality*. Sentient Publications. Boulder, CO. 2007.

Levine, Rick. *Quantum Astrology.* Levine & Associates. Redmond, WA. 1994.

Marks, Tracey. *The Astrology of Self-Discovery.* CRCS Publications. Sebastopol, CA. 1985.

McDermott, Robert, ed. *The Essential Aurobindo: Writings of Sri Aurobindo,* 2nd Edition. Lindisfarne Books. Great Barrington, MA. 2001.

Meyers, Eric. *Uranus: The Constant of Change.* Astrology Sight. Longmont, CO. 2008.

-----. *Between Past & Presence: A Spiritual View of the Moon & Sun.* Astrology Sight. Longmont, CO. 2006.

-----. *The Arrow's Ascent: Astrology & The Quest for Meaning.* Astrology Sight. Longmont, CO. 2004.

Murray, Jessica. *Soul-Sick Nation: An Astrologer's View of America.* Author House. Bloomington, IN. 2006.

Mindell, Arnold. *Quantum Mind.* Lao Tse Press. Portland, OR. 2000.

Nasr, Seyyed Hossein, ed. *The Essential Frithjof Schuon (Library of Perennial Philosophy).* World Wisdom. Bloomington, IN. 2005.

Newton, Michael. *Journey of Souls,* 5th Edition. Llewellyn Publications. Woodbury, MN. 2008.

Rudhyar, Dane. *The Astrology of Personality.* Aurora Press. Santa Fe, NM. 1991.

Smith, Huston. *Forgotten Truth: The Common Vision of the World's Religions.* HarperCollins. San Francisco, CA. 1976.

Spiller, Jan. *Astrology for the Soul.* Bantam. New York, NY. 1997.

Tarnas, Richard. *Cosmos & Psyche*. Penguin. New York, NY. 2006.

Tolle, Eckhart. *The Power of Now*. New World Library. Lovato, CA. 1999.

Uzdavinys, Algis, ed. *The Heart of Plotinus: The Essential Enneads*. World Wisdom. Bloomington, IN. 2009.

Wilber, Ken. *Integral Psychology*. Shambala. Boston, MA. 2000

-----. *The Marriage of Sense and Soul*. Random House. New York, NY. 1998.

-----. *A Brief History of Everything*. Shambala. Boston, MA. 1996.

Wolf, Fred Alan. *The Spiritual Universe*. Moment Point Press. Portsmouth, NH. 1999.

Zukav, Gary. *The Seat of the Soul*. Simon and Schuster. New York, NY. 1989.

-----. *The Dancing Wu Li Masters*. Morrow Quill. New York, NY. 1979.

Acknowledgements

Monumental heartfelt thanks to Josh Levin for serving as my editor. Your fresh eyes, ears, and wisdom helped tighten up and improve this book. How meaningful our friendship and work together continues to be. Bill Streett has once again been indispensable by providing the cover design and interior illustrations (as well as the new website!). Your precision and support is extraordinary, and I thank you Uranian comrade. Sajit Greene has been a rock-solid partner, both professionally and personally. How wonderful to bounce ideas off of someone so creative and clever. Thanks for your input and, of course, your love. To Jeff Jawer, Jessica Murray, and Gloria Star—thank you for your kind and generous words on the cover.

Many thanks to the friends, colleagues, and elders who are supporting my work: Reuvain & Patrice Bacal, Benjamin Bernstein, Robert Blaschke, Gary Caton, Sven Eberlein, Carolyn Ferber, Maurice Fernandez, Kristin Fontana, Steven Forrest, Eric Francis, Adam Gainsburg, Demetra George, Andrea Houtz, Tony Howard, Maria Jekic, Elizabeth Khan, Keith Kurlander & Emma Teitel, Rick Levine, Cathy Lindsey, A.T. Mann, Kim Mannine, Robin Manteris, Jane Martin, Ray Merriman, Kenneth Miller, Laura Nalbandian, Tami Palmer, Kelly Lee Phipps, Mary Plumb, Terri Quintel, Jim Rodgers, Betty Rosebrock, Merryl Rothaus, Sherene Schostak, Philip Sedgwick, Rick Snyder, Tiera St. Claire, Elizabeth Spring, Evelyn Terranova, Kirk VandenBerghe, Joyce Van Horne, Donna Van Toen, Dove Weissman, Medora Woods.

Thanks to all my clients and students—you help me develop my skill as an astrologer and, more importantly, my ability to be a compassionate human being. To my family (especially my son), I feel so blessed to have you in my life. And to every other significant person who has crossed my path—thank you for playing your part so perfectly.

I am happily indebted to and full of gratitude for the teachers and authors—both astrological and otherwise—who have most strongly influenced me. Byron Katie turned my world inside-out. Her simple, yet elegant "Work" is catalyzing my freedom, while providing thousands of names for joy. Adyashanti, Eckhart Tolle, and Sri Ramana Maharshi have been instrumental in opening me to wondrous possibilities and in describing the spiritual landscape with their awakened minds. The philosophical and spiritual insight from Steven Forrest, Arnold Mindell, Richard Tarnas, and Ken Wilber has also provided invaluable perspective and wisdom to draw from.

I have appreciation and respect for the field of astrology and all of its many viewpoints and approaches. I feel very fortunate to be able to help integrate the transpersonal perspective. I see astrology continuing to expand its scope and audience in the 21st Century. May it gift us all with vital insight and spiritual meaning, and may it even become a widespread paradigm that guides our way.

I want to acknowledge all of the revolutionaries and innovators, both known and unknown, who dare to push knowledge forward; you are the catalysts of evolution! Finally, I give thanks to everyone who is embracing this pivotal time frame with collaboration instead of competition, expanded perspective instead of fear, and the daring willingness to transform our existence on this beautiful planet.

Naked time unwinds beneath my mind
and from within I find the kind of beauty
only I can find
I am exactly where I need to be
I need to be exactly where I am
I am surrendering so willingly
to be the perfect me inside this now

-Amy Steinberg, *Exactly*

For more information about

Elements & Evolution and Eric's other Astrology Books

Eric & Sajit Greene's Astrology, Counseling, Workshops, and other Services

Information on Podcasts and other Media

Newsletter, Blog & Articles

Visit the website:

www.SoulVisionConsulting.com

or email: info@soulvisionconsulting.com

LaVergne, TN USA
31 March 2011
222342LV00002B/6/P